Grenada: The Jewel Despoiled

GRENADA
The Jewel Despoiled

GORDON K. LEWIS

The Johns Hopkins University Press
Baltimore and London

The Johns Hopkins University Press
701 West 40th Street
Baltimore, Maryland 21211
The Johns Hopkins Press Ltd., London

Originally published, 1987
Second printing, 1988

The paper used in this publication meets the minimum requirements of American National Standard for Information Sciences—Permanence of Paper for Printed Library Materials, ANSI Z39.48-1984.

Library of Congress Cataloging-in-Publication Data
Lewis, Gordon K.
  Grenada: the jewel despoiled.
  Includes index.
  1. Grenada—Politics and government—1974–
  2. Grenada—History—American invasion, 1983. I. Title.
  F2056.8.L48   1987   972.98'45   86-46282
  ISBN 0-8018-3422-8 (alk. paper)

To the memory of T. A. Marryshow
Grenadian, editor, patriot, federalist,
who stood for all that has been traditionally best
in West Indian life and politics

Contents

Preface

The emergence and decline of the Grenada Revolution between 1979 and 1983, ending in the calamitous events of October 1983, have given birth to an extensive book literature, written by a variety of hands—academics, political activists, journalists, government officials, "think tank" experts, and the rest. I myself have refrained from entering into that kind of immediate post-mortem analysis, since I have felt it was necessary for the dust to settle and for evidence about the events to slowly accumulate before committing myself to judgment. Now, some three years after those events, I feel that sufficient time has elapsed for the possibility of writing some long-term reflections upon the meaning of the whole phenomenon. To rush into judgment is one thing; to reflect at leisure on the ultimate consequences of what has happened is another. This book is an effort at such reflection.

The perceptive reader will see at once that the book is written, without apology, from the ideological standpoint of the tradition of European democratic socialism. It does not pretend, therefore, to be yet another title in the contemporary social sciences literature in which objectivity about method is confused with neutrality of purpose. The pretense of having no ideology in itself constitutes an ideology. But in case the reader may feel that this constitutes a bias in the reading of the story I may add the observation that the argument throughout is supported by a listing of documentary sources, collected in the notes, which, in fact, constitutes only a small proportion of the source materials that I have available. The reader may easily use those sources to arrive at his or her own conclusions. The documentation, I think, is sufficiently ample for independent scrutiny to be done without difficulty.

I do not need much space to make the usual acknowledgments. My debt to fellow Caribbeanists who have already published their own work on the Grenada affair is made evident enough throughout the text. Like most of my previous books this one has not benefited from any of the usual financial aid from the prestigious funding foundations; indeed, over the years I have developed a certain skepticism about the real worth of their contribution to academic research and publication. It gives me greater pleasure to thank the editors of the Barbados *Daily Nation* for providing me with copies of their very full reports on the trial in Grenada; and also to thank the University of Puerto Rico for letting me have time to do the work. As always, too, I thank my wife, Sybil, for her continuing help and support in innumerable ways. I might add that Grenada holds a very special place in our affections, it being one of the very first island societies that we visited in the 1950s and 1960s. Our son David shares that feeling, having published his own book on the topic (David E. Lewis, *Reform and Revolution in Grenada: 1950 to 1981* [Havana: Ediciónes Casa de las Américas, 1984]). Indeed, it can be said that, for us, Grenada is a family affair.

Grenada: The Jewel Despoiled

1

Introduction: A Caribbean Tragedy

The grim events of October 1983 in Grenada, even more than the events in the Dominican Republic of 1965, mark a crucial turning point in the history and character of the Caribbean, and especially of the English-speaking Commonwealth Caribbean. Taking place within a period of weeks, the various stages of the drama—the house incarceration of Prime Minister Maurice Bishop, his release by the Grenadian crowd, the march on Fort Rupert, the confrontation between the people and the soldiers, the murder in cold blood of Bishop and his loyal ministers, the imposition by the Revolutionary Military Council of a harsh curfew, the U.S. invasion—took on the character of a classic Greek play, with all of its dramatis personae acting out their predestined roles, at times out of conscious design but trapped at the same time in the stranglehold of Fate and Chance. On all sides, human passions and ambitions were caught up in the play of transcendental forces only at times half understood by the actors. Because it all took place in a Lilliputian West Indian society, formally independent but still exhibiting many of the pathological habits bred by colonialism, it could be analyzed in terms of the old colonial story of what Adam Smith called "the paltry raffle of colony faction." But because it also took place in a Third World territory seeking revolutionary change along Marxist-Leninist lines, it could be analyzed in Marxist-Leninist terms. And, yet again, because it was yet another scenario of the ongoing struggle between small-island nationalism and big-power imperialism, it could be interpreted in the manner, so to speak, of a Gibbon, of what takes place between the empire and the barbarian provinces.

  Whatever interpretation is favored, it is at least eminently clear that something drastically new has taken place within the English-speaking subregion. In the four years between 1979 and 1983, Grenada, of all the islands of the archipelago, was chosen to become the rendezvous of new elements. Gairyism, before 1979, marked the intrusion into the region of the habits of Latin American *caudillismo*. The overthrow of Eric Gairy in March 1979 marked, in turn, the intrusion of the Latin American habit of the *golpe de estado,* breaking for the first time the tradition of West Indian constitutionalism. The events of October 19, 1983, witnessed for the first time the resort to political assassination in the struggle for the control of the state power. The events after October 25, with the armed U.S. invasion, witnessed, again for the first time, the open and naked intervention of the American imperial power into the internal affairs of the independent nation-states of the Commonwealth Caribbean.

It is assuredly no exaggeration to say that the upshot of all this was a general condition of shock. First, of course, it was traumatic for the Grenadians themselves, a decent, warm people, deeply religious in the West Indian fundamentalist sense, gregarious, rooted in the land and the values of the land. Theirs is a village way of life more Trinidadian, perhaps, than Barbadian in its creole folk-patterns, its sharp individualism, its vivacious *brio,* its love of gossip and "ole talk," and its appetite for small-island market-square politics. Suddenly, and without warning, they were subjected to, and overwhelmed by, events that nothing in their experience had prepared them for: a murderous and fratricidal power struggle among their political leaders and an invasion by the awesome fire power of U.S. "Pentagonism," something they had seen before only in the movies. But it was no less of a shock for the neighboring West Indian islands, bound as they are as "kith and kin" to Grenadians; there are, after all, almost as many Grenadians living in Trinidad as in Grenada itself, and it is no accident that the most famous of all Trinidadian calypsonians, the Mighty Sparrow, is a Grenadian by birth. For all of them, it is almost not too much to say that the spectacle of an American war fleet and army divisions descending on them must have had the same shattering effect as the aboriginal Antillean Indians must have felt as they first encountered Columbus's galleons and the Spanish conquistadors.[1]

The long-term consequences will take time to make themselves evident. But it is not too soon to say what they will be like. The Commonwealth Caribbean has now been drawn directly into the global struggle between capitalism and socialism and, more particularly, into the worldwide hegemonic struggle between the two global superpowers of the United States and the Soviet Union. From now on, West Indians, for good or ill, are on the front line of those struggles, both as participants and victims. They have entered into a new, harsh phase of their history. What that will mean in the years to come, in politics, social life, regional relationships, even psychological states of mind, has yet to be seen. But the consequences will be there; and they will be deep, traumatic, and far-reaching. Like Orpheus in the underworld, we have finally descended into a new, dark, unknown, and perhaps even terrifying region of which we know practically nothing. It is almost as if the age of West Indian innocence had come to an end.[2]

2

The Caribbean Background

It is important to place the destruction of the Grenada Revolution within the framework of the Caribbean historical development. In one way, of course, it is something new, for it marks the triumph of the modern counterrevolution of our day. In another way, however, it is something old. For Caribbean history from its very beginnings with the conquest has been a history of violence. Its midwife has been force, not persuasion. It has not been the sort of quiet, imperceptible change from generation to generation, with precedent broadening down to precedent, each successive change flowing naturally from the other, and which explains the institutional continuity and social placidity of, say, English history. Its seminal moments have been moments of violent upheaval, of bloody struggles, of widespread social and cultural shock.

The European colonizers, at the first encounter of the Discovery, brought with them not only the violence of the European weaponry of the time but also the institutionalized violence, first of the Atlantic slave trade and then of domestic chattel slavery. The slave trade, with all of its barbarity, denuded Africa in order to populate the Indies with a transplanted, servile labor force to work the new sugar plantations. The results, as Marx observed, quoting Cairnes, displayed the essential elements of a slave economy which took out of the human chattel in the shortest space of time the utmost amount of exertion it was capable of putting forth.[1] In turn, the Europeans brought with them the violence of their imported wars, first between imperial Spain and its Protestant rivals in the sixteenth, seventeenth, and eighteenth centuries, and then, after 1898, between the United States and its rival empires in the region. There was "no peace beyond the line" as the colonizing powers injected their historic antagonisms, not only political but also religious, into the New World. The Caribbean became, in Juan Bosch's phrase, an imperial frontier.[2]

All this, in turn, generated the violence of organized Caribbean resistance to the European regimes, as, at successive moments, that resistance was undertaken by Arawak and Carib Indians, rebellious African slaves, Maroon fighters, Haitian and Cuban revolutionaries, and the rest. It is in that sense, indeed, that Grenada provides yet another noble example of that record of resistance. For the handful of soldiers and workers, both Grenadian and Cuban, who organized their pockets of resistance against the helicopter gunships and the navy bombers of the U.S. invaders in October 1983, often with nothing much more than rifles, are as much the hero-martyrs of Caribbean freedom as were, before them, all those other forces. They are in the footsteps, in a historic continuity of resistance of, speaking particularly of Grenada itself, the Carib warriors of the seventeenth century who committed suicide by hurling themselves over the cliffs of the northern island district of Les Sauteurs rather than surrender, and the small band led by the mulatto Jules Fédon, who fought the English in 1795; and, speaking more generally of the Caribbean as a whole, of the Haitian slave masses who after 1791 defeated the crack regiments of Napoleon's imperial army, and of the Cuban soldier-patriots who after 1868 held the Spanish forces at bay on and off for some thirty years. Grenada 1983 is only the latest chapter of that tremendous record.[3]

It is absolutely urgent that the peoples of the English-speaking subregion should understand this background. For in a very important way they have allowed themselves to hide from these realities. They have been seduced into believing that they live in a region of English constitutional liberties and privileges, thus accepting the myths, variously, that Queen Victoria "freed the slaves" in 1834 or that British benign colonialism "gave" them their independence in the 1960s. They thus forget that, as Michael Craton has so well demonstrated in his book *Testing the Chains,* emancipation was really the end-result of two centuries of slave rebellions.[4] They also forget that Independence was the end-result of some forty years of anticolonial nationalist struggle, including the working-class labor revolts of the 1930s.[5] Force, not will, was the basis of the colonial state; and it was ultimately force, and not will, that brought it to an end.

British West Indians, as a result, lived in a dream world. They have never bridged the gap between illusion and reality. Even their educated classes, who should have known better, have fondly believed that creole dictatorships only happen in Haiti or Guatemala, without seeing that in the form, for example, of Prime Minister Forbes Burnham's one-party police state in Guyana, dictatorships exist among themselves. Their intractable anglophilism persuades them that the English tradition will always save them. They cannot see that under the thin veneer of assimilated anglophone traditions there lies a dark underworld of violence, both in social class conflict and in ethnic animosities, which at any moment can erupt, as they did in the British Guiana of the 1960s and in Trinidad in 1970. Much of that violence has its own indigenous roots. But much of it is also imported. There are still very few West Indians who can recognize that the apocalyptic Jonestown event of 1978 was occasioned by the meeting of Caribbean religious hospitality and American social violence. A cult leader like Jim Jones believed that he could solve the problem of his aged, black, poor congregation by setting up an idyllic utopia in the Guyana jungle. Men like President Ronald Reagan, Secretary of State George Schultz, and Defense Secretary Caspar Weinberger believe that they can solve the problems of their own American imperialism by setting up a "democratic" colony in Grenada. It is not too much to say that both of those types, in their different ways, exemplify the deep, psychotic sickness of the American capitalist society, obsessed with the reality and images of power, speed, and violence. By twist of fate, the Caribbean becomes the victim of that sickness. Underneath events—Jonestown and Grenada—which appear so different there runs, in fact, a profound and close correlation. Whether they realize it or not, the English-speaking Caribbean people are now inescapably involved in that sickness, with all of its brutality and insanity. They did not learn the lesson of Jonestown. They cannot afford not to learn the lesson of Grenada.[6]

3

The Island Background

The essential point to keep in mind about modern Grenada is that it has been an underdeveloped tropical rural economy with a rigid class structure almost unchanged since the emancipation period of the early nineteenth century. All of the political movements since 1945 have been shaped by and have reflected that social structure: Gairyism itself, the New Jewel Movement after 1973, and even—despite its new Marxist-Leninist vocabulary— the People's Revolutionary Government after 1979. The well-known West Indian multilayered "pigmentocracy" generated a social structure in which class was closely related to color, so that black, brown, and white were accurately reflected in corresponding social and racial echelons. That correlation, of course, was the heritage of slavery, so that social respectability depended, in large part, on each person's racial ancestry. It was, in essence, a creole Victorian society in which everybody "knew his place." Its only saving grace, perhaps, was that in such a socially circumscribed situation everybody knew everybody else's family lineage, so that nobody could "put on airs" about who they were and where they stood in the general social-racial structure. In such a small society the vulgar democracy of social gossip made social pretensions a precarious game: everybody knew where everybody else "came from" in terms of social origin. At the same time, in a small society so class conscious it was almost inevitable that most leaders in the political game, from T. A. Marryshow in the 1940s and 1950s on, should come from the lighter-skinned middle-class elements. That was even the case with the leadership of the New Jewel Movement after it was founded in 1973.[1]

Grenada, in brief, was a small-island socioeconomic structure of a comparatively simple nature. It consisted of a *comprador* bourgeois group of estate owners and merchant import-export capitalists imbued with the in-voice mentality, hardly a sophisticated national bourgeoisie; a small shop-keeper class; a small subgroup of university people educated abroad; the lower middle-class elements of civil servants, teachers, public-service workers, police, and others, most of them ill-trained and badly paid; a tiny industrial working class which was in fact outnumbered by the vast major-ity of semisubsistence small proprietors and land workers, who were nei-ther pure peasantry nor pure proletariat but a crude mixture of both.[2] That majority of peasant farmers and estate tenants was, in fact, from the eman-cipation period right up to the period of World War II, the basic resource of the economy, constituting—as the 1896 report of the local Agricultural Commission put it—an element as vital to the island economy as was the backbone to a vertebrate animal.[3] Lacking, of course, any real independent political power of its own, that majority was also the most oppressed class of the old colonial regime. Although economically somewhat better off than the depressed sugar estate tenantry of St. Vincent and St. Kitts, as late as 1945, as the Moyne Commission report pointed out, the peasant farmers and tenants still had no defense mechanisms such as trade unions, and it was not until 1947 that the Cooperative Nutmeg Association was formed to protect the small nutmeg growers against the monopolistic power of the local dealers and the North American buyers.[4]

Social relations, in their turn, were shaped by those economic condi-tions. Grenada has a population of about 100,000, all crowded together in an island measuring 120 square miles, with a capital (St. George's) that was more a small preindustrial township than even a secondary metropolis like Port-of-Spain, Trinidad, or Kingston, Jamaica. Its general social atmos-phere was not so much one of class conflict between worker and capitalist, as in a modern industrial society, as it was one of relationships between "folk" and "elite" marked by seigneurial paternalism and political client-age. It was the "little man" against the "big boys." Grenada, like all of the other Windward and Leeward Islands, remained a semifeudal economy in which the merchants, the estate owners, and the middle-class civil servants ruled the inarticulate peasant and worker with an iron hand. Social injus-tice, not social community, marked all relationships. Work grievances, then, were not just bread-and-butter complaints as they were a simmering resentment against social indignities. As Rottenberg observed in the Grenadian case in the 1950s, a reference by a popular leader in a public meeting to a planter who is "playing white," or to the reserving of office employment for children of the "better" families, or to claims that land planted in cocoa by the workers' forefathers should by right belong to their descendants, would provoke more emotional response than a reference to the insufficiency of the daily wage rate.[5]

That general class separatism was compounded by another form of social separatism between town and countryside. A local commentator in the early 1960s noted that this was in the case of St. Lucia, typical of the small Eastern Caribbean societies. He wrote:

> The poor, barefoot, uneducated, unsophisticated, shy people in the out-districts, looked up with awe and fawning respect to the well-dressed, well-spoken and better-read city folk—the people who could boast of electricity, who met and hobnobbed with people from abroad, who went or probably might have gone to college. Castries [the capital] was St. Lucia in every way. Administrators and Governors without end continued to tour the island exactly twice during their tenure of office—once when they assumed and once when they shed the mantle of office. The out-districts were a Never-Never land where people walked silently and uncomplainingly in misery and neglect, where people waited hand and foot on leadership and direction, and the occasional word of wisdom from the city folk of Castries. That was St. Lucia only twelve years ago. It is still the image of St. Lucia that innumerable city folk still believe represents the real St. Lucia today.[6]

That, too, was pretty much the Grenada situation.

Grenada, of course, like St. Lucia and the other islands, was at that time a dependent British colonial society, suffering from all of the ravages of colonialism. It is true that, in the British colonial service, Jamaica might get a Lord Olivier or Trinidad a Sir Murchison Fletcher as governors, both of them sympathetic to the popular cause. But the smaller islands would not get that cream of the crop, and more likely would have, as colonial administrators, the failed Oxford "passman" rather than the brilliant Cambridge wrangler. They brought with them, true enough, honesty, incorruptibility, and a sense of duty and service. But this was also accompanied by their own special brand of English racial superiority, the insufferable English assumption that, without saying so vulgarly, they were the world's superior race. The Colonial Office expected them to keep "law and order," and few of them stepped outside that writ. They accepted the well-known hospitality of the West Indian planter class, and their dispatches to London invariably reflected the interests and prejudices of that class.

In response, the West Indian creole political leaderships, including the Grenadian, with honorable exceptions, accepted the subordinate role imposed on them by colonial rule. That could be seen in Grenadian politics of the 1940s and 1950s. There were men like F. B. Patterson who, although an avowed socialist, allowed the family conservatism of the old estate at Belvedere to condition his outlook on life, so that he was always known to his Carriacou constituents as "Mas Fred." There was the lawyer-politician F. B. Renwick, whose record as planter, lawyer, and newspaper proprietor probably helps to explain why a Grenadian reporter could say that the presence of a lawyer on a public platform, addressing schoolchildren and their parents on their duty to society, despite his vast knowledge of the law of torts, would cause the same amount of fear and speculation as the visible approach of a hurricane. There were, again, politicians like the dentist John Watts and the lawyer John Knight who used their middle-class prestige to build, as best they could, political parties and trade unions, which were really nothing more than personal vehicles. Finally, of course, there was T. A. "Teddy" Marryshow himself, considered by everybody who knew him, including the present author, to be a noble and honorable man. His great record of public service began as a young reporter for the old *Federalist and Grenada People* under the aegis of the patriot-editor William Galway Donovan, a Negro of Irish extraction, who combined black pride with the old ancestral Irish hatred of the English, and later went on to become the acknowledged leading champion of the federal idea. But for all that, Marryshow was, at best, a West Indian Fabian, a Royalist-Loyalist who could never bring himself to fight the colonial power except on its own polite terms. His vanity, his enjoyment of Buckingham Palace garden parties and parliamentary receptions at Westminster, and his comic pursuit of royal personages everywhere, made it impossible for him to engage the fight in any other terms.[7]

His, of course, was the dilemma of all of the West Indian leaders of the time. The dilemma was finely stated in the report of those leaders who met in Roseau, Dominica, in 1932. The report of the conference stated:

> Powerless to mould policy, still more powerless to act independently, paralysed by the subconscious fear of impending repression and therefore bereft of constructive thought, the West Indies politician has hitherto been inclined to dissipate his energies in acute and penetrating but embittered and essentially destructive criticism of the government on which, nevertheless, he has waited for the initiation of all policies intended to benefit his people, and which he has expected to assume the full responsibility for all necessary decisions. His political life has been overshadowed by a government too omnipotent and omnipresent, and has had little opportunity for independent growth.[8]

Grenadian politics and politicians, like the others, suffered from that general condition of impotence.

4

1951: Gairy, Gairyism, and the Populist Revolt

Despite the condition of political impotence, popular forces within the Caribbean were beginning yet another chapter in colonial resistance. It started with the labor riots that swept across the Caribbean in 1934–38, including not only the British colonies but also the U.S. colonies like Puerto Rico. Silenced momentarily by World War II, the riots resumed after 1945. In Puerto Rico, the unrest produced the struggle of Pedro Albizu Campos and his Nationalist party to terminate what they saw, surely correctly, as the illegal occupation of the island by U.S. imperialism after 1898. In the British West Indies it stimulated the emergence of a new group of popular, populist political leaders espousing the cause of the downtrodden masses, the "barefoot man" in Trinidadian parlance, the "sufferers" in Jamaican parlance, the "little man" in Guyanese parlance. Alexander Bustamante in Jamaica; Uriah Butler, a little earlier, in Trinidad; Robert Bradshaw in St. Kitts; Ebenezer Joshua in St. Vincent; Clement Payne in Barbados; Vere Bird in Antigua—all these leaders were thrown up, almost overnight, by the "revolt of the masses" rooted in general social, political, and economic grievances. With universal suffrage finally obtained, starting with the Jamaica Constitution in 1944, and with formal constitutional independence gained, starting with Jamaica and Trinidad in 1962, these leaders came into power, variously as chief ministers and prime ministers, supported, for the first time, by electorates participating in politics on the basic principle of "one man, one vote."

The rise of Eric Gairy, and Gairyism, in Grenada has to be seen as part of this new development. A black person of low social origin and limited education, Gairy returned to Grenada after working in the Aruba oil refineries during the wartime employment boom, and where he had learned the agitator's art. There is not much evidence that he had obtained his radical attitudes from reading the literature; almost anyone who talked with him would conclude—as I did when he was chief minister under the Crown Colony regime before independence in 1974—that he seemed to be almost tongue-tied in the presence of academics. He was certainly not like Bustamante in Jamaica, whose charm and forthrightness enabled him to take on everybody, including the "intellectuals," nor was he an intellectual in politics like Eric Williams in Trinidad since 1955. As with the other street politicians of the time, for example, Butler in Trinidad and Bustamante in Jamaica, Gairy's ideas were a curious mixture of God, Marx, and the British Empire. His program was a sort of nondoctrinal "laborism," certainly not socialism in any serious sense. Perhaps it is not surprising that Gairy's contribution to Caribbean political thought should have been his lobbying campaign, in his appearances as government leader at the United Nations, to persuade that body to investigate the phenomenon of unidentified flying objects.

Yet it would be dangerous to dismiss Gairy as simply a buffoon, as did so many at the time. With all of his limitations, he played an important role in the rising political consciousness of the Grenadian masses. Starting his political organization in the early 1950s, he presented himself as the popular champion against the white oligarchy and the brown middle class of the island society, clearly pursuing a politics of *opéra bouffe* against those elements. There is a strain of ribald irreverence in West Indian life, and Gairy brought it out into the open by his guying of prominent local personalities in his inventive market-square orations. He had a large following; for whereas Marryshow's constituency was that of the urban St. George's district, Gairy's was that of the rural folk. He himself had been slighted when the local elite tennis club would not accept him for membership, so that his own private resentments became those of his followers. When he led a group of scared estate workers into the Santa Maria tourist hotel and demanded they be served a meal, or when he told domestic servant girls to go on strike against a system of minor slavery that required them to work from 6:00 A.M. to 9:00 P.M., so that they had no time even for a bath, he was helping to destroy their ingrained deference to their "betters." He gave them a new self-respect. He gained from them in return a fanatical hero worship, because they saw in him all of the tongue-sticking defiance of the master class that they themselves could not afford to take on.[1]

Singham's book has analyzed this situation in the Weberian terms of charisma.[2] In many ways, it is a plausible analysis. Gairyism became a scenario of the hero and the crowd. He was "Uncle" Gairy. They were "my people." In Weberian terms, according to Singham, Gairy represented the charismatic leader, while the colonial administrators represented the theme of rationalistic-legal politics and bureaucratic administration. He ruled by recruiting a band of disciples dominated by his charisma; they ruled as bureaucrats within an ordered hierarchy, with their official life clearly demarcated from their private lives, and none of them being indispensable. The long struggle between Gairy and Administrator James Lloyd could be seen in those terms. Gairy's offense, from the official viewpoint, was that he systematically violated all of the rules and conventions of the legal-bureaucratic order. The violations, of course, became worse after independence in 1974, for the prime minister, as head of the new independent state, was now master in his own house. To argue—as some critics have done—that the Weberian argument does not hold because, as later events showed, the object of charisma could move from one person to another, that is, from Gairy to Bishop, is to miss the point, for there is nothing in the argument to preclude such transference of popular feeling.

The transference took place, of course, because Gairy possessed neither the moral fiber nor the intellectual capacity to transform his brand of *sans-culottisme* into a genuine social radicalism. He sought to convert it, rather, into a one-man state. Even before Independence the report of the 1962 enquiry that precipitated the British government's suspension of the local constitution had itemized Gairy's offenses: the deliberate and systematic violation of financial regulations, the browbeating of public servants, the deliberate destruction of the morale of the civil service, the illegal purchase with public monies of luxury items, including an expensive piano and a phonograph for the chief minister's residence.[3] The later Duffus report, after independence, painted an even grimmer picture: the victimization of public servants by arbitrary transfer or termination of employment; selective concessions made to favored business supporters; acts of harassment, police brutality, imprisonment without bail or trial, often undertaken by the infamous "Mongoose Gang"; the subornment of police officers, magistrates, and other officers of the law, converting them into agents of the Gairyite state; all of it adding up to a regime of terror, culminating in murder, as with the death of Maurice Bishop's father in 1974.[4] To all this was added, through repressive public legislation, the harassment of opposition media by means of the Newspaper Amendment Act of 1975, the ban in 1976 on the use of public address systems, the limits placed on trade union strike action by the Essential Services Amendment Act of 1978, and much else. Moreover, there was the systematic degradation of the legislative and executive branches of the state. The Cabinet, under the independence constitution, took over all of the decision-making power of the civil service, so that every matter from the hiring of a janitor to the building of a school had to be submitted to Cabinet, with Gairy's voice and vote supreme. The House of Representatives became a theatrical farce, with the object of the government majority simply being to ridicule the opposition, indulge in raucous invective, and vote blindly for the leader. As one observer remarked, the Grenada Parliament had become a rare caricature of the Westminster model.[5]

The populist movement, which began in 1951, could have become an agent for creative change but instead became a vehicle for destructive personalism. Power corrupts; and there can be little doubt that during these last years Gairy's character seriously declined. He lost his early radicalism, such as it was, seeking friends and cronies in the more reactionary of the group of big estate owners. He sought the help, of all places, of the Pinochet fascist regime in Chile to build up his military apparatus, in order to crush the opposition, which he saw not as critics but as enemies. Yet even that did not save him. Even the men of property of the local oligarchy finally turned against him, for he had come to embarrass them with his "squandermania," his neglect of the economy, his raiding of the public treasury, his United Nations appearances, the displeasure of London, and not least of all his sexual appetite of which some of their own womenfolk became victims, for after 1979 his successors found incriminating photographic evidence of his escapades in his palatial Mount Royal residence. Like all the little sawdust Caesars of his type, he finally brought about his own downfall.

5

1973: The Rise of the New Jewel Movement

In 1951–79 the opposition to Gairy, both parliamentary and extraparliamentary, naturally involved different groups and underwent various permutations. The two main documentary sources that describe and interpret that development are the book by the Jacobs brothers, *Grenada: The Route to Revolution,* and the Casa de las Américas prize-winning book by David E. Lewis, *Reform and Revolution in Grenada 1950–1981.*[1] It is now easy to see, in retrospect, that the struggle would end with a violent solution. But at the time, and even up to the 1976 election, all sides accepted the democratic-parliamentary route. That consensus was in fact only shattered by Gairy's paranoid view that he was engaged in a life-and-death struggle with hated opponents. It is true that the Jacobs book, in particular, tends to write about the whole experience in a tone of Marxist-Leninist determinism, almost as if the New Jewel Movement (NJM), founded in 1973, was playing the role of a revolutionary vanguard party consciously leading the masses to the predestined end. But that is a dubious thesis; it is probably more accurate to say that the NJM, like all other actors in the story, was reacting pragmatically, day by day, to events as they unfolded, including the denouement of the hastily prepared coup d'état of March 13, 1979.

Naturally enough, the initial opposition to Gairy came from the local propertied class, whose interests he challenged. Even Marryshow, largehearted as he was, was hostile to the unionizing and recruiting movement which Gairy undertook with the rural masses, marked by the successful general strike of 1951 with its "land for the landless" program. For the propertied class, Gairy was a loud-mouthed upstart whose ideas seemed revolutionary; nor did they care for his friendship with other black businessmen and budding capitalists who threatened, as they saw it, to become a new black elite in the society. Their favored political vehicle therefore became the Grenada National party (GNP) of Dr. John Watts and his ally Herbert Blaize, the Carriacou ward leader, and which held two terms of office during 1957–61 and 1962–67. During these years Gairy tended to fade as Grenada became involved in the politics of the West Indies Federation[2] and, after the collapse of the federation in 1962, the debate about the possibility of the formation of a unitary state between Grenada and Trinidad and Tobago.[3] He returned, however, in full force in the election of 1967, reelected again in 1972, and finally receiving new institutional bases of power with independence in 1974.

The real irony of this period, perhaps, is that, as both the Jacobs and the Lewis accounts show, neither Gairy's political organization, the Grenada United Labour party nor the Watts-Blaize Grenada National party constituted in any real sense a threat to the Grenada dependent capitalist economy and its class defenders. As their various public statements and programs showed, both parties supported the principle of private ownership of property, a continuing relationship with the British colonial power, general acceptance of established class relationships in the local society, and the endemic habit of elitism in the local politics. Most of the legislation passed by their respective governments favored the interests of the established dominant groups. Even the nature of their candidates for public office exhibited the same bias: thus, in the early 1951 election the six victorious candidates of the Gairy ticket were three members of the merchant-planter class, one printer, one agricultural worker, and Gairy himself as a trade unionist; while in 1957–72 the GNP fielded altogether a total of fifty-two electoral candidates, with only one of them coming from the working class.[4] Had it had any instinct of statesmanship, the Grenada dominant class would have accepted Gairy in much the same way as, at the same time, the white Barbadian oligarchy had finally accepted Grantley Adams just as the top "21 families" of the Jamaican economy had accepted Bustamante and Norman Manley. Had the Grenadian upper class done that they would have saved themselves a lot of trouble. But they failed that test. In the final resort, then, they jumped from the frying pan of Gairyism into the fire of NJM socialism.

The genesis of the NJM is of peculiar interest. It had its beginnings in the late 1960s and early 1970s, in typical West Indian fashion, in the formation of small private groups of middle-class persons, some belonging to the intelligentsia, not necessarily politically oriented, meeting to discuss the issues of the day. Such groups had proliferated in Trinidad and Jamaica during the 1940s and 1950s. They now appeared, a little later, in the Windward and Leeward Islands. But since political neutrality is almost impossible in small-island societies such groups rapidly became politicized. Involving young men like Maurice Bishop, Unison Whiteman, Kendrick

Radix, Selwyn Strachan, and Teddy Victor, as well as young women like Esther Henry, they merged into the New Jewel group and later the People's Alliance of 1976, which made them the official parliamentary opposition after the election of that year.[5]

General forces and events, both internal and external, led to that politicization. Internally, there was the increasingly authoritarian behavior of the Gairy machine, including its growing militarization. A series of events revealed Gairy's determination, as he put it, to meet steel with steel: the victimization of the hospital nurses who staged their protest demonstration in 1970; the Grenville episode of 1973 when the NJM leaders were savagely beaten by the Gairy mafia elements; the repressive actions taken against the prolonged strike of 1973–74 protesting the government's decision to go ahead with independence negotiations without adequate guarantees for the constitutional maintenance of civil rights, not to speak of a real referendum on the issue. Indeed, the popular resistance against Gairy's bid for independence showed that, for the first time, a West Indian people was not prepared to embrace the conventional popular euphoria concerning independence, for the more progressive elements had come to perceive that independence as a formal constitutional gesture had done little to change the social conditions of the "independent" territories of Jamaica, Trinidad, and Barbados, but had merely replaced a colonial condition with a neocolonial condition. Gairy certainly had no bright new plan to change the basic dependent character of the Grenada economy; and the Anguilla episode at much the same time in 1969, in which that small ward territory seceded from its major partner St. Kitts-Nevis, only to have the rebellion put down by an invading British task force, showed that at least the smaller West Indian territories had their doubts about the advantages to be gained from a merely ceremonial detachment from the British colonial empire. The cure could be worse than the disease.[6]

The external influences were equally important. The Grenadian progressive movement was influenced, naturally enough, by the general liberalizing influence of the Black Power Movement of the time, as well as by the ideological influence of the Cuban Revolution. Eric Williams had written, earlier, of the influence of English liberalism and Third World nationalism on the independence movement after 1945, commencing, in his own case, with his experience as a young colonial student at Oxford in the 1930s.[7] But this, now, was a post-Williams generation. The Rodney "riots" of 1968 in Jamaica and the "February revolution" of 1970 in Trinidad were influenced by the Black Power and militant civil rights movements in the United States, which in turn influenced the Grenada radicals. Both Maurice Bishop and Bernard Coard belonged to the group of young people of the West Indian "brain drain," encountering all of these movements in their studies abroad, Bishop studying law at London, Coard doing economics at Brandeis and politics at Sussex. Coard, in particular, had made the centerpiece of his academic studies the plight of black people in the imperialist world system—the black man in Boston, the West Indian child in Britain—and his research had convinced him that violent struggle and not liberal compromise was the answer.[8] Education, indeed, was a vital factor. In Grenada the growth of both secondary and higher education helped generate a more informed group of younger people at least susceptible to progressive ideas: between 1946 and 1970 the number of students attending secondary school increased from 751 to 4,967, and between 1960 and 1970 the number of university-degreed persons rose from 193 to 352.[9] These educational advances may not have given birth, as the Jacobs book optimistically claims, to the formation of a "radical intelligentsia." But they certainly, at least, produced a body of educated young people predisposed to question the erratic irresponsibility of Gairyite behavior.[10]

The NJM, born out of such circumstances, rapidly came to see that the general predicament required, more than anything else, a multigroup united front. By 1970, certainly, Gairy's eccentricities had reached the point of clinical morbidity. He had become, like Ramfis Trujillo in the Dominican Republic and Jean-Claude "Baby Doc" Duvalier in Haiti, the playboy of the Western world. Except for a few favored friends he had alienated every group in the society. All of the established churches resented his brand of vulgar superstition and cultism and his public identification with the dubious Rosicrucian sect. All of the trade unions, except his own, resented his interference with union matters. The middle-class professional groups, the Jaycees, the Lions, and the Rotary clubs, were affronted by his violation, as they saw it, of the tenets of honest and decent citizenship. Most important of all, perhaps, the business organizations, from the Chamber of Commerce down to the small shopkeepers, had become alarmed by his general unpredictability, his interference with employer-worker relations, his demands for payoffs, his efforts to corrupt the judiciary so that, instead of upholding traditional business class interests, it would become a tool of the prime minister's private whims and fancies. All this meant, in the final resort, that these different interests joined in the united front against Gairy. Significantly, then, the 1973 episode in which the NJM leadership was assaulted by the Gairyite police occurred when those leaders had been on an errand to Grenville to discuss continuing strike activities with the town's small shopkeepers and merchants. It is at least clear that by the early 1970s the business establishment had become convinced that Gairy was too unreliable as a supporter of their interests, just as in the Dominican Republic the business oligarchy had become convinced by 1961 that Trujillo was no longer their man and, somewhat later, the Nicaraguan business oligarchy decided that Somoza was too unreliable as a custodian of their interests. In none of these cases were the business groups by any means revolutionary. They simply wanted a rationalistic state order, free of capricious dictatorial eccentricities and power hunger, which could guarantee freedom for their capitalist interests.

The NJM manifesto of 1973 reflected those multiform concerns in the Grenada case. It was not overtly socialist. It concerned itself, in the main, with particular problems of housing, health, food, and education. It urged a program of land redistribution based on a scheme of cooperative farms, free education up to the secondary-school level, a national health plan, and the nationalization of the banking and insurance sectors of the economy.[11] This program, after all, was necessary prudence, for it is certain that most of the groups represented in the "Committee of 22" were not ready for more radical proposals. The "Committee of 22," as a matter of fact, had been set up in 1973 to coordinate the anti-Gairy struggle and was comprised of groups so disparate ideologically—from the Progressive Labor and General Workers Union to the Lions Club—that it could only speak in very general terms. It is not even certain, as the Jacobs book claims, that the principle of "democratic centralism" adopted by the NJM party could be acclaimed as an element of "scientific socialism."[12] For that principle, emphasizing the need for common accord in decision making, is really not essentially different from the principle of the Cabinet's collective responsibility in the British constitutional system. There is very little that is uniquely socialist about it. In any case, all this was academic, for by the time the decade was ending it was clear that the situation was not one of program but one, quite simply, of the physical survival of the opposition groups, and most notably the NJM. That crisis was finally resolved by the predawn coup d'état of March 13, 1979.

6

March 13, 1979: The Coup D'État

If the first explosion of the smoldering Grenada volcano was the emergence of Gairyism, the second was the coup d'état of March 13, 1979; just as the third was to be October 19, 1983, and the fourth October 25, 1983. It would perhaps be trite to say that all of those events, following each other in such a short time, reverberated throughout the Caribbean as surely as the Mount Pelée volcanic eruption of 1902 did physically. But it is nonetheless true. Especially, of course, in the English-speaking Caribbean, for such events had been common enough in Cuba, Haiti, and the Dominican Republic to be accepted philosophically almost as a way of life. It is no longer possible to hold on to the self-righteous conceit that "it could never happen here."

The immediate occasion of the coup was the information relayed by elements within the Gairy army and police forces on March 12 regarding Gairy's instructions for the assassination of the NJM leadership during his absence from the island. There has been no independent verification of this, but everything we know about Gairy and Gairyism certainly makes it not at all implausible. Three things may immediately be said of the event. In the first place, it showed the vulnerability of the small-island governments to internal subversion. As Secretary-General Shridath Ramphal of the Commonwealth put it somewhat later, "it takes only twelve men in a boat to put some of those governments out of business."[1] The very speed of the operation—the main army barracks, the radio station, and all island police stations seized within a brief twelve hours—testifies to the truth of the observation. Second, it showed how easily, too, the bullet could replace the ballot given certain circumstances. Third, and finally, the claim by the new revolutionary government in its first official declaration, that the event constituted "the seizure of state power by the Grenadian people," may perhaps be questioned, since it was in fact an act undertaken by a small group of men in the name, unsolicited, of a populace who knew nothing about it until it was over. It is true that if you plan to overthrow the state you do not undertake a public referendum to determine the support you have. But it was, nonetheless, a private action, not a popular uprising. At the beginning, then, the coup could only claim tacit consent. How, later on, that tacit consent became real active consent is the history of the following four years in which, indubitably, the new regime gained real popular support.

But when the larger considerations of the event are examined, there are implications even greater than these. West Indian reaction from the beginning was polarized between the condemnation of the right and the acclamation of the left. The right attacked the violation of constitutional legality. The left saw the event as justification of their critique of the imported British "Westminster model" of government, which they claimed was farcically inappropriate as a constitutional mechanism for solving the real problems of West Indian society; their literature on that subject had really been an elaboration of Rousseau's gibe that the English are only free at election times. Of all the long-run consequences of Grenada 1979–83 it is this ideological polarization that is, perhaps, the most damaging, converting everybody into either a friend or an enemy or, even worse, either a CIA agent on the one hand or a "subversive communist" on the other.

One of the most thoughtful assessments of the coup d'état in this general debate was that of the Trinidad Tapia Movement member Allan Harris, written almost immediately after the event. It should be noted that that movement was an offshoot of the earlier New World Movement formed by the progressive intellectual elements of the regional university, being firmly constitutionalist in its radicalism and hostile to the Marxism-Leninism of other offshoot groups. Harris, subsequently, took a cautious view of the 1979 coup d'état, which is not to say that it was timid, for caution and timidity are two quite different things. Neither unconditionally condemning nor approving, he assessed the coup in terms of constitutional due process in relation to the state of democratic institutions in the region. The forcible overthrow of a government has to be seen within the setting of the following question: how far, in fact, does the constitutional process, including elections of the conventional style, reflect the general will of West Indian societies? Not so well, according to Harris:

> In the Caribbean . . . we do not merely have what have been termed "soft states," that is, states, or governments, which lack the authority and the means to impose the hard disciplines necessary for real transformation, but, more to the point, we seem to have soft societies, or

rather societies which are soft, or hollow, at the core. This condition has usually been ascribed to the lack of a large and strong middle class. Another, perhaps more revealing way of looking at it, would be to point to the large gap between a relatively small political and economic elite and the impoverished and impotent majority of the population. This extreme political and economic inequality is sustained by constitutional arrangements which are neo-colonial in the extent to which they exclude the multitude from the corridors of power, by deeply-rooted authoritarian and personalist political cultures, and by what are frankly still colonial, export-oriented, primary-producing economic systems.[2]

Harris continues,

What is politically significant about the extremes of wealth and poverty is not simply the absence of what is called a middle class, but as importantly, the institutional void which results. The populace lacks levers with which to control the government and the government lacks the advantage of mechanisms by means of which people are mobilized for constructive action. Elections are almost meaningless in such a context. Overwhelming electoral support does not translate into the capacity for effective government if the economic margin for manoeuvre is too small and if the institutional framework is deficient. Similarly, it is almost impossible to convert widespread popular disaffection into a real political alternative at the polls, if the material and cultural means for building it are not readily available, quite apart from the legal opportunity to do so. In effect, the emphasis placed on the existence of free and fair elections as a measure of democratic freedom serves to obscure the fact that elections ought to be merely the end of a complicated social process, and that in the Caribbean it is these crucial pre-conditions which are all too often missing.[3]

It follows, the argument concludes, that democracy (meaning the institutionalization of real and effective representation for all segments of the population) hardly exists in the region. If, then, a crisis of legitimacy exists—as in this case—this is not just a matter of elections but, more, a matter of additional forms of expressing the popular will, of new institutional methods, of new social experiments. The meaning and significance of the 1979 coup in Grenada are, therefore, at least, ambiguous. The right will continue to indulge in pious imprecations about the "destruction" of "democracy," overlooking the fact that democracy had virtually ceased to exist under Gairyism. The left will continue its habit of revolutionary sloganeering, celebrating the downfall of a tyrant, without fully appreciating that the coup may be seen as the inauguration of an era of openly illegitimate power in the region. For the argument is not that elections are irrelevant, but that they have to be accompanied by new forms of representation. A great deal more is necessary to breathe new life into the dying forms of West Indian democracy.[4]

This ambiguity of attitude—sympathetic yet at the same time apprehensive—was expressed at the same time by the West Indian legal expert Justice Aubrey Fraser. His *West Indian Law Journal* article frankly recognized the inevitability, indeed the moral legitimacy, of the coup d'état, for under Gairy democracy had in effect disappeared. The formation of the infamous "Mongoose Gang" in 1970—an illegal act since Gairy had no legal authority to establish law enforcement agencies outside the provisions of the law of the state—unleashed a series of unspeakable atrocities against the Grenada citizenry, constituting a veritable reign of terror. Those aware of these facts would not then deplore the forcible and summary dismissal of Gairy from public office, and the people of Grenada seem to have wanted a change. The fundamental problem, rather, remains that of how responsibly the new rulers will observe and honor the trusteeship that the people have endowed them with. Fraser wrote:

> Whatever the method of change, it is possible for the integrity of upright men to guide the country along the paths of progress; but because the perverseness of transgressors is capable of repeating the peril from which the citizens believe they have escaped, it is urgently important to resume constitutional form . . . . The history of man's experience continues to demonstrate that in the exercise of political power the dividing line between integrity and perverseness in some countries and in different periods is made to appear so woefully thin that the blurring of the boundary inhibits early detection by the people on whose behalf that power is exercised.[5]

The argument was important. For it was not just saying, in the biblical injunction, that those who triumph by the sword shall perish by the sword. It went beyond that to underline the question, in philosophical terms, of power, its usage and abuse. All power corrupts; and often not even the best intentions of those who wield it are enough to stay that corruption. The new revolutionary government, as Fraser shrewdly saw, would ultimately be judged in terms of that truth.

A final note on the 1979 coup concerns aspects of the event that interest the military historian. It was an amateur exercise, not unlike Castro's ill-fated 1953 Moncada Barracks attack in Santiago, Cuba, to which it has been compared. But unlike Moncada the coup succeeded because, first, the Gairy forces were not on the alert and, second, the element of total surprise was perfectly executed. The forty to fifty men who took part in the attack were poorly armed with old equipment, and they could have been easily repulsed by the better-armed Gairy soldiers and police. That disadvantage was neutralized by the element of surprise. For surprise is the secret of all successful military or naval operations, as the Japanese attack on Pearl Harbor in 1941 and the Israeli Entebbe raid of 1976 show. The enemy must be caught napping. The rebellious group itself had no history of combat experience, as was also to become painfully evident with the U.S. invasion four years later. It was the element of surprise that guaranteed the rebels' success; probably to their own astonishment, they found themselves in control of the state within one brief day. They must have felt as exuberant as Mussolini's band of Fascists after their march on Rome in 1922.

Another vital element of the operation was control of radio broadcasting. Grenada, like its sister small islands, is still a radio rather than a television society. The early seizure of the main radio station meant that any counterrevolutionary force, had it emerged, would have been denied access to the general population. Fanon's well-known essay on the role of radio in the Algerian Revolution emphasized that point, and the lesson was observed in the Grenada episode.[6]

The factor of geographical size was another key to success. In each of these small societies there is only one real township, that of the capital. The social and cultural significance of that fact has already been noted. Grenada 1979, for the first time, underlined the military significance of a contained island revolution. Revolution in larger countries is a different matter; for example, in the case of the Paris Commune of 1871, the counterrevolutionary force of the army of the Second Empire was able to use Versailles as a base of attack against rebellious Paris, and it was probably one of the fatal mistakes of the Commune not to march on Versailles early on. In the small West Indian societies, by contrast, the control of the capital means effectively the control of the island as a whole.

7

1979–1983: The Revolutionary Achievement

As the People's Revolutionary Government (PRG) set up shop after coming to power it is important to appreciate the shambles they inherited from Gairyism. For Gairyite populism was not what one West Indian scholar has called the "Marxist populism" of C.L.R. James.[1] It was, rather—as already noted—a bogus radicalism geared to the private interests of the dictator and his small clique of friends, completely uninterested in any fundamental reconstruction of the society or the economy. It was "one-man, High Priest politics," as the Grenadian street parlance described it. It meant that independent Grenada in 1979 was in no better shape than colonial Grenada in 1973.

It is not too much to say that Grenada, both as an economy and a society, was in a generally disastrous condition in 1979. It was, to begin with, a stagnant economy, characterized by negative real growth rates, double-digit inflation, high levels of unemployment, and continuing deficits in the balance of payments. It was a typical raw-product export economy, selling its agricultural products—spice, nutmeg, bananas and cocoa—for low revenue to export markets whose price levels it could not control, and importing everything else at inflated prices. In more general societal terms, social services typically identified with the modern welfare state were—where they existed—backward, inefficient, and operating with a dilapidated infrastructure. One-third of the population was afflicted with functional illiteracy. For some reason Grenadians have always suffered from eye problems leading to widespread blindness, but there existed no program to tackle the problem. Middle class people regularly traveled to Barbados and Trinidad for medical and dental care; for the majority there was no serious remedial system. The average rural school was a large, wooden, zinc-roofed building with classes divided by movable partitions; students were taught by ill-trained teachers, some 40 percent of whom, according to the Brizan report of 1981, entered the "profession" for pecuniary reasons only.[2] Nor did there exist any professionally competent institutional structure to meet any of these problems; in 1979 there was not even a Ministry of Trade to deal with, among other things, the crucial problems of an import-export economy. Limited employment opportunities meant that many more professional Grenadians were working abroad than in the island itself, while escape for lower-class Grenadians meant emigration, notably to Trinidad, many of them entering illegally through the so-called rat passage of the interisland schooners.

All in all, social and economic Grenada was trapped within a global capitalist system rooted in inequity, so that, to take a single telling example, a woman worker at home cracking nutmegs for a small wage of $7.10 a day, 150 pounds a day, would finally see the finished product sold abroad at the rate of $1.00 per single ounce: the real value of her labor thus in effect constituting some 300 times her daily wage rate.[3]

The four years of the revolution were, quite simply, a heroic effort in social and economic reconstruction and, at times, transformation. All of the available sources—the innumerable official pronouncements of the PRG state agencies, Prime Minister Maurice Bishop's published speeches, the carefully documented David Lewis thesis—testify to the personal dedication and the collective enthusiasm that went into that effort, now only too easily forgotten by all of the counterrevolutionary, reactionary forces only concerned, after October 1983, to vilify and denigrate the revolution, lock, stock, and barrel. There was, to begin with, the urgent task of modernizing the capital infrastructure of the economy. That meant long-term integrated planning, with an adequate institutional framework and proper collection of statistical data on all aspects of the national economy. As early as 1981, the government carried out both a population census and an agricultural census, both hitherto uncharted areas. They became the basis for infrastructural development. Within three years the regime could report, among other things, completion of the first phase in road development, especially the Eastern Main road; the establishment of the Central Water Commission, with a much improved water supply system; a new telephone system; a new generator for electricity supply; a new radio transmitter; more than sixty-seven new feeder roads to facilitate transport of agricultural products to the port areas, always a headache for the small West Indian peasant farmer; a new stone-crusher and asphalt complex; the Cuban gift of a new prefabricated concrete-unit and block-making plant; construction of warehouses for the Marketing and National Importing Board; construction of eight fish-selling centers with deep-freeze facilities aimed at encouraging local fish consumption; new factories to produce jellies and jams from local fruits, to offset the traditional taste patterns that have always preferred imported canned foods and disdained local products; and the planned dredging of the St. George's harbor to accommodate larger ships for trade and tourism.[4]

All this, of course, necessitated a new organizational structure in the area of statistical and financial planning. The regime had to teach its electorate that everything had to be paid for. This became the responsibility of the revamped public sector. New state agencies were set up to plan and administer, among other things, the thirty state farms inherited from the Gairy regime, new agro-industrial processing plants, and the new fishing and fish-processing industry. The new Grenada Development Bank, with funds being lent at easy repayment terms to small and medium farmers and business-people with the aim of financing any project, however small, was designed to increase production and employment, while the new publicly owned National Commercial Bank established a general policy of lending half of its funds to development projects and half to the established commercial sector. The new Marketing and National Importing Board, in turn, was set up to establish import and distribution rights over products such as cement, rice, and sugar, away from the old system of private commercial wholesale and retail monopoly, thus guaranteeing fairer prices for the consumer. The success of the new public financing structure is evident from the fact that donor aid was obtained not only from friendly revolutionary Third World governments ranging from Algeria to Tanzania but also from such orthodox lending agencies as the World Bank and the International Monetary Fund.[5]

Notice must be taken of the social-welfare aspects of the revolutionary achievement as well. The effort, essentially, was to increase the social wage of the Grenadian worker and farmer. The two crucial areas in this respect were, of course, education and health, both of them in almost primitive condition in 1979. Their planned reconstruction was started in 1980. In education, three phases were conducted, respectively, by the Centre for Popular Education (CPE), the National In-Service Teacher Education Programme (NISTEP), and the Community-School Day Programme (CSDP). The CPE program included the planned abolition of functional illiteracy, the development of technical skills, the reshaping of the school curricula, and much else, some of it accomplished with the expert aid of Paul Freire, head of the World Council of Churches literacy program. NISTEP, in its turn, tackled the problem of a school system in which two-thirds of the country's primary school teachers were seriously undertrained. It introduced a popular-based and accelerated training program, avoiding the costly and elitist sort of program traditionally sponsored by the University of the West Indies, as well as laying the foundations for new free secondary education for all children. Finally, CSDP initiated the practice of bringing into the schools skilled persons, from civil servants to musicians and persons skilled in the crafts, to bridge the gulf, so typical of the old conventional West Indian school system, between the world of work and the world of learning. How successful all of these programs were can be gauged from the fact that whereas under twenty-nine years of Gairyite rule only a single secondary school was built out of public funds, a second such school had been built just one year after 1979. Moreover, whereas in the last year of the Gairyite regime only three persons had obtained university scholarships to study abroad, in the first year of the revolution the total had risen to 109.[6]

The results in health were no less impressive. Prime Minister Bishop was able to announce on the secondary anniversary of the revolution that government had instituted, among other things, an eye hospital, an intensive care unit, a maternity clinic, X-ray facilities, and a operating theater; in addition, the number of resident dentists had tripled—from one dental clinic in 1979 there were now seven. The dentistry statistics are especially interesting in light of the particular fact that before 1979 one of the very few dentists in the island, Dr. John Watts, had been better known for his political ambitions than for his professional practice, and of the general fact that adequate dental service, not only in Grenada but in the West Indies as a whole, had been nonoperative because of the peculiar white myth, going back to slavery, that black people somehow did not suffer from dental problems.[7]

The ideological aspect of the revolutionary achievement has particularly to be noted. How much of all this was "socialism," in the generally accepted sense? Further, how much of it was radical "communism," as claimed by its enemies?

Looked at in comparative terms—that is, within the general framework of British, Scandinavian, Eastern European, and Caribbean economies—it would seem to any serious observer that the Grenadian model, as far as it went in four brief years, would have to be placed more in the British-Scandinavian camp than in any other. Its main programs were those of the "moderate" social-welfare economies, where the modern state has increasingly taken over responsibility for all those services vital to the public welfare. In the Caribbean alone, all of the "more developed" countries have instituted state health services, free and obligatory education, and subsidized low-cost public housing programs. All of them, likewise, even the more conservative like Barbados, are marked by extensive state planning administrative structures in areas such as tourism and developmental capital investment, including central or national banks that seek to control the twin Caribbean problems of a business sector that has always been reluctant to plough back its profits into local capital ventures geared to creating new wealth and an affluent middle class making the external balance-of-payments problem worse by its habit of irresponsible spending abroad. Even the Grenadian policy of putting the people to work through mass mobilization institutions was not too different, in principle, from the U.S. Civilian Conservation Corps of the old Rooseveltian New Deal; and even its military mobilization of the people, "the Revolution armed," was again not too different in principle from the state policy of limited and obligatory armed service for young males as in, to take only one example, Sweden. In this sense, the Grenada model was more "social welfarism" than socialism proper, not unlike the policies of the left-wing Michael Manley government in Jamaica in 1972–80.

Even more. The PRG government in 1979, for all of its official rhetoric, faced not a theory but a condition. Low productivity, economic backwardness, a peasantry fiercely independent and, like peasantries everywhere, imbued with the property instinct, a truly appalling scarcity of available managerial and technical skills, an antiquated infrastructure: all of that meant that a giant leap forward immediately into a full-blown socialism, not even to speak of communism, would have been at once romantic and impractical. The PRG, following the early NJM policy statements, elected to follow a tripartite developmental program based on an enlarged public sector, the private sector, and a new cooperative sector. The local business groups, after all, had been an integral element of the NJM; their reward was a recognized role in the new economic regime. Both government and the local Chamber of Commerce thus worked together, with remarkable harmony when all is considered, especially in the area of tourism, centered around the construction of the planned international airport at Point Salines. The concept of the "popular front" in the anti-Gairy period was thereby carried over into the new system.

It is thus difficult to accept the curious argument of a critic like Sebastian Clark, that the "mixed economy" policy was in reality a disguise under which the new regime was really conducting a program of genuine socialism.[8] It is equally difficult to accept the argument of critics like Fitzroy Ambursley—arguing the exact contrary—that the PRG regime was really a petit-bourgeois reformist government not seriously interested in moving forward to the necessary stage of radical socialism.[9] It is difficult to accept the Clark argument because it assumes that the PRG leaders were living a deceitful Jekyll and Hyde political existence, hardly believable to anyone who knew them personally. It is difficult, again, to accept the Ambursley argument because it runs counter to all of the known environmental factors of the Grenadian situation at the time. As already noted, this was a society in which all groups, from a Marxist-Leninist viewpoint, were ideologically backward, each suffering from its own "false consciousness." In such an environment a purely Marxist proletarian revolution was clearly out of the question. So also was a spontaneous rising of the masses along the lines advocated by Rosa Luxemburg in her debate with Lenin. The Jacobs brothers had seen that clearly when discussing the tactics and strategy adopted during the Gairyite period. "The idea," they wrote, "of a whole class of people rising up on one sunny day and overthrowing the oppressor class is idealist, romantic, and obviously impractical."[10] By the same token, the idea that later on, as Ambursley puts it, the PRG government should have undertaken immediately a proletarian offensive against the dominant class as a whole, must be seen as equally romantic, an exercise, indeed, in left-wing infantilism. For, in the circumstances of the moment, the new regime needed all the support that it would garner. A proletarian offensive would have needlessly alienated all of the groups who had already given as much as could be expected of them during the long period of opposition to Gairyism.

The point is worth further emphasis. The first obligation of every revolution is to survive. It cannot afford revolutionary heroics. That is why, after 1924 in the young Soviet Russia, Stalin insisted upon the policy of "socialism in one country" as against Trotsky's advocacy of "world revolution." That is why, too, in the Cuban case, Castro played down the policy of exporting the revolution to Latin America once Ché Guevara's ill-fated adventure in Ecuador showed that the necessary mass support for such a policy was not present in the Latin American peasant masses. Ambursley's argument, then, that the PRG regime was simply a "petit-bourgeois workers' state" misses the point. It was not genuinely socialist, according to his argument, because government ministers like Lloyd Noel, Kendrick Radix, Norris Bain, and Bernard Gittens came from the Grenadian middle- and upper-class "old families";[11] this is like saying that Engels could never be a communist because he was a wealthy Victorian industrialist. It further was argued that because so many party and government members were university graduates, that too must have contributed to a petit-bourgeois atmosphere, which is like saying that because men like C. Wright Mills in the United States or R. H. Tawney in Britain were university professors they could never be socialists. Even to think of the Jamaican Richard Hart, who later became the PRG attorney general, in petit-bourgeois terms is at once absurd and insulting, for he had been known throughout the Caribbean for some thirty years as a dedicated Marxist who, since his expulsion from the Jamaican Peoples National party in 1954 had suffered much for his beliefs.

Yet the anti-intellectual tone of this line of argument is not its worst feature. More damaging, altogether, was its temptation to see the local property-owning class as the leading enemy of the revolution. As far as we know that was not the case. There is no evidence to show that they at any time undertook any serious counterrevolutionary activity; many of them cooperated readily with the new government; the episode of the so-called Gang of 26, who attempted to publish an independent newspaper, hardly showed that they were a dangerous element; and in any case the same episode showed that they were easily contained. In sum, this line of criticism was even dangerous, for it assumed that the local Grenadian bourgeoisie was the leading threat to the survival of the revolution whereas, in fact, the real enemies were, first, the outside Caribbean bourgeoisie (who had had no Gairyite experience to educate them) and, second, the U.S. imperialists, who were determined to destroy the revolution from the very beginning.

Be that as it may, it is certain that, even if only out of prudence, the revolution maintained throughout its reliance on the "mixed economy" model. Whatever differences emerged later, there is no evidence that the policy was not supported throughout by all PRG elements, including Coard who, as a trained economist and minister of finance, knew better than anyone else the harsh constraints under which the economy labored. David Lewis, writing in early 1983, saw the implications of this clearly and concluded:

> At this early stage of the revolutionary process in Grenada the issue of a Marxist-Leninist orientation within the leadership, as well as that of the possibilities for a socialist transformation of the society are, for the Grenadian masses, unreal and academic problems. That is, whereas the future of the Revolution in Grenada, and of its achievements, depend greatly on the radical nature of the process as a whole, the essence of the Revolution at this point is to effectively mobilize the Grenadian masses, to educate them, and to improve their standard of living within the process of revolutionary change. This has meant that the process of change, given the massive underdevelopment of the country's political economy, is presently restricted to what the PRG has referred to as the "national democratic state."[12]

A somewhat different way of looking at the PRG economic track record has been suggested by another Caribbean observer, Anthony Maingot. There is, argues Maingot, a significant difference between the NJM 1973 manifesto and the later post-1979 PRG pronouncements. The first is a utopian declaration based on the old hope of an active peasantry producing surplus, combined with the modern idea of small-island agro-industry, as well as a nostalgic return to a simpler and more honest past; the second postulated, quite differently, the development of a modern state with a modern administrative apparatus, and now embracing a modern airport as support for tourism, which had earlier been rejected as encouraging "national-cultural prostitution." Implicit in this, although not openly stated, is the charge that the earlier utopian dream had been betrayed to an administrative statecraft based on a centralized hierarchy of command led by the organized vanguard party. Indeed, as Maingot's article is titled, Maingot's argument becomes a requiem for a West Indian utopia.[13]

It is tempting to say that this sort of criticism is in itself utopian. It cavalierly overlooks at least three crucial aspects of the case. In the first place, it neglects to note that all revolutionary change, as indeed all revolutions show, whether bourgeois or socialist, is a matter of dynamics, not of statics. Programs inevitably change in response to fresh circumstances. Next, it fails to understand that to oppose the state is one thing, to administer it is another. Every revolutionary group discovers pretty rapidly that, once in power, it must learn to accept the pressing constraints of administrative realities; the blueprints must be adjusted to what is possible. Finally, Maingot's argument almost seems to be saying that the PRG should have remained faithful to what he calls the earlier "revolutionary aspiration and conservative nostalgia." But is that practical or feasible? It assumes a sort of pastoral socialism that has never existed in the Caribbean, nor is likely to in the future. It caters to the sort of romanticism that persuaded Albizu Campos and the Puerto Rican Nationalist party in the 1930s and 1940s to believe that before the Americans came in 1898 there existed an idyllic Puerto Rico of seigneurial coffee *hacienderos* and contented *jibaros,* which in fact never existed at all. The Grenada policies shifted from 1973 to 1980 for the simple reason that, being a Westernized society, it came to see that progress meant modernization; the only real debate was whether modernization should take a socialist or a capitalist direction. Grenada is not Shangri-la; nor should it be. To argue otherwise is to come perilously near to saying that these small Caribbean islands should resign themselves to becoming isolated and charming idyllic spots for the delight of the tourists.

===

In retrospect, the major achievements of the revolution, apart from its social experiments, were two. The first was to undertake, with some success, an economics and a politics of "breaking away," that is to say, of challenging the assumption—which had been treated almost as natural law—that independent Grenada, like everybody else, should remain within the economic and geopolitical orbit of the "Western world," which really meant the United States. That, of course, was not a Grenadian initiative. The pioneering thrust was that of Cuba after 1959, followed by the diplomatic recognition of Cuba by the Commonwealth Caribbean in the 1960s. In the economic field, it meant replacing the old neocolonial enforced bilateralism with a new multilateralism, forging trade and commercial ties with Latin American and Eastern European economies, as well as with Arab and African countries. In part, this was hard trade bargaining (selling nutmeg to Venezuela rather than just Britain or the United States). In part, it was international left-wing solidarity (although at times the solidarity was more verbal than material). In the realm of foreign policy it meant forging new friendships and diplomatic relationships with the Third World as a whole, while at the same time remaining a loyal member of the Caribbean Economic Community (CARICOM), the Organisation of Eastern Caribbean States (OECS), and the larger Commonwealth. As Bishop put it in his speech of April 13, 1979, Grenada was a free and independent country, not in anybody's backyard, and definitely not for sale.[14] Like Manley before him in Jamaica, Bishop became a frequent speaker on the international radical circuit (which may have contributed to his final downfall, for, as the record shows, it is always dangerous for Third World leaders to leave their home base unattended for too long). The new foreign policy, of course, made its mistakes, giving support, for example, to the repressive regimes of Libya and Syria, and voting against the United Nations General Assembly's condemnatory vote on the Soviet action in Afghanistan (while Nicaragua abstained). Yet it is at least arguable that the pro-Soviet tilt was in part encouraged by the relentless hostility of the United States to the new regime. Grenada rapidly discovered, like other small, weak states in the international anarchy, that beggars cannot be choosers.

The second lasting achievement of the revolution, this time internally, was to show that a Caribbean revolutionary government, with enough idealism and enthusiasm, can effectively mobilize its people in the task of national reconstruction. Few of its critics have been prepared to concede this, if only because few, if any, of them took the trouble to visit the island and take a hard, close look at what it was doing. Most West Indian island peoples have about them a general spirit of rambunctious, almost antisocial individualism which sometimes makes them antipathetic to organized discipline and hard work. Yet no one who spent any time in Grenada during those years could fail to have been impressed by their tremendous response to the revolutionary challenge. As David Lewis points out, it was not so much structure as spirit that made the revolution. Whether it was highschool students helping to educate their elders in the mass literacy drive, or young unemployed males accepting hard camp training in the army and the militia, or volunteer workers helping to build a community center in their spare time, or village women, after a hard day, attending an evening session on women's rights in the revolution put on by volunteer speakers of the National Organisation of Women (Bishop's speech of June 15, 1979, is in a way a splendid confessional apologizing on behalf of all West Indian men for the suffering imposed on women by West Indian machismo).[15] Far from being just the orchestrated acclamation of the Saturday afternoon mass rally, these activities demonstrated that a whole population was serving the common cause with zeal and dedication, unaided by the material luxuries—good roads, the family car, labor-saving household appliances, television, the office electric typewriter and photocopier, air conditioning, even the functioning telephone—that all Americans take for granted. Their zeal flagged only toward the very end.

8

1983: The Road to October

If, as Fidel Castro remarked, the revolution in Grenada committed suicide, then the key to unraveling the mystery lies in an analysis of the stresses and strains, both personal and ideological, that developed within the revolution's central agencies—the Cabinet, the party, and the party's Central Committee—during the summer of 1983. The effort to make that analysis, it has to be emphasized by way of preface, is enormously complicated by the fact that in the October invasion the U.S. counterintelligence and psychological warfare agencies sequestered a vast amount of PRG records—some 25 tons of material, according to some reports—which have been later leaked to "friendly" journalists as part of a postinvasion propaganda war against the revolution. Accordingly, what we know of that material, including minutes of PRG Central Committee sessions, is suspect, for its authenticity will be in doubt so long as it is not corroborated by independent sources. It could be, wholly or in part, systematic forgery, like the vaunted Hitler diaries, and must be used with care. It is not the least tragedy of Grenada, as Patrick Solomon has pointed out, that the story will be told to the world by the official U.S. information services.[1] It will surely be one of the first tasks of a new, properly constituted Grenada government to demand the return of all of the stolen documentation. Until that is done, the Caribbean has been thrown back yet once again into the old colonial condition, where its history is composed from the archival centers of the dominant metropolitan powers.[2]

The pieces of the jigsaw puzzle, then, must be painstakingly put together, using all the available evidence as it comes in: not only from U.S. sources, but also the reports of the surviving insiders, of eye-witnesses to the October events, of friendly outsiders who had visited during the life span of the revolution, and of the host of commentators in newspapers and journals, both in the region and outside, who have written on it. The latter category must also be viewed with some skepticism, for it includes not only all of the so-called liberals, of every brand, who with spurious hindsight have written all of their "I told you so" articles and interpretations, but also, even more reprehensible, all of the Johnnies-come-lately who have suddenly discovered that all along they were friends of the revolution, although none of them could ever be seen in St. George's at the time. The future historians of the revolution, of course, will have to take all these sources into account. It is unfortunate that they will not be able to benefit from a detailed, day-to-day account of what actually happened, written by a participant-observer, comparable to Lissagaray's brilliant account of the Paris Commune edited in his years of exile and which was translated in 1876 into English by Eleanor Marx.

All of the evidence suggests that the summer of 1983 was the decisive breaking point of the Grenada Revolution, although later interviews with surviving NJM and PRG figures such as Don Rojas, Kendrick Radix, and George Louison suggest that the leadership decomposition had begun at least a year earlier.[3] Radix is of the opinion that it started even earlier with his forced resignation from the Central Committee in 1981 on the ground of his alleged "petit-bourgeois reformist" tendencies.[4] In any case it is clear that there developed early on a split, at once personal and ideological, between the two factions headed respectively by Bishop and Coard. This in itself is no cause for surprise, for it is the history of all revolutions, bourgeois and socialist alike, that they beget rival factions and groupings vying for control of the revolution. It is human nature in politics. The very heterogeneity of the groups that made up the NJM in itself made such factionalism almost inevitable.

What is surprising about the Grenada case is the astonishing rapidity which which the factionalizing process took place. It took fifteen years for the French Revolution to travel its full course from 1789 to the declaration of the Napoleonic Empire in 1804; it took twelve years for the Russian Revolution to pass from 1917 to the final expulsion of Trotsky in 1929. The Grenada Revolution, by contrast, went from beginning to end in four short years. Its immediate cause, of course, was the internal factional struggle that finally exploded in October 1983; its final causes were the counterrevolutionary intrigues undertaken by the Caribbean bourgeoisie and the U.S. imperialists. The responsibility is thus a shared one. But the primary responsibility is that of the internal elements which provided the excuse for the imperialist intervention. As Radix has properly said, the greatest crime a revolutionary can commit is to have state power and then lose it.[5] Or, as the Nicaraguan Interior Minister Tomas Borge has added, "revolutionists cannot be assassinated, but they can commit suicide. They are invulnerable to external attacks, but are totally exposed to self-destruction."[6]

With the proviso, then, that much of the available documentary evidence comes from suspect sources, it is possible to trace the history of the internal power struggle during the summer and fall of 1983. Very early on Coard had organized his group, the Organisation for Educational Advance and Research (OEAR) within the NJM, thus setting up a "party within the party."[7] Both Radix and Merle Hodge have described how OEAR's membership was recruited from the younger elements who had only been teenagers in the formative years of the NJM and whose rigid Leninist outlook was finely honed in interminable weekend study schools in revolutionary theory, and constituting an agitprop echelon in a manner common to the history of all Communist parties.[8] By the fall of 1983, the OEAR had also gained control of the Central Committee (the crucial meetings of September–October voted overwhelming majorities in favor of the Coard proposals for joint leadership, while the final decisive General Meeting of the party's full membership of September 25 voted 46 in favor of compelling Bishop to attend, with only one vote against and one abstaining).[9] How that control was actually achieved is still not fully known. At worst, it could have been Machiavellian intrigue; Radix at least opines that Coard hid behind these younger followers and used slander, rumor, and deceit to discredit Bishop. At best, it could have been the magnetic appeal to young minds of Coard as the generally accepted brilliant theoretician of the revolution, as attested in private conversations by many who knew him. Nevertheless, it is certain that a serious interfactional power struggle developed, starting perhaps with Coard's shrewd tactic of "resigning" from the Central Committee in October 1982.

It is important to note that the foregoing was conducted in almost total secrecy. The Central Committee majority saw themselves as professional revolutionaries. For them, the revolution was the party, conceived in closed Leninist terms; as George Louison puts it, they were completely contemptuous of the people, and believed that no matter what action they took, they could eventually explain it away.[10] All committee members were ceaselessly warned not to distribute the agenda documents. Not even recognized friends, in either the Caribbean or the United States, were taken into confidence about matters, as those who attended the November 1982 Conference on Culture and Sovereignty can testify.[11] This secrecy also explains why a volume by North American academic critics generally critical of the behavior of the United States in the region, published in early 1984 but obviously being prepared in 1983, had practically nothing to say about Grenada.[12] This was caucus revolutionary politics with a vengeance; so much so that not the least shock that the Grenadian people received in

October 1983 was suddenly to discover that they had been governed by a Central Committee which they had never heard of before. It is even more astonishing when it is remembered that Grenada, like all of the small Antillean island societies, is not so much a nation as it is a neighborhood where everything, including even private lives, is a "public secret."

The presently available documentation covers the important party meetings of 1983: the Central Committee Plenary of July 18–23; the Extraordinary Central Committee meeting of September 14–16; a meeting of the Central Committee Plenary of September 23; and the Extraordinary General Meeting of Full Members of the Party of September 25. Participants seem to have included an estimated total of 300 party members, with 16 composing the Central Committee. Interestingly, many, if not all, of the 16 members of the Revolutionary Military Council, which was finally formed on October 19, were also members of the Central Committee.[13]

As one reads these minutes it is clear that the meetings were being conducted by party members and leaders who were angry, sometimes confused, and emotionally drained by a long summer of almost endless committee meetings. Radix has later testified to the toll that it all took in physical and emotional illnesses.[14] No one can accuse the committee members of not being hard and devoted workers. It might almost be said that the revolution died in committee. Whatever the case, the general temper of the minutes, looked at as a whole, is one of alarm, to say the least. The revolution, the refrain runs, is in serious crisis, indeed may almost be on the verge of collapse. The July minutes contain Louison's long criticism of the economic performance of the revolution: the failures of the key productive sectors, especially export marketing, to get moving; the extreme difficulty in mobilizing external finance; cash-flow problems; and much else. In the same meeting Ian St. Bernard carried the litany of complaints even further: there was ideological indiscipline, with few comrades taking their assignments seriously and not preparing their homework properly; party dues remained unpaid; the party secretariat was in a parlous state, with files in chaotic condition, plans missing, control cards not filed, and proper records of party work not being kept; and the propaganda work of the party was almost in total collapse, thus encouraging the apathy of the masses and the growing boldness of counterrevolutionary forces such as the Church.[15]

This general note of disillusionment was carried over, indeed intensified, in the August and September meetings. Party and government alike were accused of being in almost total disarray. Ewart Layne charged that the Central Committee had demonstrated its inability to offer real leadership. Chalkie Ventour, in support, reported that comrades were complaining of the amount of tasks, showing signs of resignation, and that some were afraid to speak up, showing timidity and fear. There was a serious drift away from the Party by the key supporters of the revolution. In some respects, too, the masses had gone backward ideologically, with their earlier support of the party's position on the Afghanistan issue being now replaced with doubts about what to think about the South Korean Boeing 747 shot down by Soviet fighter planes in August 1983. Leon Cornwall added his opinion that the "honeymoon period" of the revolution was over, and that the Central Committee had failed to develop a perspective on how the revolution must develop: "We tend to push things down comrades' throats and frustrate them." The situation was so bad that some party mobilizers were actually being chased away by residents in some areas.[16]

Until this point the discussion was general and impersonal in character. It almost sounds like an honest exercise in democratic self-criticism—for some of the participants it might indeed have genuinely been so. Every government, after all, revolutionary or not, at some point faces the problem of stock-taking. But with the September meetings there is a new tone, in retrospect ominous. The main issue was now construed to be not simply one of leadership in general but of the personal leadership style of Bishop as the political leader. Bishop remarked at the September 25 meeting that many points now being made against him had not been made in the assessments of earlier meetings. That meeting, along with the earlier September 14 meeting, was clearly called in order to "manners" Bishop. As one reads the reports a consensus emerges on the part of the critics: Bishop had become the main fetter on the revolution. It was agreed that he had great strengths, including the charisma to inspire confidence in the masses and project the image of the party abroad. According to Ewart Layne, Bishop lacked four important leadership qualities: a high Leninist level of organization and discipline, great depth in ideological clarity, brilliance in tactics and strategy, and the capacity to exercise Leninist supervision, control, and guidance of all areas of party work. Selwyn Strachan added that while brilliant, Bishop did not compare favorably with Fidel Castro, who had the ability to push the Cuban Revolution to its logical limits. George Louison noted, somewhat incongruously, that Bishop spent too much time on details and therefore lost focus.[17]

As the Central Committee saw it, the solution was the now famous joint leadership model. The model, according to them, would marry the gifts of Bishop to those of Coard, with Coard taking over responsibility for party organization, tactics, and strategy and Bishop concentrating on direct work among the masses, organization of the popular democratic institutions, regional and international work, and chairmanship of the weekly meetings of the Political Bureau. The September 25 meeting was in effect a long discussion on the implications of that model, with both Coard and Bishop (each arriving late), making their response according to their understanding of the model. Its defenders, including Layne and Hudson Austin, presented it as a form of democratic centralism: either we build a party with one discipline binding on all or a petit-bourgeois party dominated by one man. Austin was an early NJM member and loyal disciple of Bishop and later was to become the *bête noire* of the last days of the revolution. Any other alternative is "one-manism," simple opportunism. An unidentified rapporteur's report of the September 25 meeting reads:

> This is the first and most fundamental issue the party membership faces today. Whichever decision is taken will determine the future of the party and revolution, Comrade Layne stated. He went on to point out that it is either the building of a Marxist-Leninist party and the struggle to build socialism, or a petit bourgeois social democratic party and ultimately the degeneration of the party and revolution like in Egypt and Somalia. What faces us is the road of opportunism or Leninist principles.[18]

Coard and Bishop responded to this assessment in their different ways. It is interesting to note that the minutes record only a brief statement by Coard, to the effect that he accepted the joint leadership model, but had earlier resigned because he could not cope with the mountain of party and government duties hitherto imposed upon him. Bishop's responses, by comparison, take up pages and pages of the minutes:

> Bishop in response said that he assumed that the CC [Central Committee] would explain his position to the GM [General Meeting]. He added that the discussions in the CC plenary has raised concerns to him. When stripped bare and until he has completed his reflections then he can face the GM with a clean conscience. He is now relatively confused and emotional. . . . Several things . . . concern him and thus require a lot of mature reflection. He said that he shared the basic CC conclusion on the crisis in the country and party and that the source of the crisis lies in the CC. He added that he firmly believes that the more authority and power one had then the greater the responsibility and duty to accept criticism and that the overall responsibility for failures belongs to that person. He pointed out that the concept of joint leadership does not bother him because of his history of struggle especially from the 1973 merger which gave rise to NJM. He said that many comrades had criticised him in relation to his acceptance in the past in the form of Joint Coordinating Secretaries. However the masses have their own conception and perception that may not be necessarily like ours who study the science. Our history shows that the masses build up a personality cult around a single individual. He admitted that his style of leadership had led to vacillation, indecisiveness in many cases. He confessed that

maybe his conception of leadership is idealistic because of the historical abuse of power and one-man leadership. He and his contemporaries have distaste for one-man leadership and he has a strong position on this. He further pointed out that his style of leadership is in error since it calls for consensus, unity at all costs and this causes vacillation. And he is not sure that he has overcome this.[19]

The minutes in part continue:

He also said, that he is concerned about the minutes being given to the GM. If minutes are given which show what each member of the CC has said it can develop ideas of groupings and fractions and vacillations in the CC. He is afraid that it would eventually reach the masses and reaction would thus undermine the revolution and give rise to suspicions that there is a power struggle in the CC. He said that if we are to re-build links with the masses, then by solving the problem by being frank, it would undermine the confidence of the leadership. He sees this clearly and cannot understand why other CC members cannot see this. . . . He then said that he is concerned about what is the real meaning of the CC's position. He is having horrors. If it is what he is thinking, then he does not see himself as being on the CC or on the CC as a leader. . . . He is suspicious that comrades have concluded that the party must be transformed into a Marxist-Leninist party and thus he is the wrong person for the leader. He can't accept this compromise; it is unprincipled. He explained that for him to put out his strengths it must be as a result of a deep conviction, love for the poor and working people, and out of a feeling of confidence from the CC. He is not satisfied because the totality of points made is pointing him in a direction he is trying to run from. It is not joint leadership but a compromise in the interim. . . . Cde. Bishop went on to say that only he can solve the problem he is now facing because any assistance and talk about this not being a case of no confidence will be seen by him as tactical.
He further said that he is considering the option of withdrawing from the PB [Political Bureau] and CC but has not yet resolved this.[20]

What is one to make of all this? It is palpably obvious, to begin with, that the Coard people had become a hard, centralized group working to push the revolution radically leftward. The very unity and similarity of their arguments indicate a preconceived plan of action. Almost certainly it was masterminded by Coard, ambitious to become undisputed leader of the revolution (although conversations with knowledgeable Grenadians suggest that he was at times no more than a Macbeth pushed by his wife as Lady Macbeth). Be that as it may, that he remained discreetly behind the scenes in these Central Committee and General Meeting discussions reveals him as a shrewd tactician. The Coard faction was avowedly Marxist-Leninist, although much of its contribution to the discussions seems, to anyone who really knows Marxism-Leninism, as infantile and half-baked. This, of course, is not a new note in the West Indian theoretical debate: Marxism in the region goes back to the 1950s. What is radically new, as we read these marathon talk sessions, is the tone of doctrinal intolerance. For all intents and purposes, Bishop is on trial, placed before judges who identify dissent with treason; it sounds like nothing so much as the Catholic Inquisition or the Church in Calvin's Geneva, where dissent was identified with heresy. Plain speaking between comrades, of course, is typically West Indian; to "bad mouth" or "mamaguy" or "mauvais langue" an opponent is the order of the day. But this is something different. What purports to be a frank, democratic discussion between comrades really becomes a rigorous, harsh cross-examination of Bishop, emphasizing mercilessly his weaknesses and failures. He is in effect being set up as the "fall guy" of the revolution. We are back in the conspiratorial atmosphere of Arthur Koestler's *Darkness at Noon,* a very un-West Indian atmosphere.

That this was so is evident enough from the contradictions within which the accusers find themselves. Selwyn Ryan has suggested that the criticisms, made not only of Bishop but of the revolution's progress as a whole, were deliberately exaggerated in order to prepare the ground for the step forward to transforming the NJM from a loose-jointed party into a Leninist-type vanguard party.[21] It is difficult to disagree. The prognostications about the economic collapse of the revolution seem unbelievable when compared with the available statistical evidence for the economic record of 1982–83. Coard himself, as finance minister, had brought in comprehensive economic planning and had claimed that in 1982 the gross national product had grown by 5.5 percent, corroborated by the World Bank report of that year. Statistics for 1983 on particular sectors were equally encouraging.[22] Nontraditional exports, such as flour and garments, increased by 28 percent. Private remittances from abroad increased by 35 percent. Customer deposits in the local Cooperative Bank rose by 18 percent and customer loans by 10 percent. It is true that foreign exchange assets accruing from exports declined in the vital traditional areas such as cocoa, nutmegs, and bananas; but as the report of the East Caribbean Currency Authority pointed out at the time, all of the small-island economies had achieved only minimal growth in 1982, due mainly to the general worldwide fall in prices of primary commodities, certainly not the fault of any one island government.[23] None of these indicators prove that the Grenada economy was on the verge of collapse. What is more, the relationship between the public and private sectors remained buoyant, with both sectors enthusiastically working together, especially in tourism promotion. Tourism in 1982 showed only a minor decline, certainly much less than in the rival Barbados industry. The president of the local Chamber of Commerce told a visiting journalist at this time that the earlier "name calling" had stopped: "I haven't heard one unkind word against us in the longest while."[24] There is nothing here to compare with the truly calamitous state, by comparison, of the Guyana economy.

This, of course, does not mean that the Grenadian economic performance did not have its weaknesses and restraints. Finance Minister Coard himself candidly outlined them in his 1982 report presented to the National Conference of Mass Organisations. Looking successively at each sector of the economy, he underlined their shortcomings; they were suffering, as he enumerated them, from weak management, general lack of organization, bad record keeping and accounting, low worker productivity, lack of training in modern methods of production, and the use of primitive technology.[25] Yet most of those problems were inherited from the primitive colonial economy in which industry, with the technology and managerial skills that go with it, was at best in its infancy. The problems, in turn, had been compounded by the waste and corruption of the Gairyite postcolonial state and the backward nature of the private sector, which was petit-bourgeois in character, controlled by a type of businessman who—in the sharp phrase of a critic of the Jamaican economy of the time—were "bazaar merchants" rather than entrepreneurs of the advanced industrial capitalist type. The structural changes necessary to have met all of those problems would have taken a whole generation to plan and execute. Central planning in the Third World economies, whether of the socialist or neocapitalist statist types, takes time.

The claims about the impending political collapse of the revolution are even less convincing. The August Central Committee meeting was told that the revolution was facing its worse crisis ever. The mass organizations, for example, the National Organisation of Women and the National Youth Organisation, were in a state of virtual collapse. The militia was a thing of the past. Among the working class there was persistent ideological backwardness, and serious demoralization. Coard told the same meeting that the party would disintegrate completely within six months; it was dead in the eyes of the masses; the loss of state power itself was only a few months away. Only a fundamental reorganization of the party could solve the crisis.[26] Was this a true report? Admittedly, the Central Committee majority may have been privy to inside, confidential information about these matters unknown to others. But the claims seem hardly credible to anyone who visited Grenada during this period. Admittedly, the old British parliamentary tradition died hard and there was much troubled conscience about the failure to hold elections. People used to free speech disliked the curbs on independent political expression. The close ties with Cuba were not really popular, although there was little evidence to prove the more lurid rumors about how the Cubans behaved. And yet, despite all this, revolutionary Grenada remained a surprisingly open society. There were no restrictions on visitors. Tourists were welcome, indeed given the royal treatment. The occasional curious foreign journalist could wander around freely and talk with anybody, as did, for example, Michael Massing of the *Atlantic Monthly.* Not every invited academic who attended conferences— for example, the 1982 Conference on Culture and Sovereignty—was a hard-line Marxist. The revolution's social programs were undeniably popular; and the Grenada population certainly did not suffer from the acute short-ages of vital food items that prevailed in Guyana, nor did they suffer from a repressive police-army system so characteristic, once again, of the Burnham one-party regime in Guyana.[27]

Grenadians, all this is to say, stubbornly remained Grenadians. They still preferred calypso to revolutionary songs; the obligatory attendance at propaganda study periods, albeit in working hours, was generally unpopular with government workers; and people as a whole preferred to attend their local church meetings rather than party-organized affairs, although it is true that by the end the U.S.-financed fundamentalist churches in the island—as elsewhere throughout the rest of the region—had become a consciously counterrevolutionary force, attacking the PRG regime as godless and Communist. But all of this, by any means, did not add up to a mass popular discontent with the revolution as such. The honeymoon period may have been over, as Cornwall said. But this is a stage that all new regimes meet; it certainly does not mean the end of the marriage.

The conclusion seems obvious enough: the ultraleft faction had to paint a dismal diagnosis of the patient in order that they, as the doctor, could move to undertake radical surgery. The recorded meetings show that they had come to realize that they had lost control of their mass support and that they either had to neutralize the popular leader or eliminate him. It is within this context that one has to try to understand Bishop's response. His recorded remarks—it is unfortunate that we do not have his own notes and diaries to corroborate them—show him to be in a general state of emotional anguish and at times ideological confusion.[28] He clearly suspected that there was a conspiracy against him, a suspicion echoed by member partici-pants George Louison and Fitzroy Bain, who clearly voiced their apprehen-sions about the habit of caucusing into different groups. Bishop requested more time to think about the joint leadership proposal. But he would not have needed more time had he known more about the history of such concepts in, say, Soviet Russia, a history summed up in Trotsky's observa-tion that the dictatorship of the proletariat becomes the dictatorship of the Communist party, the dictatorship of the Communist party becomes the dictatorship of the Central Committee, and the dictatorship of the Central

Committee becomes the dictatorship of the secretary-general. Bishop failed to understand that the joint or dual leadership proposal was really a screen designed to conceal the fact that he was being cleverly manipulated into a position where he would be forced to resign or disappear. He wanted to take the issue to the "masses," the popular constituency; but he could not appear to realize that that could never have been accepted by his critics, since it would have spelled certain defeat for them. He argued for consensus; he did not see that to his "scientific socialist" critics that position was dismissed as "bourgeois reformism" or "right-wing opportunism." He did not perceive, as Ryan puts it, that what is historically necessary might not be politically possible in a small open economy encircled by Western imperialism. But Bishop did not possess the ruthlessness of temper—which his critics call Leninist "iron discipline"—to openly meet the challenge on those grounds; he was not the gambler ready to call the other player's bluff.

That vacillation of decisive action in the power struggle was worsened by Bishop's ideological imprecision. He told the Central Committee that he accepted the teachings of the "science," that is, Marxism-Leninism. But at the same time he reiterated his belief in the quite different West Indian political style, in which the masses develop a personality cult around a charismatic leader.[29] Any viable Caribbean political theory on politics must try to construct a workable correlation between these two models. Because he was not an "intellectual" in the Coard manner, Bishop had not worked out that correlation. His critics seized upon that as evidence of "petit-bourgeois manifestations." All in all, this is a picture of a pragmatic political leader, totally familiar with the cultural idiosyncrasies of his West Indian crowd constituency, trapped by his enemies who themselves are the victims, possibly even sincere, of a dialectical jargon far removed from those idiosyncrasies. It is almost as if the two sides were talking to each other in mutually incomprehensible languages.

But there is even more than this. Ever since the Stalinist Moscow purges of 1937–38, it has been well known how the Catholic habit of the confessional has become, in secularized form, a part of the power struggle in revolutionary movements. The frequent use of the word "confess" in the Grenada literature shows that the habit had now entered the Caribbean Third World. The delinquent comrade is cross-examined. He is chastised for his "petit-bourgeois" weaknesses (which may only mean that he retains some decency of conscience). He is obliged to confess. He is thus placed on the defensive. From time to time Bishop confesses to his shortcomings; he apologizes for not responding to the Central Committee directives. No passages in the minutes show this better than the "confession" of Comrade Fitzroy Bain:

[Bain] said he is unhappy about labelling comrades and that more ideo-logically advanced comrades put forward positions and others like him-self, who are of a lower ideological level, feel timid in the face of these. . . . He said that he knows that his ideological level is low and the other comrades have a higher ideological level but he does not like these things. He ended by saying that the comrades had well thought out po-sitions and were frank but he must say what is on his mind.[30]

Bishop himself ended the meeting of September 25 by pledging to the party that he would do everything to correct his petit-bourgeois traits. In one way, this was characteristic of Bishop, for, as Don Rojas points out, he was the most modest and least arrogant of all of the leaders, and was capable of criticizing himself publicly at a party forum in a way that Coard and others were incapable of.[31] Yet in another way it was a declaration of surrender. It is, in sum, the tone of the confessional, almost as if there is some sin to be atoned for.

It is this general inquisitorial temper, even more than the details of the debates, which has to be noted and emphasized. Everything was sur-rounded by a pervasive miasma of fear, leading to all the charges and countercharges of plots, intrigues, and machinations. Few documents bet-ter reveal the full ugliness of the temper than the letter of October 17, written by Vincent Noel, one of Bishop's supporters, after he himself had been placed under house arrest. The letter, addressed to members of the Central Committee and party, gives a vivid hour-by-hour account of what was happening, as experienced by the writer. After talking with Bishop, Noel reported that he was "stunned" to hear Bishop repeat the talk about an "Afghanistan solution" to the party crisis. Bishop claimed that he had always, until recently, had good relations with Coard and had even been apprehensive that Coard's resignation from the Central Committee in 1982 indicated thoughts of suicide. Later talks with Selwyn Strachan and Chalkie Ventour painted a different picture: of Bishop planning to kill the Coards and secretly collecting arms for his safety. Bishop, said Ventour, was a psychopath and power crazy. On retailing this back to Bishop, Noel was further dismayed to hear Bishop's account of the most recent Central Committee meeting in which members "kept pulling out their weapons threateningly during the whole meeting." Noel then added his own account of a later party meeting in which, "led by members of the Political Bureau, the meeting was a horrendous display of militarism, hatred, and emotional vilification." Things had got to the stage, further reported Noel, that Cen-tral Committee members were no longer sleeping in their homes. He came to the conclusion that the Central Committee was suffering from "an over-dose of paranoia."[32] The letter, obviously composed in much anguish, makes it clear that by this time the crisis had reached the point of no return, for there no longer existed the atmosphere of mutual trust and confidence without which civilized discourse is impossible between persons who have differences with each other. In Grenada, the moment had come for the guns of October.

9

October 19, 1983: "Bloody Wednesday" —The Guns of October

Whether he knew it or not, the last, crucial meeting of September 25 had sealed Bishop's fate. His request for more time to think about the dual leadership proposal could get him nowhere. His departure on another international tour, to Hungary and Czechoslovakia, only meant that his critics, who had now become his enemies, could all the more easily prepare the ground for the final scene of the drama. From now on, as the West Indian parlance has it, it was "ole mas," the revolution "mash up."

The chronology of events has been fairly well established. The Bishop party returned home on Saturday, October 8, one day before scheduled. Contrary to custom, no member of the Central Committee showed up at the airport to welcome the political leader, the sole welcomer being Selwyn Strachan, minister of national mobilization. Despite the fact that both Coard, as acting prime minister, and Liam James, as head of security, had a responsibility to give Bishop reports on developments taking place during his absence, neither of them did so throughout Sunday and Monday, October 9–10. On Wednesday, October 12 the Central Committee voted to confine Bishop indefinitely, under house arrest, with his phone cut off and he himself disarmed "for his own safety." Who actually effectuated that order is not known; interestingly, whereas the minutes of earlier meetings were recorded on a typewriter, the purported record of the October 12 meeting is handwritten.[1] Bishop at some point was joined by Minister of Education, Jacqueline Creft, his companion after his break with his wife Angela, who was residing in Canada. A marathon meeting of all party members met on the night of Thursday, October 13, and voted by overwhelming majority to expel Bishop from the party not on the charge, curiously enough, that he had resisted acceptance of the doctrine of joint rule but that he had deliberately circulated a rumor, through his security personnel, that the Coard faction had hatched a plot to assassinate him. The record of the meeting indicates that Bishop himself was brought to the meeting, confronted with the charge, spoke for forty-five minutes in his defense, repudiating the charge, and was then condemned for "disgracing" the party and the revolution.[2] An official statement read over Radio Free Grenada on Monday, October 17, four days later, informed the population that those decisions had been made, and advanced a long justification. Speaking of the past it said that "when members of the Political Bureau and Central Committee of the party disagreed with Comrade Bishop's opinions, he has become angry and increasingly hostile. His attention has been increasingly focussed on the question of power, and who he thinks wants to take it away from him. He has imagined conspiracies within the Central Committee aimed at removing him as leader of the country."[3] It is of interest again to note that the statement was read by the commander of the army, General Hudson Austin. Some other sources have corroborated the story of the assassination plot, which was to have been blamed by its perpetrators on the U.S. Central Intelligence Agency (CIA).[4] On Wednesday, October 19, thousands of Bishop's supporters rescued him from house arrest, almost literally carried him up to Ford Rupert, to be met and liquidated by the armored personnel carriers of the army in the early afternoon of the same day. There are a number of different eye-witness accounts of that final episode. They differ in detail and emphasis but agree on the basic, fundamental point that Bishop and his loyal colleagues were murdered in cold blood. The Revolutionary Military Council immediately declared a four-day curfew, virtually amounting to martial law; the situation culminated in the U.S.-conducted invasion of October 25.

Those thirteen fateful, unlucky days between October 12 and October 25 marked the death throes of the revolution. The road to October had arrived at its terminus. The days conveniently divide into two separate periods, October 12–19 and October 19–25. If the model of the French Revolution is used, the first week may be designated as the period of the Directory, in which the different revolutionary factions struggle to arrive at some sort of compromise; the second week may be designated as the Napoleonic stage, in which the army effectively takes over from the civilians. The two periods contribute their own different tactical mistakes and criminal errors to the course of events, so that the revolution finally meets its Waterloo with the imperialist enemy invasion. The latter week, the *semaine sanglante,* shows how the dynamic push of the revolutionary process, even in a small-island society, can within a short time spawn events, passions, emotions, and conflicts that elsewhere may take a whole generation or more to work themselves out. It is not merely the fact that, as has been said, a small island can make a big revolution. It is much more than that: the actors in the revolution, both social forces and individual persons, may unleash a series of volcanic-like eruptions which ultimately they cannot control and by which they themselves are destroyed.

October 12–19 was a week of constant and frantic negotiations, conducted both by the inside groups and visiting friends from outside. From all accounts, the Central Committee must have been in almost constant session, with meetings dragging on for five to six hours at a time. The whole island, from St. George's to Grenville, was in an uproar; rumors of plots and counterplots were the talk of the town. General Austin had already made public the alleged plot against the Coard faction; Jacqueline Creft reportedly relayed to Bishop's mother an alleged plot against Bishop. Coard had already won support in the army and had begun to disarm the popular militia, notably portions of it most loyal to Bishop. In the midst of all this, conversations appear to have continued between the two sides, notwithstanding the fact that on Tuesday, October 18, the five government ministers who supported Bishop—Unison Whiteman, Lyden Ramdhanny, Norris Bain, George Louison, and Jacqueline Creft—resigned, with Whiteman managing to telephone the media in Barbados to tell of the resignations.[5]

Two accounts have appeared so far of the history of the negotiations: one by George Louison, member of the Bishop group, the other by the visiting Trinidadian union activist Michael Als; both were mutual friends of Bishop and Coard. The Louison account is especially interesting. Although himself placed under house arrest, he was permitted, along with Unison Whiteman, to play the role of Bishop spokesman, with prolonged meetings taking place with Coard until October 18 (Whiteman was even allowed to have a breakfast meeting with Bishop as late as the very morning of October 19). The main point Louison made all through was that once Bishop had been put under arrest the party had fatally compromised the revolution. "Since at the time," writes Louison, "they were the ones who were holding the power, I said that if there was to be any compromise at all they were the ones who would have to make it. I was saying that they had to release Maurice from house arrest, and they had to restore him as leader of the revolution. The masses would accept no less than that."[6] Louison continues:

> It was very clear that Bernard [Coard] and company no longer cared about the masses of the people. We pointed out that the situation could easily develop into a civil war because the people were so incensed they would do anything to get back their leader, and therefore the party had a responsibility to ensure that no violence took place in the country. Bernard said that he didn't buy that scenario because the situation was that he could permit the people to demonstrate for any amount of

weeks, that they could demonstrate over and over. To use his exact words, "They could stay in the streets for weeks, after a while they are bound to get tired and hungry and want peace." He said Eric Williams did it in 1970 (in Trinidad) and survived. Gairy did it in '73 to us in St. George's and it could be done again. So I said, "Of course, if you are sufficiently Machiavellian. Then I suppose that could be an option."[7]

Louison reports that other options were mentioned. They included— suggested by various others—that Bishop be kept under house arrest, that he be court-martialed, that he could be publicly arraigned as a traitor to the principle of collective leadership, that he accept a self-enforced exile in Cuba. Others said that a military solution was not possible, since the Algerian Revolution showed that a popular leader like Ben Bella could not be that easily disposed of. It was Louison's distinct impression that Coard was not really interested in negotiations, that he was convinced that the people could be persuaded to accept what had been done, once they were made to understand that Bishop wanted "one-man" rule against the majority.[8] The Central Committee was stalling for time; the negotiations dragged to an inconclusive halt. The account does not mention that Coard and Bishop, as the two main protagonists, ever came together, face to face, during this period.

The Als account is less informative and more sketchy. Apparently invited by the NJM leadership, Als seems to have arrived in St. George's late in the first week. He reports having separate conversations with Coard and Bishop. Coard told him that relations between him and Bishop were "strained" and that because of the assassination rumor "things were at a low ebb." After reading Central Committee documents, Als concluded that the entire hierarchy of the party was split. The story of the rumor was widely believed, according to Als, because Bishop's security officer, Cleton St. Paul, who was known to be totally and "pathologically" (Als's word) devoted to the prime minister, had signed a statement that Bishop had started the rumor. In his single conversation with Bishop, Als notes that on being informed of this, Bishop started to sweat very heavily and the pores of his face enlarged perceptibly. Als also reports Bishop's observations that the party, with the exception of a few comrades, was against him, that he was not clear how the joint leadership proposal would work, and that handing over tactics and strategy to Coard would mean that the party would then "lean heavily" on Coard. Als adds that he discerned no real signs of personal animosity, and that both leaders expressed a desire to sit down with each other and talk. But Als makes no effort to explain why this did not happen; his reporting of Bishop's statement—"dem men tough as hell and I just as tough. We go see. They have their model and I have mine"—if correct would appear to indicate that animosity was indeed present. Als's account ends by noting that the NJM leadership had been working sixteen to eighteen hours a day for four years and that sheer physical fatigue had much to do with the outcome of events. People had simply run out of nervous energy, which was bound to affect their ability to make proper judgments and decisions.[9]

=====

The morning of October 19 must have started like any other tropical morning in St. George's, possibly the most Mediterranean of all small-island Caribbean townships, with its various layers of brightly painted wooden colonial houses crowding its *mornes,* all overlooking the Carenage and harbor area with its beautiful colonial Georgian public buildings and business warehouses. A favorite retreat of knowledgeable travelers who wanted to get off the beaten track of Caribbean tourism, there was about it an atmosphere of dreamy tropical provincialism that not even the worst years of the Gairy regime could destroy. It was still like that in the 1950s. To spend a quiet morning with the elder statesman "Teddy" Marryshow in his charming house above the Carenage, or a leisurely afternoon in the old colonial public library, or to wander around the Scottish Kirk graveyard where one could still pick up burned-out lead cannonballs of the old colonial wars, was to feel the *magie antillaise* of the small-island *ambiente.* But by the 1980s, for good or ill, and possibly inevitably, much had changed. The combined forces of the modern Caribbean revolution, unleashed by national independence, modernization, the ideologies of Black Power and Marxism-Leninism, had caught up with the small islands themselves. Some sort of historical fate had determined that Grenada should become the rendezvous of all of those forces.

Fortunately, a number of eye-witness accounts have appeared concerning the events of that fateful "Bloody Wednesday." We already know that both Louison and Whiteman had cautioned the Coard group that the people as a whole were impatient and that they could not control them indefinitely, and that they, Louison and Whiteman, were ready at any moment to call them out. The moment for that popular appeal came on the morning of October 19. The negotiations had run out; neither Louison nor Als seemed to have asked themselves whether there could in fact have been any serious negotiations between a Central Committee which had already determined that Bishop was guilty and a Bishop who was tied up, in ignominious fashion, in his official residence. It is absurd to talk about negotiations between captors and captives. In any case, the arrest of Bishop in itself effectively closed the door to the possibility of a negotiated settlement kept within the secret meetings of the party. By Tuesday, October 18, a spontaneous popular reaction had taken place, virtually amounting to a general strike. The strength of the popular sentiment was evident from the fact that efforts on the part of pro-Coard leaders to stem it failed dismally:

Selwyn Strachan was literally chased out of town by an angry crowd when he went down to the *Free West Indian* office and attempted to announce Coard as the new prime minister. Don Rojas has described the mood of the crowd:

> The response from the masses was: "Now look, man, don't give us all this crap. You lock up the man, why do you have him locked up? If you charge him with all these so-called crimes, then give him a chance to talk to us. We want to see him and hear from him. We know the man from a long time ago. He struggled for our cause. He was beaten up to the point of death by Gairy's Mongoose Gang in 1973. Where was Bernard Coard when Maurice was being beaten up in the streets? Or when Maurice's father was shot in 1974? If Maurice did anything wrong the masses will deal with it."[10]

Popular anger and frustration had by this time crystallized into the slogan "No Bishop, no revo."

The breaking point came on October 19. It was no longer possible for the party to keep the matter secret, admitted as such by General Austin himself in his radio broadcast of October 16.[11] The party had made a grievous tactical mistake in underestimating the mood of the people. Its own mass support, along with its credibility, had evaporated. It could now only play its last card of the military solution. Plans for the march on St. George's and the release of Bishop were already underway since at least the previous Monday. Sylvia Belmar has described how she was active in busing in people from the township of Grenville.[12] By noonday a massive crowd—the journalist Alistair Hughes, who was there with his tape recorder, estimates that it was between 7,000 and 8,000 people—had collected in the market square, waiting for their rescued leader, who had been earlier taken by a crowd—again estimated by Hughes at some 3,000 to 4,000 people—at approximately 10:35 A.M., an hour or so earlier.[13] The market square assembly had apparently expected that Bishop would be brought to address them. But somewhere along the line, the decision was made to move up the hill to the army administrative headquarters at Fort Rupert. Some observers have suggested that the plan may have been to take Bishop to the hospital first, since he was physically weak and exhausted; this seems plausible, since Fort Rupert and the hospital are located side by side on the same promontory. That separate march from the market square seems to have been led by Unison Whiteman and Vincent Noel. According to the evidence of policeman Desmond Gilbert, it was thought that Bishop wanted to move on to the fort in order to free Kendrick Radix, who was being held there.[14] However the decision was made, and whoever made it, it must have been a last-minute spontaneous decision; you do not hold a committee meeting in the middle of a crowd demonstration. It is in any case clear, as far as the statistics can determine, that only about a hundred or more of the original crowd would have made the journey to the final rendezvous to the fort.

What took place during the next hour or so was the final confrontation at Fort Rupert. The available eye-witness reports have described it in graphic detail. The main part of the crowd seems to have remained below, in the market square; after all, it is a hard, hot climb, in the tropical midday, even for Grenadians, up to the fort area, passing through the vertical narrow streets, past the St. James Hotel and the Scottish Kirk, to the top rise of the promontory; had the entire crowd undertaken that journey there would have been a human traffic jam of incommensurable proportions. It could only have been a handful, a few hundred at most, who made that uphill trip. The main crowd remained in the lower esplanade, where, according to the Hughes account, they were every moment being harangued by Sydney Ambrose, frantically asking them to stand firm and remain cool, until the sound of heavy gunfire from above drove them to disperse in what was obviously, by now, a situation of general panic. The Hughes account ends, at his own estimate, at 2:20 P.M., with the crowd dispersed and Hughes encountering a few wounded persons who told him hysterically what had taken place above in the fort courtyard.[15]

What actually took place in the courtyard has been described by other witnesses who were actually there, for Hughes himself, despite his journalistic curiosity, seems to have decided to remain below. Wisely so, perhaps, for he was to be arrested that same night. The events started, of course, with the house rescue. Desmond Gilbert states: "At his house, we stormed past the soldiers and went inside where Bishop was later found in an outhouse, one that is used as a security house. He was tied up with his hands stretched above his head. After he was freed he was too weak and he was only dressed in a blue underpants. The crowd shouting Bishop yes, Coard no, went with him dressed in his underpants to the market square where others were waiting."[16] Actually, Bishop did not make it to the square. Gilbert's account continues, "Bishop was so weak that he could hardly say much. He would only say, 'the masses, the masses.' When the crowd from the market square realised that he would not come to address them, the people moved to join the others going to Fort Rupert. Along the route, Jacqueline Creft who was also freed with Bishop kissed him on realising that the crowd was all for him. They were all stripped. It was only the people who provided cover by staying close to them."[17]

For what happened after that, once Bishop and his entourage had occupied the communications building at the fort, the historian of the events can rely upon at least four eye-witness accounts which seem credible: those of Sylvia Belmar, Merle Hodge, the immigration officer Peter Thomas, and an unidentified nurse. They all carry the anguished tone of the person who has entered into the valley of death and will never forget it. Thomas estimates that there were about one hundred people in the building at the time.[18] Belmar records that Bishop seemed quite weak and that two men had to hold him up in the air to show the crowd that he was still alive. Once inside the building people started rubbing him down with bay-rum. Somebody opened the canteen and brought a tub of ice and a carton of half-a-dozen Carib beers for Bishop.[19] The account of the anonymous nurse adds that Jacqueline Creft's mother came in with a basket of sandwiches and juice; the scene was joyful, friends were hugging Bishop.[20] It thus seems that the first thought in everybody's minds was to resuscitate Bishop, to give him some badly needed physical strength. But it also seems that, debilitated as he was, Bishop had a plan. Thomas reports that Bishop was seated at a table, along with some ministers and army officers, for what seemed to be official discussions. Thomas continues:

> When we entered the main building, he [Maurice] was looking around, speaking to a few people, saying hello and so on. I prepared some seats around a long table that was inside the building and after that he gave me some orders. He wrote on a piece of paper the telephone numbers of certain places and he gave me the instruction to go to the telephone company and see that the lines were opened and two lines of Bernard Coard, which he mentioned as hot lines, should be closed, so that he would not be able to get out to the public or such. I could definitely remember that he wanted two lines to the Fort opened so that he could make certain statements, that he could get in contact with some people. He also gave me the telephone line of Mr. Alistair Hughes, and he said see that Alistair's lines are open so that I can get in contact with him and he can possibly pass a message from me out of Grenada, and out to the world.[21]

Sylvia Belmar's account more or less corroborates this: "Some fellows from the Telephone Company came. Two of them. And he [Bishop] spoke to them and he told them he would like to get the lines connected to speak to Radio Grenada and to the rest of the World. So Christopher Stroude came with two guns and he gave them to those guys from the Telephone Company. And Maurice Bishop told them to take about 50 people along with them and go and connect the lines."[22]

These two accounts—relating essentially to the telephone strategy—are supported by the independent testimony of Don Rojas, Bishop's press secretary. Rojas apparently had been at the Fort Rupert meeting, but left on a similar errand on the instructions of Bishop (which effectively saved Rojas's life). At the time Maurice was killed, reports Rojas,

I was carrying out a task he himself had given to me. He told me to go to the telephone company in the city and get word out to the world the people had freed him and to communicate a number of other things he wanted the world to know on that day. First of all, that Grenadians had the capacity to solve their own problems and there was no need for any outside interference or intervention. Second, to dispel rumors that the Cubans were involved in the conflict. He wanted that to be made very clear. Right-wing provocateurs, some of the CIA agents who had been flown into Grenada on the day before Maurice's death, had been circulating a lot of anti-Cuban, anti-communist lies to the masses. Third, he wanted to call on Grenadians abroad—Grenadians living in New York, Toronto, London, and Trinidad—to support the revolution at this time, to express in whatever form they could their solidarity with the revolutionary process.[23]

Rojas, as he tells it, carried out those instructions. He found the telephone company building barricaded, but the workers inside, who were sympathetic to Bishop, opened up and allowed him to make three or four international calls, including one to the Caribbean News Agency in Barbados. Then, says Rojas, they heard the shooting taking place at Fort Rupert.[24]

Meanwhile, back at the fort—if this were melodrama and not tragedy one would almost be tempted to say, in the manner of the old Western movies, "meanwhile, back at the ranch"—events had taken their own independent course. Rojas and Thomas had carried out their missions. But Thomas, according to his report, returned to the fort, carrying with him a small arsenal of weapons, including AK-27 rifles and M3 submachine guns, kept regularly in his office.[25] Rojas, according to his report, went immediately into hiding; again with justification, for somewhat later a carload of armed men came to his house to arrest him.[26] By this time, clearly enough, it was open warfare, perhaps potentially civil war, and everybody was a potential victim. Bishop's efforts to get through to the media were already too late, for the war of words had now been replaced by the encounter of the guns.

By all accounts it was a brief encounter. The unidentified nurse, who had been brought to the fort to attend to the prime minister (probably from the hospital next door) said:

People were sitting there and then the next thing I heard was a blast. It was like a bomb. I was sitting on a chair and the woman who was standing in front of me was lifted up about three feet in the air and she fell on me and I was at the bottom and she was above me and her body was ripped apart. And then there was shelling. Just bullets coming from everywhere. So we just had to go on the ground. The army boys were talking to us and saying "Please stay down and don't lift your head up." The bullets were just coming and the place was in chaos and some of the people were praying. Maurice was on the ground and he kept saying, "My God, My God, they have turned the guns against the people. Oh my God, they have turned the guns against the people." You would hear the shelling of bullets, then it would stop for two minutes and then it would just start again. You got up to move and then you realised that you saw blood everywhere and people injured everywhere in the room with you. So I just had to lie there. Then I got shot in the arm. . . . Eventually, when all the blasting was finished, one of the other Peoples Revolutionary Army guys crawled out and asked, "Would you please cease the firing? There are a lot of injured people inside there. Oh God would you stop?"[27]

Belmar's account corroborates this.

About half-an-hour after the fellows left—those from the Telephone Company—we were in the building and we just started hearing firing from numerous guns. From the first set my daughter got shot. And Norris Bain, Maurice Bishop and all of us were head down and his wife, Mrs. Bain, bawling out in prayers. I called to her and I told her to pray more easily [quietly] for the soldiers that [were] shooting to believe all of us in the building were dead. So she slowed down on the praying and in about ten minutes time after she slowed down on the praying, they stopped firing. And a soldier who was disarmed was inside the building with us. He took a chance and he pulled the door and he ran out and said, "Comrades we surrender."[28]

The Thomas account, finally, adds some new detail to all this. He relates:

After finishing my drink, we heard shots coming from the police point area, that would be leading up towards the Fort. Heavy shots which would have come from the armoured vehicles (three were said to have driven into the crowd outside and soldiers opened fire) and the AK rifles. I heard heavy fire possibly from the armoured vehicle first and when this came closer it started ripping into the building. I heard one heavy thud of a rocket launcher come into the building. This was followed by a heavy volley of shots. When the initial fire started penetrating through the building, I ordered the crowd in the building who were at that time possibly hysterical or shocked on their feet, I saw the danger of it, noticing that the bullets were penetrating through the walls, and I commanded them, I said hit the ground and I did so myself. On falling to the ground I felt a sharp tug on my scalp and I noticed that I had got hit and was bleeding.[29]

The execution of Bishop and his ministers followed almost immediately after the surrender. Thomas reports:

I was among the last to get out. I was just in front of the ministers. We had to wait to let the civilians get out. I could remember that I was actually approaching the first armoured vehicle on the Fort with Jacqueline Creft following me, behind Jacqueline I think there would have been the Foreign Minister followed by Maurice and possibly Norris Bain. . . . I saw a slight movement to my left possibly among some shrubs that were growing on top of the wall of the Fort building. I saw someone rustle out of the shrubs and say 'hold Jacqueline Creft, hold Norris Bain, hold Uni [Unison Whiteman], hold Maurice Bishop, don't let them get away.'

On making his escape down the road, Thomas estimated that it took about two minutes before he heard a heavy burst of automatic gunfire which he assumed to be the moment of the executions.[30] The nurse's account described how she was the last woman out of the room before Jacqueline Creft: "I remember holding my arms in the air and then I heard a voice say, 'Oh, Jacqueline Creft is there. She's shaking. Hold the bitch.' When we left the room, Maurice, all the names they mention of the people that were shot, they were all alive. They were in a line with us coming out with their hands in the air."[31]

All these accounts, of course, are of near eye-witnesses. There are no accounts of direct eye-witnesses of the executions themselves, although obviously some soldiers were there. The subsequent court proceedings in St. George's under the new postinvasion government have ascertained the names of eight soldiers who were present, and four soldiers as the actual executioners. It is worth noting that the book by Payne, Sutton, and Thorndike mentions Captain Lester Redhead as being a member of the execution squad, while the Schoenhals and Melanson book adds the name of First Lieutenant Iman Abdullah. It is equally worth noting that another witness in the same proceedings, the hospital attendant Joseph St. Bernard, testified that just before the execution he saw Coard arrive at the army headquarters with a briefcase in one hand and a gun in the other. It is a bizarre picture. In turn, the witness Raymond Vincent Joseph testified that he had been a member of the execution squad along with other soldiers such as Cosmos Richardson, Andy Mitchell, and Claude Noel, as well as identifying Major Stroude and Warrant Officer Fabian Gabriel as being present at the scene, with Gabriel, Richardson, and Mitchell, "finishing off those who were not dead" under orders from Abdullah. The additional evidence of Abdullah himself helps to fill out the picture. He testified that while at the army headquarters Lieutenant Colonel Layne told him that the Central Committee had met and taken the decision to execute the Bishop group.

He instructed the prisoners accordingly and himself participated in the actual firing. According to him, Captain Redhead and Major Stroude were also present in that moment in the inner parade square at Fort Rupert. He went on to testify that after the execution he went, later on in the evening, with the bodies to Camp Fédon at Calivingy on the south coast, placed them in a pit, poured gasoline over them and let them burn until the following day, when he covered up the pit. It is an appalling confession.[32]

The crucial question for any serious student of the events is, Who started the shooting? Both the official statements of the Central Committee and the newly formed Revolutionary Military Council claimed that the Bishop faction was responsible, declaring that they would arrest and wipe out the entire Central Committee and the entire army leadership; they fired on the soldiers, killing two officers and wounding others, thus compelling the army people to return fire, during which encounter Bishop and the others were killed.[33] These are clearly self-serving declarations. They are contradicted by the various eye-witness reports. What appears to have happened was that some of the Bishop lieutenants, notably Norris Bain, as well as Peter Thomas and Vincent Noel, were in favor of using the few arms available in the communications room to make at least a last stand. But they were countermanded by Bishop. About that scene, Belmar writes:

And when he regained a little consciousness he [Bishop] called to the chief man up in the army who was Christopher Stroude, the major and he told him, "Well, the masses are here and I would not like the soldiers to shoot at them. My reason for coming here, as you know Radio Free Grenada is off the air; the telephone is also off and I would like to contact my people of Grenada and the rest of the world and when I finish speaking to them, I can die." So he then asked Christopher what he thinks: if the soldiers going to shoot at the crowd. Christopher assured him that they will not. So he said, "Christopher, that may be your wish, but I'm afraid they [the soldiers] might shoot at the masses and I would not like it."[34]

Thomas confirms this: "I remember, among the people who actually had rifles, I was the first to cock my rifle and put a bullet up into the bridge and I removed the safety catch, and when Maurice heard these sounds he commanded us 'don't fire back.' He said, 'do not fire back.' So as a matter of fact nobody from the Fort building actually fired back into the attackers."[35]

These accounts seem more plausible than the statements of the military regime. The only outside journalist who was there during the events, Dwight Wiley, attached to Radio Free Grenada on a UNESCO appointment, agrees.[36] The fact in itself that up until now the bodies of Bishop and the others have not been recovered—it is generally believed that they were destroyed either by burning or being dumped into the sea—strongly suggests willful destruction of evidence by a Revolutionary Military Council that had something to hide. It seem evident enough that Bishop, for whatever reasons—his mere physical fatigue may have encouraged a fatalistic mood—did not want to initiate a battle, and that he commanded accordingly, although he might have decided differently had he fully realized the full consequence of surrender. These conclusions seem to be borne out by the minor controversy concerning the evidence of Michael Als. A Trinidadian union activist early on disillusioned with the record of the People's National Movement, and influenced by the thinking of the local ideologue, de Wilton Rogers, Als returned from his failed trip to St. George's as negotiator between the two sides with a statement supporting the position of the Revolutionary Military Council, that is to say, that Bishop and others had died in an exchange of gunfire, and also offering what he termed a "rational explanation" on the part of General Austin. Then Austin added his own details of the Bishop group disarming the soldiers at the fort and redistributing them to the civilian supporters. Later, in Trinidad, Als retracted that account, admitting that it was based on hearsay. The retraction earned him the condemnation of both the press and his own peers as an irresponsible and discredited informant.[37] Trevor Munroe, general secretary of the Workers party of Jamaica, in a press conference on the day following the massacre, and who himself had also visited St. George's during September 26–27 as another friendly intermediary, claimed that his party had "some independent confirmation" that the Bishop group started the shooting, but offered no evidence to substantiate the claim.[38] These reports, finally, must be placed within the context of the later testimony of the Grenadian doctor Jensen Otway that he was in effect coerced by the Austin regime into fabricating cause-of-death certificates for Bishop and eight others, with no bodies being made available to him for examination.[39]

The events of "Bloody Wednesday" effectively terminated the protracted internal negotiations which had taken place from June to October. Everything was shattered by the guns of October. Two general considerations suggest themselves to the analyst of the events at this particular point in the argument. Both considerations are crucial to any further conclusions that might be made with reference to the theory and the praxis of revolution within the concrete and particular conditions of contemporary neocolonial Third World societies.

The first consideration, surely, is that political murder, anywhere, is inexcusable to any serious protagonist of serious revolutionary change. Even if the version of the Revolutionary Military Council, that the Bishop group opened fire first, were accepted as true it still remains the fact that, once made prisoners, Bishop and his colleagues were executed; it has been estimated that some 15 minutes passed between the capture and the killing. Such an act constitutes terrorism, no more nor no less, and has been outrightly condemned by even the most left-wing friends of the Grenada Revolution, including the official Cuban declarations. Nor is this just a question of how revolutionaries should behave when quarrels arise between them. It is a question, much larger, of how people in any situation should perceive the proper relationships between ends and means in the social and political struggles in which they may be involved. That lesson had been perceived by Burke—with the period of the Terror in the French Revolution in mind—in a noble passage of his *Letters on a Regicide Peace* of 1796. "The blood of man," he wrote, "should never be shed but to redeem the blood of man. It is well shed for our family, for our friends, for our God, for our country, for mankind. The rest is vanity; the rest is crime."[40] For anyone to believe that the death of Bishop and the others was not an act of criminality, or still to persist in seeking justificatory arguments for it, is to be convicted of lacking utterly any moral sensibility.

The second consideration is, perhaps, even more important. It concerns the role of the popular force in the revolutionary process. Ever since Marx and Engels, and increasingly with the Russian, Chinese, and Cuban revolutions of the twentieth century, the dialectical interplay between mass consciousness and the leadership role has been central to the theoretical discussion on the entire phenomenology of revolution. All of the leading theoreticians have agreed on the absolute necessity of the mass basis for revolution. But there have been serious disagreements on the respective roles that should be played between the mass consciousness on the one hand and the forms of party leadership on the other. That was the central issue in the debate between Lenin and Rosa Luxemburg at the beginning of the century, with Lenin emphasizing the cardinal role of the disciplined Communist party as revolutionary vanguard, and Luxemburg emphasizing the priority of the spontaneous mass uprising. Although set on a lesser scale, the events in Grenada between 1979 and 1983 in and of themselves contribute a fascinating chapter to this seminal debate.

For there can be little doubt that those events tell us much about how the relationships between people and party may evolve in the concrete environment of a small Antillean island society. In their book of 1980 the Jacobs brothers had opined, and correctly, that at that stage at least in Grenadian developments it was romantic to expect that the people one day would rise up one sunny morning to overthrow the state regime. That is why the coup d'état of 1979 was a private exercise rather than a mass uprising. But four years later, what the Jacobs brothers had seen as romantic did in fact occur. What happened on October 19, 1983, constituted a genuine people's revolutionary act. The arrest of Bishop on October 12 had somehow released a magnetic storm of mass indignation and anger that only needed a little push by the pro-Bishop ministers and unionists to become actualized into the mass release of the prime minister and the mass march on Fort Rupert, all based on the spontaneous mass motto "No Bishop, no revo." The very numerical size of the crowd tells its own tale; for if the estimate of some 10,000 people is accepted (one out of every ten Grenadians) it is tantamount to some 5 million people demonstrating in London or some 25 million people demonstrating in Washington, figures that truly boggle the imagination. The very character of the uprising also tells its own tale for, according to all accounts, it included practically everybody: party members, young people, civil servants, businessmen, housewives, even young schoolchildren. Very few of them, perhaps, would have been able to place their action within theoretical terms satisfactory to, say, a political science lecturer at the University of the West Indies. Rather, for them, it was a simple, straightforward matter that an assault against Bishop, "we Prime Minister," had become an assault against themselves and therefore against the revolution, as they understood it. It is in that sense that the only "rescue operation" that can be talked about in all of this without being mendacious is the rescue of Bishop by the Grenadian crowd. It is in that sense, too, that as surely as the Paris Communards of 1871, the Grenadian people on that day stormed the heights of heaven.

Yet even more, March 13, 1979, and October 19, 1983, are in a way two different events, qualitatively speaking. The first was a minority event, the second a majority event. Within four brief years the change within the nature of revolutionary development that Engels spoke about in his 1895 introduction to Marx's *Class Struggles in France* had taken place within Grenada itself. "The time of surprise attacks, of revolutions carried through by small conscious minorities at the head of unconscious masses, is past. Where it is a question of a complete transformation of the social organisation, the masses themselves must also be in it, must themselves have already grasped what is at stake, what they are going in for with body and soul. The history of the last fifty years has taught us that." To use Engels's phrase, the Grenada masses were "in it" in 1983 in a way that they had not been "in it" in 1979.[41]

Why is this? It surely relates to the much larger transformation in the character of revolutions that Marx himself had emphasized in a brilliant passage of the same *Class Struggles in France:*

> Bourgeois revolutions, like those of the eighteenth century, storm more swiftly from success to success; their dramatic effects outdo each other; men and things seem set in sparkling brilliance; ecstasy is the everyday spirit; but they are short lived; soon they have attained their zenith, and a long depression lays hold of society before it learns to as-

similate soberly the results of its storm and stress period. Proletarian revolutions, on the other hand, like those of the nineteenth century, criticise themselves constantly, interrupt themselves continually in their own course, come back to the apparently accomplished in order to recommence it afresh, deride with unmerciful thoroughness the inadequacies, weaknesses and paltrinesses of their first attempts, seem to throw down their adversary only in order that he may draw new strength from the earth and rise again more gigantic before them, recoil ever and anon from the infinite immensity of their own aims, until the situation has been created which makes all turning back impossible.[42]

Granted that the Grenada of 1983 was not the Paris of 1848, that the Grenada folk-people were not the urban Parisian working class, that the terms "bourgeois" and "proletarian" do not always mean the same things in different sociohistorical settings, it is still arguable that the four years between 1979 and 1983 had brought about something comparable to the almost spiritual transformation of popular mood that Marx was talking about. There was, in large sectors of the Grenadian people, a larger commitment to the revolution, a more open militancy, a serious intent to examine mistakes, a search, especially among the younger elements, to understand the theoretical presuppositions of the revolution, above all else a determination that there was no turning back. All of that must surely explain why the popular spirit in the general strike of 1974 had finally succumbed to the Gairyite state power, whereas in 1983 it was prepared to fight the Revolutionary Military Council state power to the bitter end. If to this it is argued that it is implausible that all this could have taken place within only four years, the answer, again using a phrase of Marx, is that revolutions are the locomotives of history. They unleash changes in a brief moment which may otherwise take decades to accomplish. Or—since the Grenadian people, like all West Indian peoples, are profoundly religious— one might say that, in the words of the popular West Indian hymn; "A Thousand Ages in Thy Sight Are Like an Evening Gone."

Just as military historians are tempted to look at the coup d'état of March 13, 1979, in its military aspects, they are tempted to look at October 19, 1983, in similar terms. Was there, in strict terms of military logistics, any possible alternative to what took place? Could things have been different? It is worth noting that the encounter was not just simply—as it has been portrayed by many—an encounter between an unarmed crowd and an armed soldiery. If we are to believe Thomas and Als, a sizeable amount of small arms was available to the Bishop group; what is more, the keys to the armory were available. Vincent Noel as well as Thomas and Norris Bain were, according to reports, ready to make a last stand, but were countermanded by Bishop. Bishop must have known that by giving the further command to surrender he was inviting certain death. Surrender, it could be argued, was ignominious, however much Bishop may have wanted to prevent the killing of more innocent victims. A comparison may be drawn with the Havana decision, in the later U.S. invasion of Grenada, to instruct the Cuban soldiers and workers to resist at Point Salines, an order only conditioned by the instruction that they resist only after they had been attacked. Cuban pride just could not imagine surrender without resistance. It is the same in all such encounters. Nobody, for example, criticizes General George Custer for making his last stand at the battle of the Little Big Horn in 1876; the criticism, rather, is that foolishly he allowed his column to march, without proper protection from the other two neighboring columns of the U.S. cavalry, into Crazy Horse's trap. Which, of course, was the fatal mistake of the Bishop crowd and its leaders, marching into an enclosed space where the odds were hopelessly against them. That mistake can perhaps only be excused by their belief that since the soldiers had not fired at the first encounter of the house release they would therefore not fire at the second encounter at the fort.

Had there been present at this juncture any leader with combat experience, that mistake might possibly have been avoided. Such a leader would immediately have perceived that the correct strategy would have been to keep the crowd in the market square, then perhaps to order their dispersal into the inner recesses of the town. The arms that had been taken to the fort could have been retained to arm a commando-like group of some fifty soldiers (no more than had participated in the 1979 coup) who would then have occupied strategic rooftop positions in the streets leading down, on either side, from the fort, down which, sooner or later, the Revolutionary Military Council personnel carriers (which are not armored tanks but open, uncovered vehicles) would have had to proceed in order to search out their targets. That would have meant that they would have been obliged to enter the city streets which, everywhere, are classic ambush territory. It would have meant urban house-to-house fighting, where the defenders are always at an advantage. That, after all, is the lesson both of the Warsaw Ghetto battle of 1943, where a mere handful of Jewish fighters, poorly armed, were able to hold the massed power of the Nazi Panzers at bay for an astonishing four weeks, and of the more recent 1984 street battles in Beirut, where not even the heavy shelling of the offshore U.S. naval force would prevent the Druze and Phalangist groups from regaining control of the city. If to this it is protested that such a plan would have meant carnage, the answer is, quite simply, that the carnage took place anyway, because the defenders did not undertake a serious counteroffensive. Regrettably, there was not present any military genius, like the young Bonaparte at Toulon in 1793, to see the opportunity and seize it with daring. The first fateful and irretrievable mistake had already been made, to take the crowd to the fort, there to enter their own ambush. That mistake allowed the enemy to fight on his own chosen ground. The outcome was foredoomed. In the verse of G. K. Chesterton on the Irish troubles more than half a century earlier:

Whatever we say, they have got
A Maxim gun and we have not.[43]

10

Bishop, Coard, the Ultraleft Faction, and the Military

The events of the morning and early afternoon of October 19 were followed by the statements of General Hudson Austin on Wednesday night and Major Christopher Stroude on Thursday, October 20. Stroude, curiously enough, seems to have played a double role, first appearing in the company of the Bishop group at Fort Rupert and then, a day later, as spokesman of the newly formed Revolutionary Military Council. Both statements repeated the official version of events, charging that the Bishop group had refused to continue negotiations up to the last moment, that soldiers, male and female, had been forcibly stripped of their uniforms, that Bishop had opened the armory, that the Bishop forces had fired first, and that their intent was to execute the entire party and army top leadership, all of these actions forcing the army to take defensive measures. The Austin statement announced the imposition of a night and day curfew; anyone seeking to demonstrate or disturb the peace was to be shot on sight. Both statements reiterated the warning that the Bishop group, as counterrevolutionaries, had made possible imminent invasion by the imperialist enemies.[1]

The day-to-day events of the following week, until the U.S. invasion of October 25, are clouded, and obviously require further investigation. The Revolutionary Military Council must certainly have been in daily session throughout. It was in complete control of all communications media, just as had been the PRG before it. A London source has reported that during the week before October 25 negotiations began between the Central Committee and Bishop's followers, the latter reaffirming their support for the revolution but conditioning their participation on a return to civilian rule, an enquiry into Bishop's death, and the punishment of those found responsible, and that on October 22 the OEAR faction gave in and accepted the conditions.[2] But there is no independent verification of this, and it seems unbelievable that such negotiations could in fact have taken place, since all Bishop supporters had gone into hiding. It is also difficult to believe that the Central Committee or the Revolutionary Military Council—whichever was in actual power—could have agreed to conditions on October 22, with Bishop eliminated, when they were not prepared to agree to a common accord with Bishop alive on October 18, as reported by Als based on his conversations with both sides.[3] The time for true negotiations, surely, had ended on October 12, with the house arrest. After that, surely neither side could have trusted the other. In the meantime, the Revolutionary Military Council used their control of Radio Free Grenada to broadcast, night and day, frenzied appeals to the populace to prepare for the expected invasion.[4]

≡

The social scientist who attempts to undertake some rational analysis of what occurred cannot but begin with the recognization that it involves, in all of its complexity, practically everything that goes to make the human condition. There is ambition, rivalry, the thirst for power. There is the conflict of strong personalities. There are at one and the same time high ideals and low motives. It is not a Victorian hero and villain melodrama, for all of the leading actors, starting with Bishop and Coard, are complex human beings who cannot be easily stereotyped. All of them are as much victims as instigators, caught up in an awful current of events over which, ultimately, they have no control, so that, in the final analysis, the observer, rather than allocating blame, can only perhaps feel pity and compassion. Nor, finally, should the observer feel surprise that this human and political drama should have taken place in a small Caribbean island practically unknown to the outside world. For the drama, in fact, has its roots in the period after the discovery of America in 1492 when the European colonizing powers imported their own rivalries into the region. It is no accident that both Shakespeare's *Tempest* and Defoe's *Robinson Crusoe* were located by their authors in a tropical island scene, dramatizing for their English readers the twin themes of racial prejudice and colonial exploitation which have made the modern West Indian societies, including Grenada, what they are today.

Much of the post-October discussion—by soldiers, journalists, and others—have centered around the question, Was it all due to a conflict of personae or to a conflict of ideology or of theory? To pose the problem in those terms—it appears at least to this observer—is almost meaningless, since it presupposes an either-or answer which serves to oversimplify the serious complexity of the condition. Person and ideology do not exist separate from each other. The person creates the ideology; the ideology in turn shapes the person. Only a strict deterministic structuralism will downplay the independent influence of the person; only an individualistic liberalism will downplay the independent influence of a socially determined ideology. The two intermix and interact. Both provide clues to solve the riddle of any particular historical moment.

It is palpably clear, from all who knew them, including the present author, that, although they were friends and comrades, there existed a serious difference of character and personality between Bishop and Coard. They were, of course, children of the same intellectual ferment of the 1960s, culminating in the Rodney riots in Jamaica of 1968, the "February revolution" of 1970 in Trinidad, and the advent of Manleyite socialism in Jamaica in 1972. But they were worlds apart as individuals. Coard was the self-defined "intellectual." He had gone through the usual academic mill, had written a minor classic on how the West Indian immigrant child in Britain was channeled into subnormal schools because of racial and cultural prejudice, and had also written on the similar plight of the American blacks in Boston. His education at Brandeis could only have reinforced that sense of race, for the milieu there was more liberal Jewish humanism than it was black radicalism. Coard emerged from the apprenticeship convinced of the exploited role of the black, whether British or American, in a white imperialist world. So, he was always uneasy and suspicious in the presence of whites, notwithstanding his other Marxist intellectual self. More than that he was, psychologically speaking, an introvert. He was not good at small gossip or table talk. He did not have the gift of coping with what Lord Rosebery, in British politics, once called "the Tom, Dick, and Harry aspect" of the political game. He could not set a crowd on fire, like Walter Rodney, or Michael Manley, or even, for that matter, Eric Williams. He was at his best in the private party caucus, where, as Kendrick Radix has described it, he would turn up with ninety-five carefully prepared theses for the agenda, expecting everybody to discuss them in a marathon session.[5] Like many academics, he was arrogant and impatient of criticism; so it is not surprising that colleagues who remember his stint as lecturer, at the Institute of International Relations at the University of the West Indies, St. Augustine campus in Trinidad, should remember him as a difficult person to work with.[6]

Bishop, by contrast, although a fellow Grenadian, was woven from different cloth. His former wife's account of him as a devoted family man, a leader of absolute honesty, patience, and integrity, always the one looking for consensus, completely united with the people, a man who had not chosen to be leader but rather had had the position thrust upon him, may perhaps be discounted as an overly partisan view, although her assertion that "he was always the one to bring peace, to say Okay, if that is what they want, for the peace of it we'll have it like that. That was Maurice," has the ring of truth about it.[7] Her account is supported by others. Don Rojas recalls how, on countless occasions, when proposals were brought to Bishop he would say that before a decision was made he had to get the collective wisdom of the Political Bureau or the Central Committee; or he would say, "Why don't you bounce the idea off on Bernard and the other comrades?"[8] That openness of character is apparent, more than anywhere else, in the fact that whereas Bishop was willing to appear before the Central Committee and answer the charges against him, Coard, by contrast, according to the report of an insider, arrogantly refused for one whole year to present to the same committee a thorough explanation of his resignation earlier on.[9] Others outside of Grenada have made a similar point about Bishop as person. The Latin American novelist Gabriel García Marquez recounts meeting Bishop at the 1983 New Delhi Nonaligned Movement summit conference and being impressed by his gracious manner, his impeccable English and, most of all, his sense of humor.[10] A final testimony comes from Trinidad's Prime Minister George Chambers. Despite his own serious reservations about the PRG regime he records that in the CARICOM heads of government conferences he found Bishop to be a colleague ready to listen to compromise proposals and to adhere to commitments once made.[11]

If these personality sketches are true, to that degree they substantiate the interpretation that the conflict was inherently one of personal temperament. Coard emerges as the textbook Marxist, well read in the literature of what was called in the Grenadian discussions the "science." Bishop, on the other hand, had picked up his Marxism in a less systematic way, from personal experience as much as anything else; one of his last public addresses abroad, to a Hunter College audience in New York, described how his ingrained colonialist loyalty, as a young student in London in 1963, had been shaken when he found himself the only person in a cinema audience who stood up for the national anthem, while every Englishman remained sitting (a story that also shows Bishop's capacity to laugh at himself).[12] Coard, too, in his own right was an excellent public speaker. He had the professional economist's mind, which made him a first-class finance minister. But he lacked the magic charisma of Bishop. For good or ill, the popular following made Bishop the symbolic image of the revolution, so that there grew up a bond of mutual trust and affection that no alien current could contaminate or outside force corrupt. It was not unlike the symbiotic cord that united the people and Fidel Castro in the Cuban case. Indeed, the two leaders had much in common, in terms of temperament. No one, for example, can read Ernesto Cardenal's affectionate pen portrait of Fidel in his *En Cuba,* showing him as genial, warm, gregarious, impatient with office work, always wanting to escape in order to mix with his people in the street or the farm, almost as if, in Cardenal's words, he were still with his comrades in the Sierra Maestra, without seeing much of Bishop in the same description.[13] And, indeed, if another comparison is needed, it is there in the figure of General Omar Torrijos Herrera in the Panamanian case, for Graham Greene's friendly portrait of the general reveals him as a genial, humble man of peasant stock, holding informal court with the villagers to hear their complaints, sharing their coarse jokes, and thereby reinforcing his instinctive dislike of intellectuals, city folk, and politicians.[14]

"He had a special relationship with the Grenadian people," says the insider source already quoted of Bishop, "that no one else did. He would go into the shops in the villages and sit down with them and play cards and talk and laugh and at the same time give them guidance and leadership and confidence that what we were trying to do in Grenada, this new experiment in socio-economic development of a different type in the region could work, but it could only work with the people."[15] It is not surprising, then, not-withstanding the language barrier, that a close personal friendship grew up between the Cuban and Grenadian leaders. Bishop was always "Maurice" to the Grenadian people in the same way as Castro has always been "Fi-del" to the Cuban people. Indeed, so much was this the case that it is astonishing to learn that even the old friends Bishop had imprisoned for "counterrevolutionary" activities remembered him affectionately even while they languished in prison.[16]

Leaving aside for the moment any questions about theoretical or ideo-logical differences, Bishop's position as the star of the revolution, as far as the populace was concerned, was bound to cause trouble. His critics could plausibly argue, as they did, that it ran counter to the principles of collec-tive leadership and collective responsibility. It was "one-manism"; it raised one individual above the rest, creating suspicions about personal ambition. But it is equally true, as the evidence shows, that this line of criticism, in many ways, was in itself a guise to cover up the personal ambitions of others, and especially Coard. According to our anonymous insider:

> I think the basic cause of the problem lay in Bernard Coard's ambition. It was an ambition that was very strong over the years to really be the leader of the party, if not necessarily the leader of the government, then certainly the leader of the party, to formally exercise more power than he was exercising. Now when I say formally exercise some power, let us be clear, Bernard Coard exercised a tremendous amount of power in the party even before this issue of joint leadership came up. And on most cases that had to do with party building, with the training of party cadres and the ideological work within the party and so on. . . . Maurice would defer to Bernard. So he had de facto power within the party . . . a lot of power and influence within the party. But I think what he desired

most of all was that this de facto power be formalised, and he be recognised as *the leader* of the party. Now in our situation, the party was paramount over the state. If he became leader of the party then, maybe not in name, but certainly in practice he would be leader of the revolution.[17]

Once granted these personality differences, the scene was set in the last, final year of the revolution for the ultimate power play between its leading actors. They became, at one and the same time, as if in a Shakespearean historical drama, the dramatis personae of the tragedy and the embodiment of impersonal social forces which ultimately they could not control. The history of all revolutions, whether bourgeois or proletarian, has portrayed that interplay of individual leader and general historical force. It goes back, at least in modern times, to the French Revolution of 1789. Very few of its historians have escaped the temptation to become the partisan of one of its leading actors, from Mirabeau in the beginning to Bonaparte at the end. It has been the same with the historiography of the Haitian Revolution at the same time; not even its Marxist historians, for example, C.L.R. James in his 1938 *Black Jacobins,* have been able to resist the temptation to identify with one of its leading protagonists: Toussaint, Henri-Christophe, Petión. The sheer commanding power of the leading personalities compels attention, if not admiration.

It is not too fanciful to see the Coard-Bishop relationship, potentially creative and ultimately destructive, in these terms. It is not unlike the Danton-Robespierre relationship which has been treated in the 1982 Polish-French film *Danton* by Andrzej Wajda. In that representation Danton is the life-loving, life-celebrating romantic leader who, in Jules Michelet's phrase, was capable of understanding all men and feeling all passions. He is the revolutionary who believes in the natural goodness of men, as a disciple of Rousseau, and puts his faith in the inevitable triumph of the "people." Robespierre, by contrast, is the leader as ideological fanatic, austere and committed, plunged in intrigue and secrecy, who begins by specializing in the police force as an instrument and ends by making it a final purpose. Danton's fatal blunder was to invent the Committee of Public Safety, which was then taken over by Robespierre, to be used for his own purposes in the power struggle. Yet these are not simplistic types, in the melodramatic manner of Carlyle or Dickens. It is misleading to write about the French Revolution in terms of the Scarlet Pimpernel, just as it is misleading to write about the Grenada Revolution in terms of the Central Intelligence Agency. For if Danton is the indecisive romantic, incapable of recognizing how power corrupts, Robespierre is not a monster, but a tortured mind, trapped in the purity of his ideals, torn between his revolutionary faith and his knowledge that the Terror will destroy him as surely as he had destroyed Danton. Each of them made the revolution their master, so that in the end the revolution, like Saturn, devoured its own children.

Fortuitously enough, Coard and Bishop fall into the general parameters of this historical analogy. Leaving aside the particular differences of historical time and place—for, after all, St. George's in 1983 was not Paris in 1789—both Coard and Bishop fit into the analogy. It is not that Bishop is the hero and Coard the villain. For both of them believed, with equal sincerity, in the revolution. Both of them can claim credit for the achievements of the revolution. But by the same token both of them must accept responsibility for the excesses of the revolution: the use of Draconian laws in order to repress opposition, the silencing of a free and independent press, the incarceration of political prisoners, including—if we are to believe the testimony of some—brutal physical torture.[18] Rather, within that framework, their different temperaments persuaded them to go different ways once internal dissensions arose. They both thus committed mistakes. Coard's fatal mistake was to reach for too much power too soon and, even worse, not to perceive—for all his vaunted theoretical acumen—that to move drastically against Bishop would be to destroy the revolution itself. Bishop's fatal mistake was not to recognize the danger soon enough and not to have appealed openly to his popular base in the very beginning, so that in the end he was outmaneuvred by his opponents.

Trying to be fair to both sides, a group of North American friends to the revolution comes to the conclusion that the larger guilt was that of Coard. This violent and shocking ending, the authors of *Death of a Revolution* state, "strongly suggests that the conflict between Bishop and Coard went beyond the issue of popular democracy versus party control, and that personal animosities—jealousy, ambition, vindictiveness—were a crucial part of the equation." They continue, "Indeed, it appears in retrospect that a deep and long-brewing power struggle was also at work. The statements about Bishop becoming swollen with power and grasping for 'one-man leadership' appear unsupported in fact, and probably reflect Coard's personal fear and jealousy of Bishop's popularity with the masses." Furthermore, Bishop's "close supporters who have survived to tell his side . . . argue that Coard wanted to remove Bishop because of Coard's own 'thirst for power.' " Yet according to these authors, Bishop also "apparently let his fears of Coard's intentions distort his response to the question of party leadership, which was not in itself an illegitimate issue. . . . To sum up this tragic struggle, it seems to us that while a case can be made on both sides of the leadership issue—party control versus Bishop's populism—the executions of the leadership cannot be justified by anything, and effectively ended both the revolution and any hope of staving off the long-feared United States attack." [19]

Culpability, after all, is one thing. Crime is another.

As the foregoing quotation indicates, it is probable that the personal factor was not only present, but also perhaps paramount. It indicates that there were also issues relating to the theory and practice of the revolution. Granted—as has already been argued—that a conflict of personal power and ambition lay at the root of the matter, it is simply inconceivable that much of the prolonged discussion that went on in the closed meetings of the party organs during the 1983 period had nothing more to it than that. The record of that discussion surely shows that many party members were sincerely concerned with the state of the revolution, and with the general question of the direction, including strategy and tactics, in which they thought the revolution should go. West Indians, as anybody who has known them for any length of time will appreciate, are not dupes or fools although they can sometimes be naïve, which is quite a different thing. Because of their long colonial and anti-colonial tradition, or even, for that matter, because they are, for the most part in terms both of internal and external migration, a widely traveled people, they are a highly sophisticated political people. The PRG Central Committee minutes reflect that truth.

It has been the thesis of some—Rojas, for example—that no fundamental ideological differences existed between Coard and Bishop, only nuances or minor differences on approach, questions of methodology and tactics and maybe of leadership style.[20] But this, in a way, is to beg the question, for means and ends cannot be so neatly separated. There comes a moment when differences about tactics and strategy become qualitatively transmuted into differences about ultimate purpose. If, for example, differences arose about the pace of the revolution, with some wanting to push forward more rapidly from the "national democratic" stage to the "socialist" stage and then on to the "communist" stage, such differences could hardly be regarded as merely concerning tactics; they would directly concern the very nature of the revolution itself.

It is perhaps possible to determine where differences of a potentially ideological character did in fact not exist. It has been suggested, for example, that some differences arose out of the fact that whereas Bishop and his people early on came out of the Black Power tradition, Coard derived his ideological outlook from Jamaican Communist currents and possibly from Moscow.[21] But this is fanciful speculation, and disproved by the well-known facts about the intellectual formation of both men in the 1960s. Or again, it has been suggested—and picked up avidly by the outside international press after October—that Bishop was a "moderate" and Coard a "hard-liner," especially in the crucial area of foreign policy. But again there is no hard evidence to prove this. Bishop's open letter to President Reagan of March 26, 1981, was at once an earnest plea for improved relationships between the two countries and a spirited protest about continuing U.S. destabilization policies against the island regime;[22] but there is no evidence that the letter did not express the official government view, including that of Coard. And if, again, there is any credence to be placed on the view that, in 1983, after his visit to the United States, Bishop was preparing to be "soft" on the foreign policy issue, even perhaps to "sell out" to the United States, a reading of his collected speeches during the period does not bear out that particular slur at all. Those speeches, indeed, reveal an increasingly emphatic anti-American and anti-imperialist stand, as Bishop obviously comes to realize that any kind of rapprochement was impossible with the ultrareactionary Reagan administration, whatever might have been the case earlier with the Carter administration.[23] Again, there could have been no room for any serious disagreement between Coard and Bishop on this matter. The humiliating treatment meted out to him by the Washington people during his visit there in June 1983 must have persuaded Bishop, beyond any doubt, that peaceful coexistence was impossible.[24] Coard, reputedly more influenced by Moscow than Havana, could not have disagreed.

It has been said that Elizabeth Tudor's sixteenth-century foreign policy was Protestant at home and Catholic abroad, based upon the imperative need to appease Philip of Spain as long as possible before the ultimate attack came in 1588. But once President Reagan had made his Caribbean trip in April 1982 and denounced Grenada as a Marxist "virus" it was clear that no Elizabethan policy of appeasement was practical for Grenada. Any leader, Bishop or Coard, who had advocated such a policy after that date would have committed political suicide. In sum, there seems to have been an almost total consensus in St. George's about the foreign policy of the revolution. This conclusion is supported by the fact that Bishop's Washington visit was approved by the Central Committee, albeit with some misgivings, and that the subsequent analysis of the visit prepared for the NJM Political Bureau was satisfied with the results.[25]

If, then, it follows, there were differences that approached the theoretical or the ideological, they have to be found in the internal dynamics of the revolution itself. For if, as Marx pointed out in the passage already quoted, all revolutions, both bourgeois and proletarian, have their distinctive characteristics, it is equally true that each particular revolution possesses its own peculiar idiosyncrasies, related to the historical time and place in which it takes place. The Grenada Revolution, thus, took place in a tiny Caribbean island society with its own special sociocultural traits: its ethnic character as a black society, its inward-turned social propinquity, its general life style where everything personal becomes political and everything political becomes personal. There is here very little of Durkheim's urban anomie or Weber's institutional impersonality; after all, you can walk from one end of St. George's to another in an hour. That is why so much of the post-October analysis, both by radical friends and hostile critics abroad, has missed the atmosphere of the *ambiente* in which the events took place. In English terms, it is village life, in American terms, small-town life. It would take an Agatha Christie or a Sinclair Lewis to do it full justice.

The prolonged discussions of the Central Committee and general party meetings have already been examined. What do they tell us about possible ideological conflict within the PRG? If one leaves aside the purely personal ambitions that must have provided much of the motivation, it is demonstrably clear that serious differences about ideology were present. The ultraleft faction set those differences in terms of, first, the theory of "stages" of the revolution, and second, the theory of the appropriate tactical vehicles of revolution. Both were intertwined, because it is impossible in real life to separate the theory of "stages" from the theory of "vehicles."

With reference to the issue of "stages," the ultraleft faction somewhere along the line decided that there was too much vacillation in pursuing full-scale communism. Its view was presented in the plenary meeting of October 1982:

> The Party stands at the crossroads. Two routes are open to the Party. The first route is the petty bourgeois route which would seek to make Comrade Bernard's resignation the issue. This would only lead to temporary relief, but will surely lead to the deterioration of the Party into a social democratic society, and, hence, the degeneration of the Revolution. This road will be an easy one to follow, given the objectively based backwardness and petty bourgeois nature of the society. The second route is the Communist route. The route of the Leninist standards and functioning. The route of criticism and collective leadership. The Central Committee reaffirms the position taken by the General Meeting of September 12 and 13. The Party must be put on a Leninist footing.[26]

All is stated in proper Marxist-Leninist terms. But what strikes the reader is that it is in fact un-Marxist in its astonishing naïveté. It violates practically every rule that Marx and Engels, and after them Lenin, had laid down about the whole general problem of transitional stages, as society moves from capitalism to communism. Marx and Engels had never seen socialism or communism as an ideal for which a fine blueprint could be drawn up, but as the product of the laws of development of capitalism; and the forms which socialism might take would therefore only be revealed by a historical process still unfolding. In his definitive *Critique of the Gotha Programme* (1875)—which was later accepted by Lenin, in his *The State and Revolution* (1917) as the authoritative statement on the subject—Marx distinguished between two phases of communist society. The first phase is the type and form of society that will immediately follow on the heels of capitalism. It will necessarily carry the marks of its origin: the new ruling class of workers will still need the state apparatus to resist counterrevolutionary forces; popular mental and moral states of mind will still be colored by bourgeois ideas and values; and income, although no longer derived from the private ownership of property, will need to be calculated according to work done rather than according to need. This will be followed, over an indeterminate period of time, by the "higher stage" of communist society, under which the state will wither away, new concepts and attitudes of work will develop, and wealth and income will be distributed according to the motto "from each according to his ability, to each according to his need." None of this would take place overnight, for the transition from capitalism to communism may well require a historical time period as lengthy as that which witnessed the transition from feudalism to capitalism.

The various statements of the ultraleft PRG faction in the Grenada case show clearly that its members had not read their Marx carefully. Marx, who in his own right was a superb sociologist, recognized that what the French call *mentalités collectifs* change at a glacial pace; the new society cannot in any way transform them immediately. His Grenada disciples, on the contrary, were Marxists in a hurry, speaking of a "communist" society as if it was just around the corner. They recognized that their society was still possessed of a petit-bourgeois communal psychology. But it was at best a theoretical perception only. They did not in any serious way adjust their tactics and strategy to the reality of those petit-bourgeois elements: that this was a society still composed of a peasant majority clinging to the idea of individual landownership, a tiny working class only embryonically industrial working class in the Marxist sense, and a middle class thoroughly West Indian in its individualistic values. In terms of economic structure, four years of social reform programs had not in any serious way attacked the land problem, so that a tiny set of wealthy estate owners still existed. Even more: the ultraleft members themselves were in many ways petit-bourgeois still; as Don Rojas has put it, "Even the class composition of the party itself was petit-bourgeois basically—radical petty bourgeois people who had evolved beyond their own class and become proletarianized." [27]

Rather than attempt to meet these issues in any constructive theoretical manner, the ultraleft group elected to adopt a rigid and dogmatic line of action that can only be termed pseudo-Marxist. It might have learned something, for all the reading in the "science" that its members did, by reading Fourier's early writings on a "socialism for the peasant," instead of fondly believing that the Grenada "masses" were some sort of modern industrial proletariat. It did not correctly understand that the struggle for socialism, anywhere, must be a protracted struggle, requiring patience, understanding of weaknesses, a recognition of the concrete, objective conditions that retard the growth of the new socialist consciousness. Somehow or another, it became convinced that the Grenada pace was too slow. It thereby committed the fatal mistake of speeding up the pace without ensuring that it had behind it the understanding and support of the mass populace in that move. It therefore committed the same mistake that the Soviet Russian leadership made with its forced collectivization of the farms in 1932 and that the Chinese leadership made with their "cultural revolution" of the 1970s. Both of those decisions cost the Russian and Chinese revolutions dearly, because, being decisions made from the top rather than from the bottom, they entailed a tragic loss of human talent and ability the true dimensions of which we still do not know. In the end-result, then, the Grenadian ultraleft forgot the lesson that both Marx and Lenin, in their different ways, had ceaselessly taught: that the revolutionary process, at every stage, must have behind it the sympathetic undertstanding and informed support of the masses.

The PRG debate on the theory of "vehicles," as distinct from the debate on the theory of "stages," reveals a similar purblind attitude. For the Coard group the appropriate vehicle for the new push forward was to be a revitalized party along strict Leninist lines. The way forward, in the words of Leon James at the Central Committee meeting of September 14, was to take an honest, cold-blooded, objective, and scientific approach to the situation. The key phrase was "iron discipline," which really meant complete ruthlessness in dealing with a leader like Bishop who was seen as weak and vacillating. The "science" demanded nothing less.[28]

This, on any showing, was the central and crucial issue of the matter: the role of the vanguard party in the revolutionary process, and its relationships with, first, the masses and, second, the state apparatus. It was, as in all situations in the contemporary world of mass nationalist liberation movements, an important and legitimate issue demanding discussion at the highest and most sophisticated level. But there are certain things that have to be noted about the evolution of that discussion in the Grenada context. In the first place, there is no one, single, orthodox route to revolution. Each national process must adjust the "science" to its own special circumstances. That had been sufficiently recognized by observers both before and after October 1983. The Jacobs brothers wrote:

There is no "orthodox" or "correct" or "traditional" route to revolutionary change, just as there are no definitive, complete and inviolable theories, if only because reality changes all the time and the frontiers of knowledge keep expanding. To argue, therefore, as the dogmatists and the bourgeois intellectuals do, that for socialist revolution to occur we need the existence of a Marxist-Leninist vanguard party which mobilises the politically conscious urban proletariat for the purpose of seizing state power and establishing the dictatorship of the proletariat at one stroke, is to chase after phantoms, and, of course, create self-fulfilling prophecies.[29]

Selwyn Cudjoe, writing in late 1983, made a similar point:

One may wish to ask whether the NJM were too overcome or overburdened by the strict rigidity of the Leninist position and whether it was modified sufficiently to suit the special conditions of Grenada. Certainly, after the Vietnamese and Cuban wars of national liberation, the role of the party vis-à-vis its military component and its relationship to the general populace needed greater theoretical clarification. After all, Grenada with its relatively homogeneous population, does not represent the same degree of heterogeneity as the Soviet society. . . . In the [Russian] context, the insistence on the inviolability of the party's line, its rigidity and inflexibility under most circumstances are understandable, if not necessarily acceptable. The dominance and the rigidity of the party can be seen as necessary if there is to be any coherence of and for the society at all given times. Grenada, on the other hand, is a small society where everybody knows everybody else, where all the people speak the same language, have been subjected, more or less, to the same conditions of slavery, colonialism and imperialist exploitation. . . . The insistence on the guiding role of the party, yes. Its rigidity and turgidly imported line remains a questionable proposition.[30]

As these citations show, it was the fundamental contradiction between the uncritical acceptance of a model borrowed from outside and the empirical realities of the local situation that became the Achilles heel of the ultraleft faction. It led them, inevitably, into disastrous mistakes of analysis and tactics. The contradiction spawned even more contradictions. There was the contradiction between looking at the administrative weaknesses of the revolution and then blaming Bishop for it all, a thoroughly un-Marxist procedure. There was the contradiction involved in the charges brought against Bishop, for, on the one hand, they accused him of "personality cultism" and of spearheading a conspiracy against the Coards, while on the other hand they accused him of indecisive and weak leadership, charges that are diametrically opposed. There was the further contradiction of presenting themselves as the pure custodians of the Marxist gospel and then inventing a curious concept of dual, joint leadership that cannot be discovered anywhere in the Marxist texts; it is almost as if one were to identify the Papal Schism of medieval Europe, with one Pope in Rome and another in Avignon, as having its origin in the universalistic teachings of primitive Christianity.

As this situation came to a head it was, then, an irreconcilable clash between the doctrine of party authority and the doctrine of popular sovereignty. This does not mean that Coard was the protagonist of the first and Bishop the protagonist of the second. Things are never that simplistic. For Bishop himself had worked within the party for four years, accepting all of its secrecy, in the same way as he had accepted the incarceration of former friends and colleagues as political prisoners. As some other commentators have pointed out, there is a real danger of developing a Bishop cult, which can only have the result of even further mystifying the why and the wherefore of the events. Bishop himself, after all, was not completely an innocent. He could share the ultraleft extremism as much as anyone else. It is, for example, difficult to read his angry speech of February 15, 1980, in which he criticized an intercepted letter by a priest of a Catholic order as constituting an attempt at counterrevolutionary destabilization on the part of the Church, without feeling that he had not really understood the letter. For to any careful reader, the letter sounds like an earnest effort for church-state cooperation on the part of someone who clearly shares the modern ecumenical effort to foster a Marxist-Christian dialogue. As everyone knows, the real religious counterrevolutionary efforts came, not from that source, but from the North American fundamentalist churches which flooded the island with their cheap, reactionary pamphlet literature. Bishop, here, was barking up the wrong tree. And for him to end that speech with the simple-minded declaration that the people look to the Church for spiritual guidance and to the government for political leadership is to deny not only the modern ecumenical debate in which both Protestants and Catholics are beginning to emphasize the radical character of the social teaching of the Christian churches, but also even to deny the legitimacy of the early English Victorian movement of Christian Socialism out of which it rose. Camilo Torres, the Latin American priest-turned-revolutionary, of all people, would have been astonished to hear a fellow revolutionary assert that the Church had no place in politics.[31] This particular episode, indeed, showed a lack of ideological sophistication on the part of the PRG leadership. The revolutionary process ought not to travel too far and too fast ahead of the existing popular consciousness, lest it lose touch with the masses. As one Caribbean liberationist theologian has observed, it was undoubtedly a major failure on the part of the leadership to play down the religious factor in Grenadian society, thus making it easy for its enemies, both within and without, to charge it with being a godless revolution of atheistic communism.[32]

It is, then, not just a case of Bishop, the innocent populist, pitted against Coard, the Jesuit dialectician. Bishop, as much as Coard, could talk doctrinal nonsense when it suited him. It is much more to the point that, despite the inconsistencies of thought and action of both—to which, like all human beings, they were entitled—Coard, at bottom, was Leninist, and Bishop, at bottom, populist. Coard thought, essentially, in Leninist (sometimes perhaps Stalinist) terms; perhaps that explains the curious fact that throughout the party debates there are no references at all to the local Caribbean political thought, almost as if its architects—Frantz Fanon, Aimé Césaire, Eric Williams, Cheddi Jagan, Juan Bosch, Pedro Albizu Campos, C.L.R. James, Jacques Roumain, Fernando Ortiz, Jean Price-Mars—could have made no meaningful contribution to the issues that confronted the Grenada ideologues. Bishop thought, essentially, in West Indian populist terms, as is evident enough from his collected speeches, where throughout he obviously prefers to speak in terms of particular groups—the students, the peasants, the women—rather than in the more abstract terms of "bourgeoisie" and "proletariat." It is in this sense that, ultimately, Bishop was nearer to the subjectivist reality of the Grenadian people. Coard, by any measure, had become divorced from that reality, for only that can explain why he could have made such a fundamental error as to miscalculate the mood of the Grenadian people and to adopt such a contemptuous attitude toward them in the final act of the drama. The critical analyst of the whole affair is almost driven to ask himself: if Coard was the brilliant ideologue as he has been portrayed, how could he commit such a disastrous error of judgment? One is tempted to agree with Rojas that the explanation lies in the fact that Coard allowed an avalanche of rampaging ultraleftism within the party to grow out of control and distort his judgment.[33]

Various other insider-participants have described the atmosphere of those last months of the revolution. There was clearly a coordinated plan on the part of the Coard group to lay the groundwork for a takeover of the revolutionary leadership. Ministers such as Jacqueline Creft were demoted from their party membership. The existence of a so-called right-wing faction was identified, much to everybody else's surprise. Everybody, both in government offices and party organs, was recruited into the compulsory study groups, which were really exercises in ideological indoctrination. Party cadres were advised to catch up on their reading, which included, among the favored texts, the book of 1974 by the Soviet academician K. N. Brutents, *Present-Day National Liberation Revolutions: Some Theoretical Questions.* Indeed, so demanding did the study obligations become that the administrative and managerial tasks of the governmental system were seriously interfered with, thus further complicating a general situation where the revolution, throughout its whole life, was harried by a calamitous shortage of trained personnel in those fields. It is almost as if the revolution became buried in study. The parliamentary talkers took over from the administrators. Both sides probably took a close look at their military support; it has been said that the Coard group moved to disarm members of the army and militia regarded as being "unreliable." Both sides also probably talked with foreign friends; it has been averred that the Coard people talked with the local Russian embassy people, although, as related by Castro later on, the Bishop people did not talk with their Cuban friends.

All of this—and especially what went on during the *semaine sanglante* after October 19—urgently requires investigation by future historians. What is at least certainly known is that the internal power struggle had been at least a year in the making; Bishop's Antiguan friend Tim Hector has related how he, Hector, warned Bishop as far back as November 1982 that there were discernible signs of a temper of "bureaucratic Stalinism" in the PRG ranks. In response Bishop became angry and insisted that there was no room for "isms" of any kind in the revolution, leading, as Hector remembers, to a cooling of their relationship. Hector's more general comment is that Bishop, with a lawyer's training, was overcautious in demanding proof of charges which, together with the fact that he had never really had any interest in the history of socialism as an idea, overdisposed him to seek consensus with the Stalinist elements beyond the point when consensus was possible.[34] The historian can only wonder whether things might have turned out differently if Bishop had listened more seriously to a friend's warning. Hector's account, once again, serves to give credence to the general opinion that Bishop was ultimately betrayed by his own essential decency as a person, by his tendency to trust people too much, to believe that consensus could solve all. In the Shakespearean quotations that Hector uses, Bishop thus came to play the role of Othello to Coard's Iago.

Cudjoe, in the piece already noted, draws an interesting analogy between the Grenada power struggle and what happened, in a somewhat similar fashion, in the People's National Movement and the government of Trinidad and Tobago in 1958–60. On that occasion the two men involved were Eric Williams, as prime minister and party political leader, and C.L.R. James, the Trinidadian Marxist, with James being called home to Trinidad from Ghana in order to help in the development of the national independence movement, as editor of the party newspaper. The arrangements broke down three years later. James, with his self-image as the theoretician of the world revolutionary struggle, had imagined becoming the theoretical leader of the movement, leaving Williams as political leader. If that maneuver, as Cudjoe presents it, is to be seen as somehow similar to the Coard takeover in the Grenada case, it is useful to understand why it failed dismally. The reasons were clear even at the time. First, Williams could never have been dislodged because both as West Indian scholar and consummate politician he towered over everybody else, including James (who made the mistake of treating Williams as if he, Williams, were still James' early pupil at Queens Royal College in the 1930s). Second, Williams, psychologically, possessed and was possessed by an "inward hunger" for power and recognition which would brook no rival, and it also made him superb at manipulating men for his own purposes, as his successful political career shows. By contrast, James, for all his vaunted portrayal of himself as master strategist and tactician, never matched that record, all of his directly political adventures—including his later organization of the Workers and Farmers party in Trinidad—being stillborn. Williams knew, cleverly, how to get rid of people he could not get on with simply by ignoring them, as he did with James. Third, there was the factor of ideology. The dominant note of the Trinidad movement, in those days, was black middle-class nationalism, of which Williams was the incomparable theoretician. By contrast, James was an international Marxist, an exponent of socialism, for which Williams—and of course the Trinidad electorate which he led—had no room.[35]

There are, then, certain similarities and differences between the Trinidadian and Grenadian cases. In both cases, there took place an intense debate about the role of the party in the respective movements, as Williams's address of 1958, "Perspectives for Our Party," shows.[36] In both cases, two leading figures, so different from each other, struggled for the national leadership. In both cases, too, any really serious working cooperation between those involved hardly seems credible, in the Grenada case because Coard's ambition would not have tolerated it for long, in the Trinidadian case because the mere thought of anybody riding in tandem with Williams's massive egocentricity is on the face of it laughable.

But the differences outweigh the similarities, if we are to use these two cases as a comparative case study. Bishop, as prime minister, did not possess, for good or ill, the gifts of Williams, either the historical scholarship or the authoritarian personality. It is true that, as much as Williams, he was the adored popular hero of the movement. But Williams would never have made the mistake, as did Bishop, of playing that trump card too late. Finally, the most important difference was that in Trinidad there existed among everybody a consensus on the rules of the game: both Williams, for all of his authoritarian temper, and James, for all of his very real Marxism, took for granted the system of parliamentary democracy inherited from British colonialism. It was Coard's decision at the last moment, to use the weapon of military force that made all the difference in Grenada.

To these considerations, we should add that any discussion about the respective roles of government and party, or the respective roles of "political leader" and "theoretical leader," must recognize that it cannot be the same in the small West Indian island societies as it is, say, in the advanced Western European constitutional democracies. For in Britain or France it is readily accepted that party and government, although belonging to the same national movement, inevitably live separate and largely autonomous existences; that is the case with the British Labour party when Labour is in power and with the French Socialist party when the socialists are in power. In small ministates it is different, and it has to be different, if only because the same few leading personalities run and control both government and party. It is therefore difficult to accept Cudjoe's assertion that the distinction between the "political leader" and the "theoretical leader" is a "very simple though necessary distinction." [37]

With the formation of the Revolutionary Military Council on October 19 the revolution entered into its final, brief stage. Here there is yet a further analogy with the French Revolution of 1789. That is the moment when the revolution enters into its Napoleonic phase. In a prophetic passage in his *Reflections on the French Revolution* Burke had warned that as each successive stage of the revolution produced more chaos there would emerge a military adventurer to impose order. As that prophecy came true, Napoleon in fact reaped that harvest of the failure of the Dantons and the Robespierres. It is now clear that in the week between October 19 and October 25, with Bishop gone, the military men such as Hudson Austin and Liam James and Ewart Layne took over tactical control. It is immaterial, in one way, whether they were being used by Coard or whether Coard was using them. The material fact is that it was now military, not civilian rule; and in such circumstances he who holds the gun calls the shots.

The Revolutionary Military Council, of course, was not a brand-new outfit composed of newcomers. Some of its members were members of the Central Committee, including Ian St. Bernard, Ewart Layne, Christopher Stroude, and Leon Cornwall, so that there was a certain degree of continuity. George Louison is of the opinion that Liam James, in charge of the police and intelligence forces, and Ewart Layne, as Political Bureau chief in the army, wielded the real power, with General Austin trailing behind them.[38] The opinion is shared by Russell Tyson, another government worker who also knew them all; he strongly believes, he says, that Austin was thrust into his position as a front and could never have led the country or the army as has been alleged, and that in reality Cornwall, Stroude, and Layne were the "point men" at the helm of the army.[39] These opinions make sense, for it is the experience of most modern revolutions, starting with the Russian Revolution, that it is the figure of the party political commissar attached to the military forces who controls the decision-making process. In the Grenada case, we do not know too much about the leaders of the Revolutionary Military Council as persons. It is possible that some sort of personality transformation might have taken place with some of them throughout the years of the PRG regime. It is of interest to read the observation of Lloyd Noel, one of the PRG political prisoners, speaking of

Austin, "I never saw him as a hardline military man, but a likeable, charming chap who worshipped the ground Maurice Bishop walked on." [40] The observation has to be set against the report that Austin, a former prison guard, had earlier been removed from command of the Fort Rupert prison because of charges of ill-treatment of prisoners.

Whatever the case, these men personified, in the Grenada case, yet another feature of so much of the contemporary Third World: the emergence of the military strongman, for example, Samuel Doe in Liberia, Jerry Rawlings in Ghana, Desi Bouterse in Suriname, Idi Amin in Uganda. He comes into power by a coup d'état plotted in the army or air force camps; sometimes deliberately "wastes" his predecessors and opponents; promises to put an end to the old civilian regime with its corrupt politicians and squabbling political parties; vows to return to camp once order and national moral purity have been restored; and all of it usually accompanied by a rhetoric of half-baked revolutionary language, and seemingly without any understanding of the general economic and social conditions that occasioned the corruption and the squabbling in the first place. The signal contribution of men like Austin and James and Cornwall to all of this razzmatazz was to seek to legitimize their new power by citing the need to prepare for a U.S. invasion which they themselves had in fact invited by their own actions. It is also worth noting that this type of leader usually appears in newly independent countries where there is little, if any, long-standing tradition of a professional military elite shaped by training, institutional pride, and a respected place in the national society, not to mention honed by combat experience. It is not surprising, then, that among the new Grenada military leaders there was no Bonaparte at Austerlitz, or, for that matter, General Custer at the Little Big Horn. The military leaders rapidly disappeared on October 25, with Austin reportedly vanishing into the "bush" with a handful of hostages, to be later captured and now imprisoned.

One final, and indeed crucial, question remains. Was there a Central Intelligence Agency involvement in the collapse of the revolution? As one analysis has pointed out, granted the well-known history of CIA plotting against regimes seen as anti-American, the suggestion that there were no CIA agents in Grenada at the time of the coup and the invasion is, on the face of it, preposterous. It is inconceivable that the American intelligence services would not have been present, in one way or another. There is, in fact, some circumstantial evidence to prove the point. The mainland press reported on the presence of a former U.S. consul in Laos masquerading as a student at the St. George's medical school, as well as a ham radio operator, also at the medical school, who transmitted coded messages about troop movements. There could also have been CIA involvement in the earlier fire and bombing episodes that were directed against the revolutionary government. It is likewise not unreasonable to assume that the CIA had managed to place an informer at the level of the Central Committee. It has even been suggested that there might have been *agents provocateurs* present in the crowd that released Bishop, which might explain the mystery as to why the crowd moved to the fort rather than to the market square.[41] The same source has speculated that the identity of the informer, if such existed, may become known when it is seen who fades from sight among the twenty prisoners when it came time for their scheduled trials.[42] It is of some interest to note that of those prisoners, Ian St. Bernard was freed from the major charge of murder in August 1984, with twenty other prisoners of the original forty-eight having been released earlier.

11

The Counterrevolution Prepared: The Role of the Caribbean Bourgeoisie

It is no exaggeration to say that large and important elements of the Caribbean bourgeoisie—that is to say, of the English-speaking Commonwealth Caribbean—were suspicious of, and hostile to, the Grenada Revolution from the beginning. The suspicion and the hostility, of course, were by no means total. The more left-wing elements of the regional academic intelligentsia welcomed the new regime enthusiastically, while even the non-Marxist, liberal elements were sympathetic. Many members of the other middle-class professions also gave their support, although sometimes with reservations, including the eminent jurist Aubrey Fraser.[1] At the regional intergovernmental level, again, all of Grenada's fellow members in CARICOM soon proffered diplomatic recognition of the new regime, based generally on the accepted precept of international public law that, except in special cases, internal changes of government, even by force, do not justify refusal of such recognition, and based, more particularly, on the doctrine of "nonintervention" in the domestic affairs of member states as enunciated and accepted in the charter treaties of both the CARICOM organization in 1973, and OECS in 1981.[2] As a member of both of those regional bodies, as well as of the regional university, Grenada was thus enabled to continue after 1979 as a sovereign state participating fully in all of their activities, including summit conferences of CARICOM held in 1982 and 1983.

Grenada also remained a member in good standing of the Commonwealth of Nations, with Prime Minister Bishop attending Commonwealth summit meetings like that of 1983 in New Delhi. The constitutional lawyer, indeed, will note the curious fact that while the PRG regime abrogated in toto the Grenada Independence Constitution of 1974, it did not declare itself a republic, as did Trinidad and Tobago after 1962, but on the contrary, by special proclamation retained a nominated governor-general in the person of Sir Paul Scoon, who, as a ceremonial figure in the archaic manner of the old British Crown Colony system, remained as the representative of the Queen in St. George's. It is not the least of West Indian cultural anomalies that many West Indians retain an affectionate regard for Britain even in their most revolutionary moments. There is little doubt that both Coard and Bishop would have been delighted to have received the Queen on a state visit.

All of this, in sum, shielded the new Grenada from any sort of regional ostracism. It is true that the other CARICOM and OECS governments were concerned about the regime's failure to honor its early promise to hold elections, and that the concern was rooted in a concept of what "democracy" meant, far different from the interpretation of "democracy" entertained by the new Grenada leadership. But that philosophical difference, basic and fundamental as it was, was somewhat ameliorated by a general regional temper of "live and let live," formalized in the acceptance by the CARICOM summit meeting held at Ocho Rios, Jamaica, in November 1982, of the doctrine of "ideological pluralism" (first enunciated in the U.S. Linowitz Report of 1976); the Ocho Rios Declaration forthrightly stated that while "the emergence of ideological pluralism responds to internal processes and is an irreversible trend within the international system, we are committed to ensuring that it will not inhibit the processes of integration."[3] The declaration thus reflected the very real sense of regional community.

Throughout these years, then, although the common foreign policy envisaged in Article 17 of the 1973 CARICOM Chaguaramas Treaty had not materialized, there did take place a positive coordination of foreign policy moves between member states. The importance of that fact, from the viewpoint of the present argument, is that a number of those moves involved CARICOM support of Grenada against U.S. hostility. There was the U.S. attempt in 1981 to block the plans of the European Economic Community to help in cofinancing the construction of the new international airport project at Point Salines, not to mention bringing pressure to bear on both the World Bank and the International Monetary Fund to vote against funding aid for other Grenadian technically viable projects. There was, worst of all, the affair of the Caribbean Development Bank in the same year when the United States offered the bank a $4 million loan for "basic human needs" in the region, on the explicit condition that Grenada be excluded; all of the CARICOM members closed ranks to refuse an offer made in such divisive terms. The Caribbean regional sense, in these matters, was stronger than U.S. economic sabotage. Indeed, it is worthy of note that the real threat which faced that regional sense was not the Grenada "human rights" issue but the "minitrade war" which broke out in early 1983 among the "more developed countries" of Trinidad, Barbados, and Jamaica, as each one resorted to protectionist measures—monetary manipulation, increased import licenses, differential trading rates—to protect its own market and thus frustrate the goal of a regional common market.[4]

Yet when all this has been recognized, it is nonetheless the case that it did not prevent the development, step by step, of an anti-Grenada propaganda campaign on the part of the West Indian propertied classes and the more conservative of the regional governments which represented their interests, notably the Barbados of Prime Minister Tom Adams and the Jamaica of Prime Minister Edward Seaga. Notwithstanding the fact that both of those governments called themselves "Labour"—another West Indian colonial anomaly—they were in fact conservative in their domestic policies and almost slavishly pro-United States in their foreign policies. They, and the neocolonial bourgeoisie whom they represented, could not stomach socialism in any form, not merely the parliamentary socialism of the Manley years in Jamaica between 1972 and 1980, and certainly not the more radical-sounding socialism of the Grenada regime. They engaged Bishop in angry debate at each summit conference; and the "war of words" which erupted in early 1983 between Bishop and Adams, going down into the gutter of West Indian "robber talk," revealed not only the ideological differences but also the personal animosities which informed the encounter.[5] There was no question, of course, of breaking off diplomatic relationships. But diplomatic harassment was always possible, and Grenadian ministers and governmental personnel were regularly subjected to humiliating treatment as they passed through the Barbados airport.[6]

This set the pattern for more systematic destabilization efforts at the nongovernmental level. Chris Searle's book on that subject has to be read with caution, for it is a doctrinaire and completely uncritical defense of the PRG regime, self-righteous in tone, and perceiving every critic of the regime, however mild, as a CIA agent. But much of what it says has been documented from other sources. There were terrorist acts within Grenada itself, such as the fatal Queens Park bomb blast of June 19, 1980, and the gunning down of four young men in St. Patrick's Parish on November 17, 1980. There was evidence that U.S. mercenaries, in collaboration with Gairy, had planned to make Grenada their main target in a Caribbean expedition, with U.S. financing. More systematically, there is little doubt that an extensive mass-media propaganda blitz was undertaken in the region to discredit as much as possible the achievements and purposes of the revolution. Grenada, like Jamaica before, became the target of an avalanche of hostile and critical reports, ranging from the Voice of America radio station in Antigua, *Newsweek* and *Time* magazines, the American

Security Council Foundation, such leading regional newspapers as the Barbados *Advocate* and the *Jamaica Daily Gleaner,* both the *Trinidad Guardian* and *Express,* not to speak of the U.S. Information Service.[7]

In documenting all this Searle sometimes tries to prove too much. He reproduces, for example, Bishop's address of April 17, 1982, in which the prime minister cites a research analysis done by the Media Workers Association in Grenada on the content of regional newspapers between June 1980 and December 1981, showing that of a total of some 1,570 articles on Grenada about 60 percent were downright lies or distortions. This appears to imply that the other 40 percent might have been favorable, a conclusion which is supported by any independent reading of the same press at the time.[8] The *Trinidad Express,* for example, carried many articles by university people in defense of the revolution, permitting expression of divergent opinions, which is more than can be said for the state-controlled media in Grenada itself. And if the same paper periodically ran lists of political prisoners held in St. George's that is no more than what Amnesty International always does. The *Express* also, for that matter, carried from time to time interviews with Bishop himself.[9] Nor is it quite fair to include the *Washington Post* and the *New York Times* in the list of hostile press magnates, for they belong, as everybody knows, to an American liberal tradition; both of them led the press campaign, after October 1983, in exposing the hypocritical emptiness of the Reagan administration's excuses for the invasion. And coming back to the regional press, it would surely be difficult for any fair-minded reader to believe that the *Express,* for all of its editorial opposition to the revolution, ever sunk to the level of sheer vulgarity, personal libel, and scurrilous irresponsibility that marked the *Jamaica Daily Gleaner* in its venomous vendetta against Manley and his socialism in the 1970s.[10] Domestic quarrels, perhaps, are always more savage than international squabbles.

With these provisos, however—albeit they are important—Searle is right to insist that during this period Grenada became the target of a concerted media assault which can only be explained by the fact that the PRG regime had elected to follow a revolutionary path out of tune with the mainstream ideology of the region. They were marching to the sound of a different drummer, and the West Indian middle class, notoriously neocolonialist in its mentality, did not like the sound. Like the Cuban middle class after 1959, they saw Bishop, like Castro, as a traitor to his class. Or, to be more charitable, they saw him, as Bernard Coard's elder brother Robert, living contentedly in the United States, has said of his brother, as "a bright kid . . . very committed . . . but a little misguided perhaps."[11] But charitable or not, their paranoid fear of "communism" made it certain that in the long run they would not be prepared to live with Grenada as they saw it.

Until the events of October 1983 erupted, the various programs of destabilization had to be content with basically very little success. More than
anything else—as already noted—the Grenada regime was protected by the
universally accepted doctrine of "nonintervention." That doctrine, indeed,
had been invoked immediately after the coup d'état of 1979, by the Trinidad government, with its then minister of external affairs citing the so-
called Mexican Estrada Doctrine of 1930, which gave definitive expression
to the view that it is not the business of any government to pronounce
moral judgment on any particular regime or on the nature of any governmental system that any other state may adopt. Diplomatic recognition, it
follows, does not imply moral approval or disapproval; it simply responds
to that respect for sovereignty which is at the heart of all international
relationships.[12]

But the events of October 12 and 19 changed the whole picture, almost
overnight. The regional community, of which Grenada was a member, was
compelled to reexamine the "nonintervention" doctrine, and for that reason alone Grenada will become a classic case study in the law books. It may
fairly be said that, as the anguished public debate and the frenzied diplomatic negotiations were conducted in that two-week period, four alternative lines of action presented themselves: (1) a rigorously observed "hands
off" policy, on the ground that Grenadians had a right to resolve their own
internal problems by themselves; (2) a policy of agreed upon and immediately enforced economic sanctions, in order to bring pressure upon the new
Revolutionary Military Council to moderate its behavior and accept some
measure of conciliation; (3) a "rescue operation" to be undertaken by the
available forces of the Caribbean Community; and (4) a "rescue operation"
to be undertaken by the same force, but with the invited participation of
the United States.

Merely to state the first option, which was recommended by President
Burnham of Guyana, was to reject it.[13] In terms of international protocol, of
course, it was correct. But it was immoral, for it would have had the effect
of abandoning a fellow West Indian people to a ruthless military regime
against which they were powerless; as in the earlier case of the Spanish
Civil War, it would simply have allowed the stronger side to prevail and do
as it pleased. The case was cogently stated by the regional university
lecturer Trevor Farrell. "Non-intervention," he wrote, "is not, and cannot
be an absolute principle. There are other circumstances in which intervention in another country is justifiable. . . . There are circumstances in which
the principle of non-intervention clashes with the principle of people's right
to life, and the latter principle must take precedence over the former. The
intervention of Nyerere's Tanzania in Uganda to halt Idi Amin's butchery
was, in my view, supportable. An intervention by, say, a powerful Nigeria

against the white racist regime in South Africa can be supported. An intervention to halt the murder by a Hitler of millions of Jews would be supportable." [14]

The same case was propounded by A.N.R. Robinson, chairman of the Tobago House of Assembly and former minister of external affairs in an earlier Trinidad government. "As one who has been engaged for the last ten years on the international scene in seeking to establish an international criminal jurisdiction," he said, "I take into account that such acts as genocide are regarded as international crimes. Consequently, if genocide is being committed in a country then I would not rule out the use of force collectively, so to speak, in order to stop that crime being committed, wherever it is being committed. . . . If I take up that position then I cannot say I accept as an absolute principle non-interference in the affairs of other states. But the exceptions must be clear." [15]

The second option—that of imposed sanctions—was seen not so much as posing problems of principle, as posing problems of practical applicability. Sanctions were recommended by the CARICOM heads of government who met in Port-of-Spain on the weekend of October 21–22. But it is well known that sanctions rarely work. They are slow, take time to induce effects, and cumbersome to apply. They rarely bring the targeted country to heel, as is evident from the U.S. economic sanctions against Cuba and the U.N. sanctions against South Africa. Even more, it is extremely difficult to maintain them collectively; there are always countries that will refuse to accept them or at least evade them, as the South African case shows. Sanctions of a social or cultural character are even more problematical; interestingly enough, the most recent example of this is the increasing readiness of many black West Indian cricketers over the last few years to break the international sports quarantine of South Africa by accepting invitations to play in that country in response to handsome salaries. Not surprisingly, the idea of sanctions in the Grenada case was dropped almost as soon as it was raised. Besides, it was argued, why make the Grenadian people suffer for something for which they were not responsible; was it not a situation, in the words of another West Indian commentator, of the people against the oligarchs?[16]

It all came down, then, to a choice, bitter enough for many, between a "rescue operation" manned by local West Indian governments, or even including governments of the larger worldwide Commonwealth of Nations, and a "rescue operation" including the United States. Apart from the tiny, marginal Communist groups of the region—who saw nothing wrong with leaving the military regime in power in St. George's, almost as if nothing had happened—it is fairly safe to say that the main body of liberal and progressive opinion in the region was in favor of a regional-Commonwealth intervention. Both Farrell and Robinson, already quoted, supported the option; as did also a wide spectrum of others throughout the region, including—not to make it an exhaustive list—Patrick Solomon, Lloyd Best, Neville Linton, Michael Manley, Errol Barrow, as well as (as far as can be made out) Prime Ministers George Price of Belize, Lynden Pindling of the Bahamas and George Chambers of Trinidad and Tobago. As one reads their various statements their collective position seems to center around four basic points: (1) it was useless to seek to try to save the revolution, which was already dead; (2) the urgent and necessary task, indeed duty, was to save the Grenadian people from more bloodshed; (3) any intervention, once all avenues of diplomatic negotiations had been exhausted, had to be restricted to the regional-Commonwealth governments, for this was a family matter; and (4) at all costs, the United States must be excluded from any such joint venture. Basic to this position was a general fear of the U.S. superpower and its geopolitical ambitions in the region.

That fear was summed up in Trevor Farrell's contribution:

The American record is clear. They, in truth and in fact, care nothing about human rights in the non-white world, as demonstrated by their support of South Africa, Somoza, Pinochet's Chile, the Shah of Iran, Duvalier and countless others. Furthermore, racism is endemic in white America. . . . There is a distinction between an invasion force and a peace-keeping one, even though the latter may have to end up fighting. It was not inevitable that Austin would resist an international intervention force, but faced with a punitive American force, the regime was bound to fight.[17]

As events turned out, it was the fourth option—of an American invasion force, albeit operating under the fiction of a U.S.-led "joint force"—that was finally taken up. So, the option of a genuine multination peace-keeping force—for which, after all, there was a precedent at the same time in the genuinely international Lebanon peace-keeping force—was turned down, as was also the option, concurrently, of pursuing diplomatic overtures with the Austin people. It was a victory, without doubt, for the more conservative and pro-U.S. elements of West Indian public and political opinion. The opinion thus made possible the first direct U.S. interventionist act in the English-speaking Caribbean; for the previous episode—that of the destabilization of the left-wing Jagan government in British Guiana in 1964—had involved the Americans only indirectly, with the major role being played by the British Harold Wilson Labour government. The Americans had now entered by the front door. As Farrell put it succinctly, "Coard gave the Americans the Grenadian revolution on a platter, and we in the rest of CARICOM, then laid the table for them to eat it up." [18]

Why was that decision taken? The answer to that question can only be provided by an examination of what took place between the CARICOM and OECS countries in the period immediately preceding the invasion of October 25, including what took place between some of them and the United States. Properly speaking, it is a theme for the diplomatic historians. In large part, it will be found that it is a story of secret agreements secretly arrived at. For this is the former British West Indies, where newly found diplomatic practices are still colored by the temper of the British Official Secrets Act. The historians will have to turn to Washington for illumination, where the Freedom of Information Act makes it easier to pry information out of the federal agencies, including the Federal Bureau of Investigation and the CIA. It is not the least of the ironic and laughable paradoxes of the whole Grenada affair that U.S. participation makes it that much easier for the diplomatic historian, as well as the sharp investigative newspaper reporter, to find out, in detail, what actually happened.

That, of course, may take some time. After all, it is only now, by means of information finally provided by the CIA, that the American public is beginning to learn the full extent of the involvement of the U.S. intelligence agencies in the overthrow of the Arbenz regime in Guatemala in 1954. Yet we know enough of the Grenada-related negotiations to obtain a more or less clear picture of what went on, if only because there occurred a serious division of policy strategies between the various CARICOM leaders, so that each one has felt compelled to offer publicly his or her own apology. It makes, to say the least, a fascinating story.

The events of October 12, and certainly of October 19, presented the leadership of the regional community with a foreign policy crisis the like of which had never been seen before. Obviously, something had to be done. An outraged and shocked regional public opinion demanded action. The bald facts of the response to that demand are readily identified. The OECS convened an emergency meeting in Barbados on October 21 (although Barbados is not a member). It proposed a number of actions against Grenada, including refusing contact with the Revolutionary Military Council, suspension from OECS membership, and severance of all air and sea links. In informal statements given to the press after the meeting, both St. Lucia Prime Minister John Compton and Dominica Prime Minister Eugenia Charles said that a decision would have to wait for the plenary meeting of CARICOM heads to be held in Trinidad the following day.[19] Shortly after the OECS meeting ended, the prime ministers of the Eastern Caribbean Defense Pact (Barbados, Dominica, Antigua, St. Vincent, and St. Lucia) met in private caucus. After that, the CARICOM meeting convened on the following Saturday evening in Port-of-Spain, completing its sessions the next day, Sunday, October 23. Soon after, Prime Minister Chambers of

Trinidad held two press conferences, the first in his capacity as chairman of the meeting and the second as prime minister of his own country. As chairman, he announced two CARICOM decisions, first to suspend Grenada from the body and second to honor the OECS proposals of imposing economic sanctions and severing all communication links. As prime minister, Chambers said that he was opposed to external intervention as a solution, that the problem was a Caribbean one, and that he favored Trinidad joining other Caribbean forces to restore law and order in Grenada.[20]

The historian with a morbid sense of humor will note that that fateful weekend meeting took place at the Trinidad Hilton Hotel, the so-called upside-down hotel, due to its peculiar architectural layout. When the U.S. invasion came just two days later, everything did indeed turn upside down, with open disagreement as to what actually took place during the meetings. A story of intrigue and double-dealing was revealed. The next few weeks witnessed a barrage of public accusations and counteraccusations, extraordinarily undignified even by West Indian standards, where "mauvais langue," "mamaguy," and "robber talk" are taken for granted by a tolerant public.

The "war of words" was curious indeed. It began on the very same day of the invasion with the statement to the nation by Jamaican Prime Minister Edward Seaga, who certainly lost no time. The statement declared that at the OECS meeting of October 21 the members had decided under the authority of Article 7 of the OECS Treaty to take collective defense action against Grenada, whose military government possessed armed capabilities and a military infrastructure capable of undertaking acts of hostility against other Caribbean states; the members had also decided to request assistance from "friendly neighbouring states" in that endeavor. The statement went on to claim that Bishop himself was a "moderate" and that other Caribbean countries, unnamed, had "stood aside" from the OECS action.[21] This announcement was followed on the same day by the statement of President Burnham of Guyana, which said that the CARICOM meeting of the weekend had originally arrived at a consensus determining that any resolution of the Grenada crisis should be wholly regional in character, should not violate international law, should have no extraregional military intervention, and should have as its primary purpose the restoration of normalcy in Grenada. It went on to describe how, later in the meeting, the OECS countries refused to accept that earlier consensus and resolved that Grenada should be "deemed" to have been expelled from CARICOM, making it clear that outside intervention was contemplated.[22] The Trinidad and Tobago prime minister's statement of October 26 corroborated the Guyana statement: certain heads of government maintained, in the latter part of the CARICOM meeting, that there was now no consensus on the previously agreed proposals—which included the immediate establishment of a broad-based civilian government in Grenada, acceptance of a fact-finding mission, and negotiations to be begun with the St. George's regime—and that there now could be no official contact with the Grenada regime. The statement ended with the reiterated Trinidad position that it could not agree with measures involving the use of force as a first resort.[23]

These, so far, were disagreements couched in proper diplomatic language. That tone, however, rapidly disappeared under the stress of events. Prime Minister Chambers told his Parliament on October 26 that the invasion came as a "complete surprise" to him and that the first official notification he received of it was from the U.S. ambassador in Port-of-Spain through the Trinidadian minister of external affairs, and that up to the present moment he had received no notification from any CARICOM member country of any intention to request assistance from the U.S. government to intervene militarily.[24] Prime Minister Adams of Barbados responded by claiming that he himself had advised the Trinidad ambassador to Bridgetown, Basil Pitt, of the decision to invade; Pitt denied that such an explicit statement was given to him, confirming same to his prime minister later; Adams angrily accused Pitt of being a "liar" and, later, claimed that a tape recording of the conversation was in his possession (although it has never been made public).[25] Prime Minister Chambers's lengthy statement to his People's National Movement Women's League of November 6 made it clear that he felt he had been misled by his CARICOM partners and that it had left a bitter taste.[26] Anonymous government sources angrily declared that it was all "deceit and double-cross" and that the governments supporting the invasion had wanted to "play macho" with the issue.[27] Other governments joined in. President Burnham of Guyana, on the same day of the invasion, accused the OECS group of instigating and/or supporting outside interference in the region.[28] The OECS leaders responded with their own accusations against Guyana. Jamaica's Seaga claimed that "traitors among us" leaked the decision to invade to General Austin immediately after the Trinidad meeting and only stopped short of naming Burnham as the culprit.[29] Dominica's Charles later pressed for the exclusion of Guyana from CARICOM, adding that she suspected Guyana "had been paid to obstruct." [30] Later on at the New Delhi Commonwealth summit, Adams derided Burnham as a "figure of fun" and "a cross that Guyana has to bear." [31] Burnham replied to all such charges by continuing to insist that the OECS countries had acted as "puppets and stooges" of the U.S. government.[32] It was, altogether, to use the Trinidadian expression, "ole mas." A highly unedifying episode, it starkly showed how much the new Caribbean nation-states have still a lot to learn about the old art of diplomacy.[33]

What really happened? We now know enough to feel fairly certain that Prime Minister Chambers's feelings about being "let down," if not "deceived," were in large part justified. Adams has admitted that he spoke three times by telephone with Chambers over the weekend, but did not broach the question of invasion because he "could not trust the security of the conversation on the telephone," a rather lame excuse.[34] All the more reason, one would have assumed, why Adams should have attended the Port-of-Spain meeting himself rather than sending, as he did, his foreign minister to head the Barbados delegation, which rather seems like adding insult to injury. Seaga, in turn, has admitted that the proinvasion CARICOM members made their plans in "great secrecy" and said nothing about the plans to the others at the same Port-of-Spain meeting "because we did not want anything to leak out," which hardly displays a spirit of trust or confidence.[35] If they distrusted Burnham why at least not talk confidentially to Chambers?

But this is not all. We now also know that the OECS countries, plus Barbados and Jamaica, had already been engaged in secret and urgent conversations with the Americans well before the Port-of-Spain meeting, and of which the four dissenting CARICOM members—Trinidad and Tobago, Guyana, Belize, and the Bahamas—knew nothing, although they must have suspected for certainly since October 19 invasion had been the talk of the town. Adams's statement of October 27 makes it clear that the decision to intervene immediately with force, thereby scuttling any possibility of a negotiated settlement, had already been reached by the OECS countries, along with the outsiders Jamaica and Barbados, on October 21, with an invitation for participation being sent to the United States, and that staff discussions were held with the U.S. Marine Corps, as well as visiting U.S. officials such as Ambassador Francis McNeil and Major-General George Crist, special emissaries to the eastern Caribbean.[36] But it is now known that the request to the United States was in fact drafted by that country's own state department and then ferried down to the relevant countries, thus contradicting the implication of Adams's statement that the request was prepared in Barbados.[37] What is more, Seaga has subsequently revealed that the October 21 discussions were attended by Charles Gillespie, deputy assistant secretary of state for inter-american affairs, notwithstanding the fact that no formal request for U.S. participation had yet been made.[38]

The story of a request for assistance from the Grenada Governor-General Sir Paul Scoon—Scoon has said that the letter was sent on Sunday, October 23—also deserves some skepticism, for although Prime Minister Charles corroborated the account, adding that she was the first person to be approached by Scoon,[39] the letter could not possibly have been sent or delivered until after the invading forces had landed on October 25, and after Scoon had been taken the following day on a U.S. helicopter to the USS *Guam* for two days. In any case, he later told reporters that he had not been aware of the possible involvement of the U.S. forces until they landed in his front garden.[40] That particular story about the Scoon role is so hard to believe that a local West Indian newspaper ran a teasing and facetious column by Austin Clarke about it.[41]

Certain conclusions suggest themselves:

1. It is clear that the OECS countries, along with Barbados and Jamaica, and in collusion with the Americans (whose presence was at least questionable, since President Reagan's acceptance of their "request" for assistance was not formulated until October 24), entered the Port-of-Spain emergency meeting under false pretenses, agreeing to discuss alternative plans when in fact they had already determined on a U.S.-led invasion. It was farcical, to say the least, perhaps almost cynical.

2. The effort of President Reagan, in his joint television conference with Prime Minister Charles, to present the case as one in which the U.S. administration decided over a weekend to accede to a request from the West Indians just strains credibility.[42] You do not put together a massive naval task force in two days. In any case it is now documented that the United States had decided on intervention much earlier. Adams himself has testified that—speaking on October 15—an official in the Barbados Defense Ministry had been approached by an unidentified U.S. official who raised the possibility of U.S. assistance to mount a "rescue" operation.[43] Meanwhile, the U.S. ambassador to France, speaking rather imprudently, stated that the U.S. invasion had been planned at least two weeks earlier.[44]

3. At no time during the crisis was any serious effort made to solve it by negotiation with the Grenada regime. The regime's diplomatic note of October 23 to the U.S. embassy in Barbados declared that it intended to form a broad-based civilian government and that it wished to continue its historically established ties with all friendly countries.[45]

Whether sincerely meant or not, the invitation to talk was not considered, despite the fact that both Prime Minister Chambers of Trinidad and Prime Minister Milton Cato of St. Vincent were in favor of meeting with General Austin's people. It was argued that one does not talk with murderers; to which the answer surely is, if that is the case then why did not the United States and the OECS countries break off diplomatic relationships with the Bouterse military regime which just a brief year earlier had committed a similar crime of deliberate murder of political opponents in the neighboring Caribbean country of Suriname? Two wrongs, of course, do not make a right. But the difference of response to the two episodes, which were so remarkably similar, strongly suggests that there were special political and ideological reasons for the Grenada invasion.

The last point, concerning the possibility of a negotiated settlement, merits elaboration. The Grenada Revolutionary Military Council diplomatic note of October 23 indicates, with its deferential and almost fulsome language to the Americans, that the Austin regime realized that it had backed into a corner from which it could not escape. Austin and his people were talking with everybody—Sir Paul Scoon, Michael Als, the director of the American medical school on the island, even the U.S. officials who briefly visited the island on Monday, October 24 (ostensibly to discuss the possible evacuation of the U.S. medical students, although it might have been a spy mission, since President Reagan's decision to invade had been made the night before). Communications were still open; it was not the Austin regime but the OECS command that canceled all LIAT airflights at the same time.

It is in the light of these factors that one must consider the opinions of two prominent West Indian personages, neither of whom can be regarded as a flaming revolutionary: A.N.R. Robinson, the leader of the Tobago House of Assembly, and Sir Shridath Ramphal, secretary-general of the Commonwealth in London. Ramphal's opinion was short and succinct. "Grenada," he is reported as saying, "wouldn't have happened if other little island states hadn't been frightened into over-reacting," adding that "it takes only twelve men in a boat to put some of these governments out of business." [46] The remarks imply that other, less coercive measures might have been considered. Robinson spelled out such other measures more elaborately. "I think," he has stated, "there was a great deal of room for diplomacy. . . . The international concern could have been somewhat assuaged, I am not saying completely satisfied, by bringing in the Commonwealth, which is a wide organisation consisting of many states which are not committed to any particular ideology, and certainly not having that antagonism, that the East-West cold war image that the United States and Russia would have; and I think that an international observer, like Sonny Ramphal, would have been eminently suited to be brought into a situation of that kind." [47]

It is worth noting, with respect to Robinson's remarks, that in support of his argument he cited his condemnation, in his former capacity as Trinidadian foreign minister, of the British unilateral use of force in the 1969 Anguilla secessionist matter. More generally, his advocacy of the use of special observers of intermediaries in such situations is a widely used mechanism in international disputes: the United States itself has used it, in the form of presidentially appointed diplomatic "troubleshooters," from Averill Harriman to Philip Habib, in the post–World War II period. It is regrettable that this device was not given a chance in the Grenada situation, and that, even more, the whole idea of diplomatic negotiation and personal diplomacy seems not to have been seriously considered at any time.

Negotiation, indeed, including proper consultation with interested parties, was conspicious by its absence. Both internally, with respect to the Commonwealth Caribbean, and externally, as already noted. Internally, most of the island parliamentary oppositions complained that they had not been properly consulted or informed. The deputy chairman of the Tobago House of Assembly complained that the Trinidad and Tobago government, while calling on religious leaders and representatives of foreign governments for consultations, had never attempted to obtain the views of the Tobago partner-government.[48] The complaint was echoed by the opposition in Trinidad itself, even although its spokesmen agreed essentially with the "principled stand" of Prime Minister Chambers.[49] In Barbados, in turn, the opposition resented being treated "shabbily" in the matter of the parliamentary debate on the issue of a regional defense force, and chastised Prime Minister Adams for his impolite and undiplomatic behavior in the Pitt matter.[50] The opposition nonetheless supported the government's decision to approve the invasion although, curiously enough, its leader bitterly criticized the decision in an article in a U.S. magazine.[51]

The whole sorry story, altogether, is one of evasive excuses, half-lies, ex-post facto rationalizations, "secret agreements secretly arrived at," and, to be the most charitable, imperfect communication between all concerned. It is possible to avoid falsehood, wrote Robert Louis Stevenson, and yet not tell the truth. It is in that sense that the Caribbean governments who joined in the invasion did not tell everything to their colleagues who felt unable to lend their support. It is also in that sense that the Americans dissembled when—as in the statement by the Department of State of January 24, 1984—they asserted that until October 21 they had been planning unilaterally and only shifted into a multilateral mode after being approached by the OECS countries.[52] It is that sense, finally, that both President Reagan and Prime Minister Charles took liberties with the truth in their joint television appearance of October 25 insofar as they failed to tell all of the facts, which have subsequently become common knowledge, surrounding the decision to invade.

12

October 25, 1983: The Empire Strikes Back

With its penchant for bellicose titles, the United States named its Grenada operation "Urgent Fury." Like the Japanese invasion of Pearl Harbor in 1941, it was undertaken without benefit of a formal declaration of war. That the Pentagon was determined that nothing would go wrong was evident from the awesome fire power of the invading task force: the 18,300-ton USS *Guam,* carrying up to twenty helicopter gunships, the 39,300-ton USS *Saipan,* carrying up to twenty-six gunships, accompanied by six other vessels, the chief of which was the 79,300-ton aircraft carrier *Independence.* With the fleet was the Twenty-Second Marine Amphibious Unit, more than 400 marines equipped with helicopters and assault ships, capable of landing five M-60 tanks, thirteen amphibious armored vehicles and jeep-mounted antiaircraft missiles. Alongside them were the commando-like Seals and Rangers. These would be reinforced after the initial predawn assault by 5,000 paratroopers of the Eighty-Second Airborne Division flown in from Fort Bragg, North Carolina, by A-141 Galaxies and C-130 Hercules transports. Backing up all this was a huge stockpile of war material in Barbados—small artillery pieces, tanks and armored personnel carriers, jeep-mounted missiles, bulldozers, forklift trucks, and advanced communications equipment, all of which gave the impression, as one British journalist on the spot observed, that the U.S. forces had been in Barbados for months.[1]

By comparison, the defending force was meager indeed, consisting of the People's Revolutionary Army (PRA), the popular militia, and the Cubans. The 1,000-odd members of the Cuban-trained PRA were the best equipped, with AK-47 and AK-17 automatic rifles, light antiaircraft weapons, military trucks, rocket launchers, and a few armored personnel carriers. The militia, initially, had been much larger, but many had been disarmed by the Revolutionary Military Council as pro-Bishop sympathizers.[2] The 784-strong Cuban contingent was mainly construction workers, although with some military training, as is the Cuban custom; but according to official Cuban statements, later accepted as correct by the U.S. government, no more than 43 were military. In other words, the defending forces were outnumbered ten to one, had no air support or heavy weapons and, to make matters worse, had very little support from a population demoralized by the events of October 12–19. They might have benefited from an injection of Cuban military assistance. But that was ruled out by Havana on the grounds that it was, in any case, an unequal struggle; that the Grenada military regime, guilty of assassinating Bishop, was not worthy of support; and that the logistics of ferrying aid through a Caribbean sea effectively controlled by the U.S. Navy were insurmountable.[3] Possibly only an act of nature, like the bad weather in the English Channel and the North Sea which devastated the Spanish Armada in 1588, could have saved the day. But, despite the fact that October is within the Caribbean hurricane season, there was no providential hurricane to harass the North Americans. It was a case, all in all, as in Hugh O'Shaughnessey's book title, of the sledgehammer and the nutmeg.

And yet, curiously enough, the invasion was not the walkover that the Americans seem to have expected. As a military operation, it was a seriously flawed exercise. It took three days, longer than expected, to achieve a complete victory, with unexplained delays of troop movements on the ground. The "counterinsurgency" and intelligence units failed to anticipate the resolute resistance from the PRA. Reagan administration sources pointed to the "surgical precision" of the operation, a claim marred by the mistaken raid on the Richmond Hill mental hospital which killed more than thirty patients; that sort of mistake sprang, more generally, from the excessive reliance on air power which had been honed to perfection in the Vietnam War. In modern war, apparently, the foot soldier, the infantryman of World War I, is no longer in the front line but rather in the second line protected by preliminary naval shelling (as in Lebanon) or preliminary air assault (as in Grenada). There were serious intelligence miscalculations, whether deliberately made for propaganda purposes or not. Most notorious was the estimated number of Cuban fighters on the island, which in three days plunged from more than 1,200 to fewer than 200.[4] The later investigation by the U.S. House of Representatives Armed Services Committee identified poor operational planning as the reason for, among other things, hundreds of U.S. troops milling around not knowing what to do, the consequence, perhaps, of pouring too many combat personnel into too restricted a space. Earlier the same committee had identified similar serious errors in judgment, especially in security measures, which led to the October 23 truck bombing of the U.S. Marine headquarters in Beirut.[5] Stories of marines in Grenada equipped only with tourist maps, not knowing for several days whether the PRA was on their side or not, expecting to find a Cuban soldier under every bed, and treating their West Indian allies almost as if they were the enemy, throw serious doubt upon the quality of any briefing that they might have received.[6]

Much of this confusion was accompanied by, and in part caused by, the Reagan administration's strict control and indeed cynical manipulation of the press throughout the operation. All of the official sources—the White House, the Pentagon, the State Department, the National Security Council, the admirals and generals—disseminated inaccurate, unproven assertions, false statements of fact, and deliberate distortions, all known euphemistically as "misinformation" and designed to put administration actions in a favorable light. The administration was able to do that—starting with official denials up to the eve of the invasion that any such action was planned—because it imposed an extraordinary and unprecedented restriction upon the flow of news. For the first two crucial days no reporters were allowed to go to Grenada so that—apart from the monitoring of the ham radio transmissions[7]—the only information available to the American public came from official government reports and commentaries, that is to say, government-managed information.[8]

The result was that in the Grenada War there took place a separate and minor battle between the professional soldier jealous of security and the newspaper reporter intent on getting a story. It was frustrating, acrimonious, sometimes comic. A whole press corps, American and foreign, was sequestered in Bridgetown, Barbados, kicking their heels, and trying to cope with the type of glib, fast-talking public-relations type who seem to become press secretaries in U.S. governmental offices. It is a breed unknown, for example, in British government. Their job, essentially, is to cover up for their bosses. The attitude, in turn, of the military and naval commanders was one of outright hostility, summed up in Admiral Joseph Metcalf's threat at one point, perhaps in jest, to fire upon unauthorized press boats that tried to reach Grenada.[9] But it is known that such boats were in fact harassed by buzzing navy planes.

The account given of his adventures by Don Bohning, one of the few U.S. correspondents who knows the Caribbean well, is revealing. Along with a few other correspondents, he persuaded a scared and apprehensive Barbadian boat captain to ferry them out to Grenada where they were loosely detained by the Grenadian army and then detained by the Americans at the St. James Hotel in St. George's. During their stay they had the opportunity to disprove at least two of the Pentagon official releases; that the correspondents had been "evacuated" from "an area of heavy fighting" and that armed Cubans holding out in Richmond Hill were overrun by attacking U.S. troops. To the contrary, reported Bohning, there was no heavy fighting, and the Richmond Hill prison was in fact "liberated" by three of Bohning's colleagues who simply walked quietly into the unguarded prison and freed ten political prisoners, including the Grenadian journalist Alistair Hughes.[10] Similar serious inaccuracies abounded concerning the number of U.S. troops involved, the rate of casualties on both sides, the nature of the stockpiled caches of arms discovered at the airport, and the capture of Bernard Coard.

All of the official explanations for the censorship policy—that the Reagan administration was concerned about the safety of reporters and camera crews, that it was urgent to maintain the element of surprise, that the generals in Grenada demanded a news blackout—are not convincing, as all of the media representatives later charged. The Grenada regime knew about the invasion beforehand; it is not in the U.S. tradition for elected officials to take orders from unelected generals; most of all, it has been standard practice for reporters and photographers to accompany the forces in all modern wars, from World War II to the Korean and Vietnam wars, with them signing waivers absolving the services of responsibility for their security; nor has there been a single verified instance of operations being in any way compromised by leakage of vital information on the part of correspondents in the field or their editors back home.

Indeed, the figure of the intrepid war correspondent, risking life and limb for the news, has been a part of all modern conflicts since the U.S. Civil War: the young Winston Churchill in South Africa, Edgar Snow in China, Edward Murrow in wartime London, Herbert Mathews in Cuba, not to mention the war photographers, starting with Matthew Brady in the U.S. Civil War and most famously represented by Joe Rosenthal's picture of the U.S. Marines raising the Stars and Stripes on Iwo Jima's Mount Suribachi in World War II. If, as the saying goes, a picture is worth a thousand words, a thousand words from the reporter on the spot, often challenging the official versions, is vital to a democratic society that finds itself at war. Looking at the Grenada media shutout, it is difficult to resist the conclusion that it was undertaken deliberately in order to boost President Reagan's scenario of an enemy Grenada full of thousands of Cuban soldiers armed to the teeth poised to export Communism to the rest of the region.

Apart from the combined military-naval campaign, the Reagan administration undertook at the same time a well-orchestrated propaganda campaign to justify the act of invasion. The "misinformation" concerning the "requests" from Governor-General Scoon and the OECS countries has already been noted. That "misinformation" was really an ex post facto justification of an intervention planned even before the death of Bishop; the Inter-

American Bureau of the State Department began pressing for the invasion on October 17, advocating a takeover of the whole island, on the pretext of evacuating the 500-odd students at the American medical school, the purpose of which was "a show of American resolve to the Caribbean and Central American region and the world," and to "rid the island of its radical leadership."[11]

Three other leading themes, used to justify the invasion, appeared in the propaganda war. They were, first, the theme that the students of the offshore medical school in the island, as U.S. citizens, were in immediate danger; second, that the arms caches discovered proved that the PRG regime intended to use them in order to export its brand of revolution to its neighboring island states; and, third, that Grenada had become a Cuban-Soviet colony acting as surrogate for the export of Communism.

The first theme, ostensibly humanitarian, did not fit the facts of the case. It was the classic so-called hostage excuse. But there is firsthand evidence of the sequence of events which invalidates it, particularly evidence provided by Peter Bourne, son of the dean of the St. George's medical school and himself a visiting member of the faculty. After Bishop's house arrest, Deputy Prime Minister Coard gave Geoffrey Bourne assurance about the safety of the campus, with the same assurances being offered by Commander Austin after October 19.[12] On the Wednesday before the invasion the school's New York office received a call from Millan Bish, the U.S. ambassador to the Eastern Caribbean, asking the school's deputy head, Dr. Charles Modica, to come down to Barbados and publicly request the United States to intervene in order to protect the medical students. Dr. Modica refused.[13] The same day, reports Peter Bourne, he himself received a call from a school trustee, a conservative Republican, who said that the Reagan people were asking the trustees to say that the students were in danger.[14] On that same weekend Dean Bourne helped arrange an on-site visit by two U.S. embassy counselors in Barbados, one of whom, Ken Kurse, reported that he perceived no danger to the students.[15] On Monday Austin opened the local airport and some students, as well as the same two U.S. counselors left. It is also known that the Revolutionary Military Council had granted permission for a Canadian chartered plane to remove Canadians wishing to leave, and that by order of the Barbados government such flights were not permitted to depart. Dean Bourne was later "called in" by the State Department and retracted his earlier opinion.[16]

It is worth adding that subsequently not a single medical school student has claimed that he or she was in danger during that period, although they might have been tempted to do so since most of them were "right thinking" Americans. Anyone who knew the school before the October events, situated on the magnificent Grand Anse beach, will remember that sometimes it looked more like a typical southern California beach scene than a serious educational undertaking. This is not to say that the student body was lazy and not dedicated to study; it is merely that the attraction of the beach was always there. And, as one U.S. Peace Corps volunteer who was on the spot has noted, one never saw the American students working during their free time in the village health-care programs as did the Cuban doctors and dentists.[17] In any case, it may fairly be concluded, the situation was far from being Entebbe or Iran, where hostages were being held against their will by a hostile enemy state. In the end, it thus became, ironically, a matter of the U.S. armed forces "rescuing" a body of American students from the consequences of a U.S. attack.

The West Indian observer, indeed, might almost be justified in asking, Even if it were beyond a doubt a situation in which American lives were at stake (which was not the case), would not the invasion have amounted to a U.S. military operation to rescue a group of American citizens who constituted a white enclave in a black society, an image with definite racist overtones?

The second justification advanced—that Grenada had become an armed camp—had some merit, but not much. It is true that the PRG had organized an armed militia and an army on a scale hitherto unknown at least in the Commonwealth Caribbean. The scale was too large to meet the needs of controlling the local population, but certainly it was too little to have constituted, in Prime Minister Charles's words, a threat to the security of the people of the Eastern Caribbean states. A leading West Indian jurist, writing anonymously, has claimed that by reason of its nonlegitimacy the Revolutionary Military Council regime had become a "mercenary" regime.[18] But neither he nor Prime Minister Charles has provided any evidence, then or subsequently, of any known plan on the part of the regime to undertake "mercenary" attacks upon any neighboring state, including Prime Minister Charles's Dominica. The matter of the arms buildup in Grenada is also open to some skepticism. In his October 27 speech, President Reagan claimed that three warehouses of military equipment, including one with "weapons and ammunition stacked almost to the ceiling, enough to supply thousands of terrorists," had been uncovered. Reporters inspecting the warehouses the next day said that this seemed an exaggeration, that the equipment might have been as appropriate for defense against an invasion as for export of terrorism, and that in any case although there was much Soviet-made weaponry the warehouses were no more than half-full, with much of the equipment being antiquated. As one U.S. reporter put it, there were lots of "Saturday night special" pistols, but very little modern weaponry.[19]

Once these self-serving propagandistic excuses thus evaporate, it becomes even more difficult to accept the more sweeping assertion, again made by President Reagan, that Grenada had become "a Soviet-Cuban colony being readied as a major military bastion to export terror and undermine democracy," and that "we got there just in time" to prevent Cuban occupation of the island. This claim has been accompanied by later background briefings to the effect that it was all part of an even larger plot in which "hard-line" pro-Soviet and pro-Cuban elements, in league with Havana and/or Moscow, overthrew Bishop in order to sabotage his alleged new pro-U.S. political moves. Once again, no concrete or believable evidence has been published, then or now, to substantiate these surprising accusations. To accept them would require us to believe that every one of the pronouncements of the Cuban government—that it knew nothing of the internal PRG power struggle, that it denounced the murder of Bishop and his colleagues, that it refused to send armed assistance to the revolutionary Military Council—are all hypocritical lies. It is, in truth, to enter into the almost paranoid fantasy world of the espionage novel, almost as if all world politics can only be understood through the lens of a book by Ian Fleming or John le Carré.

It is of some interest that the Jamaican officer heading the Caribbean contingent of the invading forces ventured the opinion, although speaking guardedly, that the Grenada arms were probably not intended for the purposes of exporting the revolution, subverting neighbors, or training terrorists.[20] Further, all of the abortive attempts in the last few years to overthrow a small-island government have not been proven to have originated in Grenada and in fact have been plotted by, in the case of the Grenadines, a small group of disgruntled Rastafarians. In the case of Dominica, they were plotted first by a small element in the local defense force led by a former prime minister with alleged ties to South Africa, and second by a small group of soldiers of fortune operating out of New Orleans with ties to the Ku Klux Klan. It is perhaps not unfair to conclude that the justificatory arguments for the Grenada invasion were, in Wendell Bell's phrase, "the use of false prophecy to justify present action."[21]

Not since the Russian invasion of Afghanistan has an act like the U.S. assault on Grenada won such almost unanimous condemnation from the world community. Only four OECS states voted for approval of the United States in the Organization of American States discussion. The United Nations General Assembly voted 108 to 9 condemning the action as a violation of the U.N. Charter.[22] Countries ideologically estranged voted together in the General Assembly majority vote: Russia and China, Ecuador and Cuba. Governments normally pro-United States voiced their criticism, also complaining of lack of adequate consultation by Washington. That was particularly the case with Britain, whose Foreign Office has always cherished the concept of a "special relationship" between London and Washington; Prime Minister Margaret Thatcher's injured remarks made it clear that she thought the concept had received a serious setback,[23] reminiscent of Churchill's complaint in 1952 that he had only learned the details of the hydrogen bomb explosion at Eniwetok Atoll through reading a British newspaper report of a speech made by the chairman of the Joint Congressional Committee on Atomic Energy. However, it might be noted that in this case Prime Minister Thatcher, perhaps, as the Americans say, received her comeuppance. For the Washington policymakers had never really forgiven her for seriously compromising their Latin American relationships in the Falklands War of 1982, which is why they only belatedly finally came down on the side of London rather than Buenos Aires. It was hardly for Thatcher to complain a year later in the Grenada matter.

The Grenada action, perhaps more than anything else, raises the fundamental issue of the rule of law in international relations. What Washington called a "firm legal foundation" for the action turns out, on examination, to be not very firm at all. The case rested mainly on the invitation of the OECS countries acting under the mandate of the 1981 treaty. But the crucial Article 8 of that treaty restricts OECS competence in areas regarding an 'external aggression' and then only in accordance with the right of individual or collective self-defense recognized by both U.N. Charter Article 51 and the Organization of American States Charter. Furthermore, Article 8 specifically requires unanimous agreement among member states before any action can be taken; and there is nothing in its language to justify the use of a preemptive strike force.[24] Both the rule of unanimity and the limitation to actions responding to "external aggression" were thus clearly violated. To that must be added that three of the OECS members—Grenada itself, St. Kitts-Nevis, and Montserrat—did not vote for the invasion, while three of the countries that did join the action—the United States, Jamaica, and Barbados—were not OECS members. The possible illegality of the "request" of the countries involved has already been noted, to which must be added the possible illegality of the "request" to intervene by Governor-General Sir Paul Scoon, for, as British constitutional authorities have noted, the notion that a governor-general within the framework of Commonwealth constitutional law has a reserve power personally to invite a foreign country to invade his nation by force, without first taking the advice of a government minister or the Queen (through the channel of the British prime minister) is unprecedented and directly in conflict with constitutional authority.[25]

It is beyond argument, in sum, that the invasion constituted a gross violation of both territorial integrity and political sovereignty, both of which, as legal concepts, lie at the very heart of modern interstate relationships. It completely bypassed the obligation imposed by both the Organization of American States and U.N. charters for recourse to those bodies before unilateral action by force is taken by any member state against another, when they are in dispute with each other. Adding insult to injury, the U.S. invasion went further in the sense that it was undertaken in response to a "request" by one party to another to intervene in the domestic affairs of a third party which was not consulted and certainly would not have agreed if so consulted. As a group of American lawyers has also noted, in previous cases of U.S. action undertaken against countries seen as hostile—the Cuban missile crisis of 1962 and the invasion of the Dominican Republic in 1965—Washington in both of those instances consulted with the Organization of American States (OAS). President Kennedy obtained unanimous OAS approval for his quarantine of Cuba in 1962, and President Lyndon Johnson obtained subsequent OAS approval for his Dominican Republic action in 1965. By contrast, President Reagan's disinclination to obtain such approval from the OAS, plus his failure to adequately consult or inform allied governments, seemed to many to constitute an almost deliberate transgression of that "decent respect for the opinions of mankind" which has always been so much at the heart of the American republican ideal.[26]

The various rationalizations of the invasion put forward by Washington have already been examined. But it is perhaps worthwhile rehearsing them at this point in the light of the larger considerations of international public law here mentioned. It is a sacred principle of international relations which dictates that no foreign forces can ever enter the territory of a state unless properly invited by the duly constituted authority of that state to help defend it against some clearly defined external threat. Nor may that principle be violated on the ground of the legal and moral qualifications, or absence of them, of any particular government or regime, for that would imply that judgment of some sort or another may be passed upon the internal affairs of other nations. This is a position that received its definitive expression in the Mexican Estrada Doctrine of 1930. If that doctrine is correct, then the U.S. excuse for the Grenada invasion—that it was undertaken to restore "democracy" in the island state—becomes unacceptable, first, because it assumes a right to moral judgment which no one state can claim and, second, because it gives carte blanche to any state to invade another whose system of government it deems as "undemocratic." The word "democracy" in the modern world means different things to different people; it cannot then be employed as a fit yardstick for aggressive action.

Nor can such action be justified on the ground that there has taken place a breakdown of authority in a state system, a principle summed up in Brownlie's injunction that "territory inhabited by people not organised as a state cannot be regarded as *terra nullius* susceptible to appropriation by individual states in case of abandonment by the existing sovereign."[27] The doctrine is pertinent to the other U.S. rationale that such a breakdown had occurred in Grenada, which now possessed, it was asserted, only the "semblance" of a government after the events of October 19. But that in fact was not the case. Sovereignty was still intact; there was no condition of civil war, as in Lebanon at the same time; and General Austin and his colleagues were in full control of the state power, as their ability to impose a prolonged curfew on the entire citizen body showed. Austin himself was talking with everybody at the time—Michael Als, medical school deputy head Modica, Governor-General Scoon, and even, through his colleague Major Cornwall, with the U.S. consular officials who were visiting the island—with all the authority of an established head of state. It is true that it was a dictatorial regime, guilty of heinous crime. But, again, as the Estrada Doctrine emphasizes, that in and of itself does not, in international law, justify armed external intervention to put things right. As Prime Minister Thatcher put it succinctly, you just cannot walk in everytime there is trouble.[28]

Respect for sovereignty thus must remain the operational principle of the behavior of states in their relationships. Otherwise, we enter too easily into international anarchy. There is, however, a longstanding legal exception to the prohibition of transboundary force in situations where a genuine humanitarian reason can be advanced for interventionist action. There is an emerging norm of customary international law which recognizes that in such situations the doctrine of nonintervention should not be employed in an absolute sense; it must give way to reality. The recent cases of the 1976 Entebbe raid, the 1980 Iran hostage rescue attempt, and the 1979 Tanzanian intervention against Uganda's Amin regime, all accepted by international public opinion as being justified by the particular circumstances of each case, show how political law must give way, so to speak, to natural law, where the lives of innocent people are at stake.[29]

This, on the fact of it, might seem to provide sufficient justification for the U.S. Grenada invasion. But, as has already been noted, the "hostage rescue" excuse did not really exist as a reality based on fact. To the evidence already cited we might add, even more convincingly, the evidence of members of the U.S. congressional fact-finding mission that visited the island soon after the invasion. After quoting Dr. Peter Bourne to the effect that the American students were never in any danger, Congressman William Clay of Missouri quoted from Stokes's diary: "I asked all present [in Grenada] if they could give me the name of any American they were aware of who at any time was harmed, injured or treated as a hostage. No one could name a single person. It was interesting that this entire group was unanimous in their opinion that the Americans should have intervened."[30] It is also interesting, one might add, that the entire congressional team, with the single exception of Congressman Ronald Dellums of California, were of the same opinion.[31]

This leaves the "hostage" excuse invalid insofar as it refers to the U.S. argument about the American student body on the island. It has greater validity, of course, if it refers to an interventionist action to save the Grenadian people as a whole, who were in effect hostages of the Revolutionary Military Council. Such action would have entailed a genuine "rescue mission" undertaken by a Caribbean peace-keeping force, and excluding absolutely any external participatory force. That was the position at the time of the dissenting countries involved in the OECS meetings. It has also been the position since, of at least the more progressive elements of the regional public opinion. It would have matched perfectly the Entebbe-Iran-Uganda analogy. It would almost certainly have meant less bloodshed, for there is much reason to believe that the Revolutionary Military Council might have surrendered readily to a rescue force of fellow West Indians, whereas it could not have done so confronted with a U.S. force because everything that the revolution had stood for dictated resistance to the imperialists.[32]

In summary, although the principle of humanitarian intervention has certainly acquired status in international law, at the same time the law has hedged it with restrictive conditions. Early on, the *Caroline* incident of 1837 emphasized that the doctrine of anticipatory self-defense could only be invoked if the party appealing to it was able to show that it was obliged to take the action that it did to ensure its own safety and that it was left with no alternative.[33] Judge Max Huber's opinion in a later case in the Court of International Justice (1925), while upholding the doctrine, limited its application to cases where a state does not possess the means of protecting aliens or where foreign nationals have actually suffered injury or harm.[34] A later academic authority has noted, speaking within the framework of new international agencies such as the United Nations, that in such pressing cases every effort must first be made to persuade the United Nations to act and intervention must be solely for the purpose of securing the safe removal of threatened nationals. The clear thrust of these cases and opinions is to condemn the Grenada action.[35]

In point of fact, the U.S. action bypassed or ignored practically every alternative method of resolving the problem. No alternative plan, involving either consultation or negotiation, was seriously considered. And it was not seriously considered because the larger framework within which it might have been adopted—that of continuing negotiation between all sides involved—was also not seriously considered. This is, indeed, the crux of the matter. For it is the very bedrock of international law which insists that in dispute with others, nation-states must oblige themselves to submit to processes and procedures of negotiation and arbitration before resorting to the arbitrament of armed force. Not only did the intervention in Grenada willfully bypass the United Nations and the Organization of American States structures, at the same time its planners gave little time or thought to the possibilities of negotiation with the St. George's regime. The possibilities did exist. Certainly by October 22, Governor-General Scoon had been asked by Austin to stay on in his office as governor-general and help form a broad-based civilian government; Dr. Geoffrey Bourne had persuaded Austin to allow representatives of the U.S. embassy in Barbados to come to the island, which they did; U.S. citizens who wanted to leave had been allowed to do so; and Dr. Modica's poll of the school students at Grand Anse and True Blue had revealed that only 10 percent wished to leave (the cynic might add that they were, after all, enjoying a pleasant Caribbean work vacation; why spoil it?).[36]

Stokes's diary further confirms that there was opportunity for negotiation talks right up to the eve of the invasion. He reports:

On Monday, 7 November, we met with our embassy officials, who had participated in negotiations with the People's Revolutionary Council after Bishop's death. Official Ken Kurze verified that Bourne had contacted them at Austin's urging and set up the first of several diplomatic meetings. He said Major Cornwall of the Revolutionary Council gave them assurances of the students' safety. Kurze said he and other embassy officials met with Cornwall over the next four days. During that time they were given access to the students. In addition, Cornwall, representing Austin, had been in touch with diplomatic personnel from the British High Commission and the Canadian and Venezuelan Embassies to assure the entire diplomatic community that they were in control of Grenada and that there was no danger to the international community there. There is no doubt that these types of diplomatic negotiations were going on and in process at the time of the invasion.[37]

That the opportunity for further and more thoughtful diplomatic discussion was not taken can only be explained by the fact that neither the OECS countries nor the United States were seriously interested in the possibility. Accounts provided by White House and State Department officials showed that Washington's attitude was one of skepticism, because finding someone to trust in the new revolutionary government was like "a floating crap game."[38] But the issue was not whether men like Austin could be trusted; it was, rather, that no earnest effort was undertaken to find out if that was true or not. You do not refuse to negotiate with another person because you distrust him, for it is in part because you do not trust him that you are in dispute with him. The evidence strongly suggests that the Americans were unwilling to negotiate because their plan to destroy the revolution had been a long-standing one, going back certainly to the U.S. 1981 maneuvers in the region in which the Caribbean chapter of the "Ocean Venture" exercises included a simulated invasion of the Puerto Rican island of Vieques under the suggestive title of "Amber and the Amberdines," a barely disguised reference to Grenada and the Grenadines.[39]

The Grenada invasion, on any showing, illustrates all of the dangers involved in the temptation to overplay military force and underplay diplomatic initiative. The dangers were sufficiently advertised at the time by two wiser voices, Jean-Luc Pepin, the Canadian external affairs minister, and Michael Manley, the leader of the opposition in the Jamaican Parliament. Pepin observed,

> It is vital to me that countries have an obligation to exhaust all avenues for peaceful solution. . . . It is also difficult for us to believe that you had to have a full-scale invasion, or rescue as the Americans call it. Any group of countries planning an invasion must think of the consequences. For example, any revolutionary group, X, Y, or Z, could take over Anguilla; or even South Africa could undertake an invasion with justification of a neighboring black country . . . so we must think of the consequences."[40]

Mr. Manley, speaking more directly to the OECS discussions in October, made a similar point: "If I had been Prime Minister of Jamaica, I would have insisted at the meeting under George Chambers' chairmanship that we explore the possibilities which Chambers believed to have existed for working out a rapid, tough, negotiated settlement that forced the military to back down, to substitute a proper civilian Government and to bring justice to the people who killed Bishop. I would have backed Chambers to try that first, and decisively, and then see what happens."[41] That alternative route was never traveled because, as Manley writes elsewhere, it was a U.S. political act carried out for political reasons, part of a historical political agenda that has to be traced back to the Monroe Doctrine.

13

The Imperialist Ideology and Mentality

As Michael Manley's remarks, quoted in the preceding chapter, imply, no one can fully understand the Grenada episode, in all of its ramifications, without considering the general background of the United States as a new world power, beginning in 1898 with the Spanish-American War, and developing with increased rapidity after 1945, when World War II finally established the nation as the leading protagonist of the "Western world." Its massive productive capacity and advanced technological skills as the world's leading capitalist economic system have now made it, apart from Soviet Russia, the leading world power, able to impose its will upon other nations with scant regard for moral scruples or international law. To this must be added the geographical fact that its sheer distance from any other nation willing, or able, to threaten it, has rendered it invulnerable for all serious purposes; although the advent of the intercontinental missile as well as the escalation of international terrorism now places that invulnerability in doubt. Again, apart from Russia, there is no other power capable of challenging any hegemony the United States wishes to assert; for both Britain and France emerged exhausted after World War II and have not yet recovered, while the postwar emergence of Japan as an ambitious trade rival has merely meant commercial competition unaccompanied by any military threat. America, in a word, stands at the top of the world; and the belligerent rhetoric of its leaders, especially since the Vietnam War, reflects a new national mood in which those who control its destiny feel that they are now entitled to dispense justice and leadership to the rest of the world in the manner of the old colonial powers of a previous age.

It is important to note what this has meant for America itself. It has meant, to begin with, the total eclipse of the isolationist temper of the young republic in the beginning. No one who observes the anxiety of the country in its early history to proclaim its extra-European status as a new democracy different altogether from effete European feudalism, the emphasis of its early statesmen upon the danger of "entangling alliances," the eagerness with which it sought, by the Monroe Doctrine, to be free from the impact of foreign nations in the hemisphere in which the pioneer leaders believed the American destiny to be set, and the profundity of the early isolationist spirit, can help noting the irony of America's present position, more than 200 years later. Paine's famous warning that "it is the true interest of America to steer clear of European contentions" has given way to a new, bold interventionism literally all over the world, so much so that U.S. national politics today are more and more those of foreign policy, with domestic affairs relegated to a low, secondary status. It is safe to say that the psychological foundations of the old isolationism, very much alive as late as the 1930s, are now pretty much eroded. The real choice, then, for Americans is not between withdrawal and participation. Rather, it is between an aggressive nationalism which seeks safety by domination, and dedicated participation in a New World effort to outlaw bellicose behavior and lay the foundations of a new world peace.

No one who has watched the developments in foreign policy and behavior since the 1950s is entitled to optimism on this point. The onset of the Cold War sowed the seeds of fresh conflict. The terms of the American-Soviet debate gradually deteriorated, for if in the beginning the Churchillian concept of the Cold War saw it as a rivalry between the two new global powers which had to be set within the framework of a "balance of power," or even a "balance of terror," in order to maintain an uneasy yet peaceful coexistence between the two, some forty years after Churchill's speech of 1946 the Cold War has become converted into the doctrine of an open challenge (based on a new arms race) to Soviet power, with the end of destroying it. In part, this change grows out of the traditional American hatred of Communism, so that President Reagan's denunciation of Russia as an "empire of evil" is really a logical extension to foreign policy of Senator Joseph McCarthy's assault against all of those Americans who were seen as being "soft on Communism" in the 1950s. In part, again, it is a new version of the traditional American distrust of the Old World, this time seeing Russia as a sort of savage, Slavic society outside the pale of civilization. In part, yet again, it is an expression of the American temper of earnest self-righteousness which chastises transgressors. Even American presidents are not immune to that temper. It has been said of Ernie Bevin, the British foreign secretary after 1945, that he treated the Russians as if they were a recalcitrant branch of the Trades Union Congress. President Jimmy Carter, in similar fashion, treated them as if they were children in a Southern Baptist Bible class in Plains, Georgia, while President Reagan seems to treat them as if they were a tribe of hostile Sioux or Apaches in the Indian Wars of the late nineteenth century.

But all this is simply, as it were, the psychological content of the new American imperialism, which does not explain all. Far more fundamental as a reason is the vast structural transformation which has changed the small community of 1789, largely agrarian, into an industrial capitalist state, now entering into the stage of state finance-capitalism, with the old distinction between private and public sector, so characteristic of free-enterprise capitalism, giving way to new formations of bureaucratic power. The national economy is thus increasingly a state economy governed by the network of interlocking directorates between big government, big business, and, to a lesser degree, big labor. Its more characteristic economic instrument is the multinational corporation, which is only multi-national in the sense that its operations, whether in oil or tourism or petrochemicals, is literally worldwide, but national in the sense that the major part of the immense profits revert to the U.S.-centered headquarters. Its more characteristic political instrument is the vastly expanded national administrative machine, backed at once by a new "imperial presidency" and a "new federalism" which have sharply curtailed the historic role of the individual states in the decision-making process. If one adds to this development the phenomenon of rural depopulation, along with the unplanned growth of the big cities, the massive immigration influx with Asia and Latin America replacing Europe as the traditional source of new ethnic groups, and the escalating consumerist habit in the U.S. population as a whole, replacing the old revered work ethic with a new play ethic, the picture is complete of a new, modern empire looking more and more like the Roman Empire of the ancient world.

Since capitalism, by its very nature, is inherently expansionist, and since imperialism, the last stage of capitalism, is even more so, this has meant that the American empire, like all empires before it, has been characterized, certainly since the period of the U.S. Civil War, by a history of overseas economic penetration and overseas military adventurism mainly designed to protect and expand that penetration. The record is well known, and has been frequently documented: the various interventions in Mexico, Cuba, Haiti, the Dominican Republic, the illegal formation of the Panama Republic to facilitate the U.S. canal interest, the incursions into Nicaragua, all of them designed to make the Caribbean "the great American archipelago"; to which must be added the organization of dependent "banana republics" like Honduras and the diplomatic encouragement and support of a long list of Caribbean and Central American neofascist satellite regimes deemed "friendly" to U.S. interests, including Somoza's Nicaragua, Batista's Cuba, Duvalier's Haiti, and Trujillo's Dominican Republic, a policy even pursued during the interlude of Franklin Roosevelt's "Good

Neighbor" policy in the 1930s and 1940s. Alongside all of this was the search for naval bases, sometimes imposed by treaty, as with Guantanamo in Cuba, and sometimes obtained by friendly exchange with other colonial powers, such as the 1940 bases-for-destroyers deal between Britain and the United States in the British Caribbean islands. It meant, among other things, the effective Latin Americanization of the Monroe Doctrine which, originally intended as a defensive declaration against further European colonization in the hemisphere, became transmuted into an offensive principle for the active pursuit of U.S. interests. It thus became, in Juan Bautista Alberdi's phrase, a doctrine of intervention against intervention, and a grave threat to that idea of Pan-Americanism which, even since Simon Bolivar, has been a sacred article of faith of the Latin American political mind.[1]

But all of this, so far, was nothing more than what the older colonial powers had done, notably in Africa and Asia; although it was, nonetheless, a grave betrayal of the fond dream of Americans that somehow democratic America was different from monarchical Europe. After 1945, however, new elements have entered into the American search for hegemonic power, and it is vital to note them. In the first place, since 1945 the search has become global, so that there is no region in the world in which the United States does not declare that it has a legitimate interest and concern, leading, if necessary, to active intervention, as the Korean and Vietnam wars show. Second, whereas the old imperialism sought its ends by physical domination of a country, as with France in Algeria and Britain in India, the new imperialism is of a more modern type which uses economic rewards to achieve the same end. American financial aid, in all forms, thus becomes a whole new political enterprise, for its very wealth makes it possible for America to lavish dollars on its client states on a scale quite unknown in the older empires. This, essentially, is the so-called Puerto Rican model, where the massive injection of transferred federal funds into the island economy ensures Puerto Rican loyalty to the U.S. cause, despite the fact that Puerto Ricans are second-class citizens in the Union.[2] Alternatively, preferred trade advantages may be used, as in the Caribbean Basin Initiative, to foment a similar loyalty in formally independent nations.[3] Third, the new hegemony is marked by all of the new and sophisticated usages of psychological warfare and counterinsurgency tactics that have entered the scene as the modern state has turned to mass propaganda to obtain its ends. This includes, among much else, espionage; deliberately manipulated mass media news; the politicization of sports, as in the matter of the Olympic Games; a variety of "destabilization" plots against unfriendly or hostile governments, ranging all the way from clandestine military aid to domestic opposition groups, economic sabotage, diplomatic harassment, naval blockade, monies paid to friendly opposition parties, diplomatic nonrecognition, and planned assassination of government leaders. All of this, in turn, is conducted with a sophistication and subtlety which makes the old "big stick" tactics look crudely amateurish by comparison. Fourth, and finally, there is a new temper of ideological combativeness masquerading as a holy crusade against world Communism which, to say the least, does less than justice to the American liberal tradition.

There is no doubt that since 1980 those elements of the U.S. ruling class who believe in this kind of aggressive nationalism are in ascendency. They are intoxicated by the scale of American power. They are fanatically ideological to the point where they seem to have forgotten the pragmatism that has always been such a strong force in American thinking. They see all the ills of the world, simplistically, as being caused by a wicked Communist plot and so they fail to understand that the turn to Communism on the part of much of the Third World is due to a chronic condition of underdevelopment, poverty, disease, and hunger; so much so that they themselves become the victims of the conspiratorial mentality they castigate in the Russians. They cavalierly overlook the fact that the rise of Euro-Communism has overtaken the myth, which they still hold to, that Communism is a worldwide monolithic system, and that certainly in Latin America the traditional Communist parties are suspect in the eyes of many of the region's radical governments and insurgent groups. In every foreign-relations problem with which they are concerned, then—détente, the arms race, arms control negotiations, the Central American and Middle East imbroglios, outer space technology—they see Soviet Russia and its allies less as fellow members of the world community and more as evil and unscrupulous enemies who must be destroyed or at least taught harsh lessons.

This mentality has meant a number of developments which challenge not so much the Soviets as the American democracy itself. It has meant—not simply since 1980 but going back to the very beginnings of the Cold War—the growth of a permanent and large-scale militarism embodied in a new powerful military caste, large professional defense forces, and increased stockpiles of the latest weapons, which are constantly renewed and replaced as the outcome of research. This new militarism has laid the foundations for a close alliance between the military leaders and big business, if only because it breeds what Congressman Thomas Downey of New York has aptly called a "cult of procurement" whereby the Pentagon warlords, with the help of a contracts-conscious Congress, spend more and more on an ever-increasing arsenal of weapons.[4] This, in turn, breeds a new politics in which the average representative or senator is forced into an acceptance of that program, for it will be rare for any one of them to resist a military-naval contracts program which brings thousands of jobs into his or her state. In other words, what President Dwight Eisenhower in 1956 apprehensively called a new "military-industrial complex" has now drastically changed the direction and nature of U.S. national economy. It has meant the gradual replacement of the welfare state with the warfare state. For a welfare economy is rarely compatable with a military program that seeks to secure invulnerability against the possibility of total war, which today really means the nuclear holocaust. The military program not only involves the acceptance of values which alter customary priorities, but it even subordinates the market economy, the main pillar of the American economic system, to its urgent demands. Almost for the first time in peace, the American people and leadership thus confront the issue of "guns versus butter."

The very future of America as a democracy rests on that issue. For empire and democracy are irreconcilable opposites. Sooner or later, the one must yield to the other. A military caste is utterly alien to everything that "Americanism" has stood for. Deliberate preparedness for a thermonuclear war shocks the American people, as the national response to the 1983 television movie "The Day After" has shown. As things now stand, America, in the words of one Puerto Rican political scientist, is an "imperial democracy," with its basic traditional values still intact but placed under severe stress and strain by the new militarism.[5] It is certainly too early to agree with the thesis of the Dominican Republic writer-politician Juan Bosch that the United States is already controlled by *pentagonismo,* with the decision-making power already passed from the politicians to the soldiers.[6] It is also true that the so-called Vietnam syndrome—that is, an attitude of extreme wariness on the part of the decision makers about getting into a situation that might escalate into another Vietnam—is still a powerful deterrent, as the various congressional moves in recent years to apply the terms of the War Powers Act to Reagan administration activities in Nicaragua, El Salvador, Honduras, and Lebanon show. But it is a plausible hypothesis that the administration's acceptance of those moves, although frequently violating the congressional intent by clandestine and illegal activities, may just be part of a general policy in which it is testing the accuracy of the "Vietnam syndrome" assumption before deciding on its future course.[7] Be that as it may, the larger question still remains. Can the drive for world hegemony be, in the long run, compatible with the maintenance of democratic institutions in American life? If it is true that the American people want peace more than anything else—an assumption still unproven—will not the readiness of their ruling class to ignore that sentiment ultimately, and inevitably, lead to the imposition of a police state so the ruling class can have its way? It is in that sense that the American democracy faces its most agonizing crisis since 1861.

There is one final point in this discussion of the imperialist ideology and mentality. Many of President Reagan's liberal critics since 1980 have been tempted to reduce the problem to the dimensions of presidential personality. The president, it is said, is a "trigger-happy cowboy," belligerent, impetuous, perhaps even paranoid. But this is to see history and politics, in typical bourgeois style, as a game of individuals and not of forces. It is true, admittedly, that given the vast powers of the U.S. presidential office, the person makes a difference. It means much whether the executive is a Woodrow Wilson or a Warren Harding, a Calvin Coolidge or a Franklin Roosevelt. It is also true that President Reagan, in his person, is not exactly the cream of the crop. Like Sinclair Lewis's Babbitt, he is a child of small-town, Midwest America, and in his values he has never really outgrown the background of his Illinois boyhood. He has its virtues, for he is a devoted husband, a solid family man, and basically a decent person; even his enemies concede that his real sense of humor is a welcome change from the religious solemnity of his predecessor. And yet it is a limited personality. It is a *Reader's Digest* mind, tempted, in the tradition of the small-town, homespun philosopher, to reduce every great problem to a well-turned joke. As a former film actor and skilled in the television art, he thinks all the time in terms of the public image that he presents, almost as if he were still playing a role in those B-rated movies which were his main claim to fame in the history of Hollywood. As, too, a former liberal, he has all of the stridency of the relapsed believer who has found a new creed. Like his predecessor, he is an outsider, this time not from Georgia, but from California, so that he does not really understand the Washington political game, least of all the necessity for a president, by constitutional mandate, to deal with Congress as an equal. It is almost as if, for Reagan, the White House is a Hollywood movie set of the 1940s or even perhaps the "little house on the prairie." Add to all this the fact that the American political system, unlike the British, often puts into the White House a successful presidential candidate who has had no training in and little experience of foreign affairs and the picture is complete of a small man catapulted into a great office.

Yet when all this is conceded it tells us little except that President Reagan is that kind of man. The picture has to be seen within the framework of the larger, impersonal forces at work. It is not simply a matter of an aberrant president. The first thing to remember is that the road to militarism precedes 1980, going back at least to the decision of President Kennedy, the "shining prince" of Camelot of the liberals, to begin the serious interventionist policy in Vietnam, and that it was followed by the support of succeeding presidents, both Democratic and Republican. The second thing to remember is that 1980 simply witnessed the intensification of a program already under way, but with the difference that it was now in the hands of the more reactionary elements of the U.S. ruling class, classified as the "ultraright" and "Moral Majority" groups. Historical verisimilitude demands it be recorded that the "liberal" elements of the Eastern establishment themselves participated, during their own administrations, in the militarist policy, and that during that earlier period it was only the individual "mavericks," such as the late Senator Wayne Morse of Oregon and the late Senator Frank Church of Idaho (both, interestingly enough,. from the far Western states) who defied public opinion in their stand against the Vietnam adventure. A ruling class is a ruling class; and in the American instance it is a matter of a ruling class both of whose elements, liberal and conservative, are responsible for the present American condition. It is as grossly simplistic to blame President Reagan for everything that goes on in Washington as it is to blame Bernard Coard for everything that went on in St. George's.

General causes are always illustrated by particular events. In that sense, the Grenada action of 1983 furnishes rich illustrative detail to fill out the general considerations just analyzed about the American imperialist ideology. As a political action it was accompanied by all of the braggadocio of the conquering hero—that the United States could "dish it out," "stand tall," show all the virility expected of a strong nation. President Reagan was portrayed as the John Wayne hero who arrives on the spot at the crucial moment to save the honor of the corps. In part, it was an action designed to stave off the fear of the Washington planners that Grenada could become another embarrassing Iranian hostage crisis. In part, it was undertaken as a token revenge for the bombing of the marine headquarters in Beirut; Washington needed a quick victory to forget the humiliation of that episode. The observer who cherishes irony will note the fact that there is a Mount Lebanon in the Grenada foothills; one might wonder what a marine would have thought had he had time to climb it. There was the same obsession with the Communist bogey in the charge that Grenada was about to become a Cuban-Russian colony and that the new airport was to be used as a military airstation, neither of which have ever been documented. There were the further charges, based on seized documents, that the Grenada regime had signed pacts of mutual assistance, including military aid, with Eastern European countries, almost as if, as an independent sovereign state, it had no right to do so, thus reflecting the imperialist position that no country within the imperialist "sphere of influence" has a right to an independent foreign policy that may be construed as threatening the imperialist interests.

As a military-naval action Grenada also provided nice instances of the foibles of the new militarism. The vulnerability of high-priced technology, reflecting the American belief that there is a technological solution to every problem, showed itself in the fact that in one brief week of fighting a tiny, weak, and demoralized opponent a total of eight helicopter gunships, including the expensive and sophisticated Blackhawks and Cobras, were lost. There was the obsession with sheer numbers, in that a total of more than 6,000 personnel were deployed in an operation that could probably have been successfully conducted as a small commando raid in the manner of the British and the Canadians in World War II. The mixed-command structure, involving complicated intercommunications between all different services, also, as everywhere, created problems; the Americans, despite their Vietnam experience, have never really mastered the art of the small jungle-warfare commando group, operating outside the control of headquarters, which penetrates deep into the heart of enemy territory, guided by the sort of idiosyncratic leader like Orde Wingate in Palestine and Burma. The American conviction is that anything great has to be big. If ever they become involved in the future in another conventional war in, say, the Amazonian jungle or the Carpathian mountains or Central Africa they will have to learn to readjust the basic premises of their military thinking. They might even have to learn the meaning of the Duke of Wellington's dictum that the art of war lies in knowing when to retreat and how.

These general observations are borne out by the report of the Military Reform Institute, presented to the House of Representatives Military Reform Caucus, on the Grenada action. According to the report, the original plan, which called for a *coup de main* by quick-striking navy and marine units, was changed in order to allow army participation, which resulted in a "pie-dividing contest" among all the services, and consequent imperfect overall planning. The desire of the specialized forces command to show off its elite groups was ironic, since their actual performance did not justify their claim to be the nation's military elite; only one of the four missions undertaken by the navy commando unit was a success; the crack antiterrorist outfit, Delta Force, failed miserably in its assault on the Richmond Hill prison; and the high loss rate of helicopters against an opponent with no antiaircraft missiles was an aspect of the entire operation which, in the words of the report, is not easy to pass over. The report adds two other comments. First, the slowness of army operations was probably due to the decision to deploy a frontal, linear approach to the Cuban defense instead of a more elastic approach which could have used infiltration tactics. Second, too many of the elite units apparently were affected by a "cowboy syndrome" which assumes that *machismo* is what defines a good soldier. In the Grenada action, this resulted in "cowboys" who were tempted to fight the enemy frontally when they could go around him, and they also "came unglued" when faced with the unexpected.[8] The report, certainly, is not a blanket indictment. But, as Representative Jim Courter of New Jersey pointed out in his foreword, it raises troublesome questions about many aspects of the invasion from the viewpoint of tactics and strategy.[9]

Power breeds arrogance. Every empire exhibits that disease. In the Grenada action the U.S. politico-military leadership sported their own variant of the disease. Generally speaking, and obviously, there was the primordial arrogance of the mere fact that they imposed their will upon a smaller people without consent, and in so doing inflicted upon them a degree of suffering that the American people, never having been occupied by an enemy force in any war, has never itself experienced. As George Santayana once put it, the American has never yet had to face the trials of Job. That immunity from suffering expressed itself in the more particular statements of arrogance in the Grenada affair. There was the arrogance of the American commanders on the spot who, disdainful of their Caribbean allies, refused to allow them to join in combat and assigned to them the lowly tasks of simply providing police and guard duties.[10] There was the arrogance of the remark of the White House press secretary that a count of Grenadian dead was difficult since he understood that Grenadians immediately buried their dead because of the tropical climate, thus betraying his ignorance of the fact that for Grenadians, as a Catholic people, that would have been an abhorrent practice.[11] There was the arrogance of President Reagan's callous remark, when asked by reporters how he reacted to the condemnation of his invasion of Grenada by more than a hundred nations around the world, that it "wouldn't disturb his breakfast."[12] There was, too, the arrogance of Secretary of State George Shultz's remark, full of the businessman's attitude, that Grenada was "a lovely piece of real estate."[13]

This, of course, was the arrogance of official America. But there was also the arrogance of unofficial America, that of the press and the politicians. There is no doubt, of course, that the Grenada invasion was seen by both public and mass media as a proper and popular exercise of national power, accepting uncritically the president's version of a strike against a dangerous Communist outpost in the Caribbean, although most Americans had never even heard of Grenada before, or even knew where it was. Even more, it unleashed a mood of euphoric nationalistic jingoism just as the British attack on the Falklands a year before had set loose a similar jingoistic response in the British public. The headline of the *New York Post*— "Yanks Seize Terror Island"—was typical.[14] Not even the traditional "liberal" press was immune to that temper. Even when the press was critical, as were both the *New York Times* and the *Washington Post,* it saw the event in terms of the global East-West struggle rather than something that concerned, more than anything else, the issue of Caribbean political sovereignty. This was also the case with leading European papers, for example the *London Times* and the Paris *Le Monde.*

This general mixture of jingoism, ethnocentrism, and just plain misunderstanding of what Grenada meant could also infect the American "liberal" elements. For, when the chips are down, the American liberal turns out to be more American than liberal. When the American way is challenged the liberal becomes as chauvinist as the rest. The Grenada invasion provided examples galore. Charles Krauthammer of the *New Republic* dismissed the Grenada Revolution with disdain. "Revolution," he wrote, "is a large idea and Grenada is a small island. Of such incongruities comedy is made," adding that "the idea of revolution has devolved of necessity upon that part of the world to which it is least suited."[15] The editor of *Caribbean Review,* based in Miami, and who is supposed to know a little more about the Caribbean, added his own inane remarks that the Revolution was simply something conducted by "middle class bred chest-beating heroes" whose discussions were simply "alienated group therapy" and that "it would be funny if it were not so deadly."[16] In a similar vein of crude misunderstanding Arthur Schlesinger, Jr., while upbraiding the Reagan administration for its over-readiness to resort to armed force on flimsy excuses, could only see Grenada as a scenario where "one set of Marxist thugs had murdered another set some days before."[17]

Others joined in this chorus, liberals, former liberals, neoliberals. Max Lerner, one-time ardent New Deal reformer now turned all-American conservative, could write of Grenada that "the island was under the control of Cuban 'advisors' who had engineered one military coup, set up a Communist Revolutionary Council, then killed the Prime Minister and replaced him with a more manageable communist," thus buying the Russian-Cuban conspiracy theory without providing a shred of evidence to support it.[18] Norman Podhoretz, editor of the neo-conservative anticommunist magazine *Commentary,* and whose autobiography *Making It* shows the price some Americans are willing to pay in order to achieve success in the New York literary jungle, supports the Grenada invasion as the use of military power to "protect our democratic friends in the region generally and to further the cause of democracy in Grenada in particular. We are also taking action against the strategic threat that has been posed to us by the gradual transformation of Grenada into a base for Soviet and Cuban military operations." Here again the press was buying the Russian-Cuban conspiracy theory without providing any evidence.[19] As a final example, Sally Shelton, ambassador to the Eastern Caribbean during the Carter administration, and by reason of which she becomes yet another instant expert on the region, also supports the invasion, albeit with some reservations. She justifies her stand to an interviewer on the curious ground that "one does change as one gets older."[20]

It is easy, in a way, to understand these sentiments coming from both the "conservatives" and the "liberals." The more conservative element, after all, only reflects the fact that the U.S. imperialist camp was behaving, logically, in its own interests, so liberal indignation becomes rather an empty gesture. It was a response appealing to the "tell it to the Marines" syndrome, in which it is argued that wars have to be fought all-out to be won, that the marines are the heroes of that strategy, and that any American group that differs from that view, as do some of the more progressive churches, is composed of people who "love atheism and loathe America."[21] The conservative thinks in terms of some sort of global Armageddon, best illustrated in the Grenada case by the astonishing remark of a U.S. Army colonel, located in St. George's for the purpose of training an expert squad of counterinsurgency fighters. He stated: "The Third World War has begun . . . and Grenada is the front line."[22] In this mind-set, the marines are perceived as the Praetorian Guard of the American "way of life." They are a special breed who, in the time-honored military tradition of the soldier, never give a second thought to an order; theirs is to do or die. "Whether on active duty, retirement, out of the service, dead or alive, in the air, on land or on sea," writes one former Marine sergeant, "we are all united from the Halls of Montezuma to the Shores of Tripoli." It only remains to be noted that the author of that jingoistic letter was a Puerto Rican, who, like all Puerto Ricans, is a second-class citizen denied the right to participate in the U.S. congressional and presidential elections. The colonial is frequently the most vociferous champion of the empire.[23]

The response of the more liberal elements is also easy to understand, although somewhat less excusable. For American liberalism has always accepted the basic premise of the national business civilization, content to challenge and criticize its particular abuses only, never its central principle of profit making as the sine qua non of the total socioeconomic-cultural order. So, traditionally, it has been a single-issue politics, in which different groups concentrate on their particular nostrums, whether it be civil rights, the abortion issue, "gay" rights, the feminist movement, "small business" as against "big business," and so on. Consequently, on the Grenada issue the "liberals" attacked the matter as simply an expression of the Reaganite reactionary elements instead of merely yet another extreme symptomatic expression of American capitalism in its imperialist phase. The liberals are thus circumscribed and limited by their ideological immaturity. They cannot understand socialism, in Grenada or elsewhere, because their framework of reference and vocabulary of politics have never included socialism, not to mention communism or Marxist-Leninism. The liberals are the victims of the intellectual backwardness of American political life. They thus bow to every wind that comes along because they have no solid philosophical anchor. The consequence is moral bankruptcy whenever the liberal's patriotism is challenged by the socialist position, no better illustrated than in the case of Speaker of the House of Representatives Thomas "Tip" O'Neill, who initially strongly condemned the Grenada invasion and then recanted once he realized that the American public, displaying a strong streak of chauvinism, approved of the action.[24]

Of all of these liberal groups perhaps the most interesting is the group which, in one way or another, was directly involved in the invasion. The curious case of Sally Shelton has already been noted. Peter Bourne's involvement has also been noted; to which may be added that it is now known that, apart from the drug scandal which forced his resignation as special White House adviser on drug abuse in 1979, he had been active in providing debriefing reports to the CIA after trips to Southeast Asia and Pakistan.[25] His collaboration, with his father, in writing a position paper in the last days of the revolution to advise General Austin on how to distance himself from the Bishop government and accede to U.S. demands, as well as how to bring Grenada "back toward democracy," indicates a self-serving deviousness, to say the least.[26] To these examples must be added that of Robert Pastor, former Carter National Security Council member—who most certainly must have lent his support, in that capacity, to the destabilization moves undertaken against Grenada in the last years of the Carter administration—who collaborated with Bourne and Shelton in the secret dealings with Austin and Coard toward the end.[27] There was also the elusive figure of Ashley Wills who, as political officer at the U.S. embassy in Barbados during the period of the PRG regime, played out the role of "liberal," to the extent of organizing forums at the local university, and who at the very end was discovered by reporters as "political adviser to the United States operation" on board the USS *Guam*.[28]

This type of person, speaking of all of them, is peculiar to the American political system. Except for the career official, they are not professionals but rather outside political players. Usually located in a university "think tank" or a prestigious corporate law firm or a private philanthropic foundation, they keep close to Washington, waiting for the political party of their preference, Democratic or Republican, to come into office. Their liberalism may indeed be untarnished. But their driving ambition is to become, if not secretary of state or National Security Council adviser, at least powerful at the next level; if not that, they become shadowy figures, advising behind the scenes. They can produce a Cyrus Vance, combining solid principle with dull personality, or a Henry Kissinger, marrying brilliant intelligence with paranoid vanity. One way or another, they play an important role in every episode like the Grenada invasion.[29]

As this game is conducted, the Washington political jungle only too often persuades the actors to give principle a second place to power. Not even as fine and high-minded a person as Adlai Stevenson could bring himself, as U.S. ambassador to the United Nations, to make a public protest against the 1961 Bay of Pigs invasion. The art of resignation from

public office on a point of principle becomes more and more rarely practiced. It is significant that no such resignation took place on account of Grenada. It was thus left to the small radical groups to make the proper protest, including the congressional Black Caucus, even although at times it was a mild enough protest. The mainstream of the national political life, whether it called itself "liberal" or "conservative," seemed not even to have recognized that anything had occurred that even called for a protest.
===

Yet when the Grenada action is thus debated, it is important to realize that it is only the latest example in a whole conceputalization of the place of America as a world power. The concept goes back to the very foundation of the republic itself and is encapsulated in the doctrine of Manifest Destiny, whereby America has justified its claims to national expansionism and, later, to world hegemony. The doctrine has consisted of a series of rationalizations by which America has justified expansionism and hegemonic ambitions to itself. The rationalizations have been varied and numerous, as Weinberg's definitive study shows.[30] There has been the biological argument that "inferior" races must be brought into "civilization," the Darwinian argument that self-preservation makes acquisition of further territory necessary, and the further argument, in the same vein, that it is the "law of nature" for a people to expand and that when expansion ceases, death supervenes. Or there is the argument grounded in "natural right" ideas which justifies expansion into other people's territory by propinquity, or by the necessity for security, or by the mere idea that a neighboring nation that is seen as "anti-American" cannot be permitted to continue as a nation. Or, even more, there has been the argument that justifies expansion for reasons inferred from the facts of geography, not seldom coupled with an inferred knowledge of the "great purpose of human events" or even the Jeffersonian assertion that America is the "last great hope of earth." Expansion has been justified with the argument, notably in the case of the Indian tribes, that the superior ability of the American to use the lands he has coveted thereby justifies their seizure; the claims to California and Texas were based on the same rationale. This kind of argument even justifies the right to economic imperialism, in which the occupying country is seen to hinder the development of the wastelands; that was the justification put forward by President Theodore Roosevelt in the matter of the Panama Canal. The same kind of argument has been used, in a broader sense, to justify the politics of "Dollar Diplomacy," summed up in President William Taft's observation, with the Caribbean specifically in mind: "It is essential that the countries within that sphere shall be removed from the jeopardy involved by heavy foreign debt, and chaotic national finances, and from the ever-present danger of international complications due to disorder at home. Hence, the United States has been glad to encourage and support American bankers who were willing to lend a hand to the financial rehabilitation of such countries."[31]

There are three other elements in the doctrine of Manifest Destiny that ought to be noted. The first is the idea of the "white man's burden," by which it becomes the obligation of the United States to civilize the "backward" peoples, to spread Christianity, to rescue native peoples from "barbarism," such as the rule of Spain in Cuba and the Philippines. These were the strong elements in justifying the Spanish-American War of 1898. Such obligations have been less marked after that period, as the United States itself has become a multiethnic society, so that, today, cities like Miami are almost predominantly Hispanic communities. But the prejudice dies hard. During the Vietnam War, Vietnamese became "gooks," while in the immigration movement from the Caribbean, Puerto Ricans have become "spiks." The use of racist stereotypes has always been endemic in the mentality of white majority America, and there were many expressions of it on the part of U.S. soldiers in the Grenada action. It might even have been present in the American "liberal" response to the invasion, as many "liberal" commentators seemed to find it comic or absurd that a group of black Grenadian revolutionaries should have undertaken an earnest discussion of Marxist-Leninist theories.

The second element of Manifest Destiny is the theory of the United States as the wielder of an international police power by which it preserves law and order within the general sphere of its interests, which increasingly becomes the whole world. Acting as this sort of international policeman, successive U.S. administrations have deemed it their duty to quell revolution, to restore governments of its own choice, to reorganize a country's financial structure, to "destabilize" governments seen as hostile or unfriendly, and even to undertake full-scale war, as in Vietnam, in the name of a holy crusade against Communism. In all of this, the United States remains the final judge of what constitutes "communism" or "democracy." In the end result it has meant that Washington has supported a series of regimes and governments only because they purport to be "anti-Communist," whereas in fact their nature has violated everything that in the American experience has been known as democratic: the Somoza regime in Nicaragua, the reactionary army regimes of Honduras and El Salvador, Duvalier's Haiti, Trujillo's Dominican Republic, the regime of the Shah of Iran, the South Korea regime, the Marcos regime in the Philippines, and many others. None of those regimes, by any stretch of the imagination, can be called democratic. Yet they have received the aid and friendship of the United States on the sole ground that they have been prepared to uncritically support Americans in whatever the United States chooses to do in the international arena. Furthermore, U.S. administrations, with some honorable exceptions, often have acted in open defiance of world opinion.

The third and final element of Manifest Destiny is the view that America is destined to be the leader of the world. Many diverse streams have contributed to the formation of that outlook. There is the sense, from the very beginning, that America is not like other nations, that it is a new republic set against effete Europe, and therefore it is superior to them; every visitor, from Alexis de Tocqueville to Lord Bryce, noted how powerful and pervasive that spirit was in the national psychology. There is the religious contribution, rooted in the Puritan heritage, which deeply believes that America is the handmaiden of divine purpose in the world. There is Social Darwinism, applying, frequently incongruously, the concept of the "survival of the fittest" to the arena of international political affairs, a concept which leads only too easily to the argument that America must not appear weak and that it must display its strength and power, otherwise it will be supplanted by its rivals in the survival race. There is, finally, the appeal to the principle of naked power, which of course is contradictory of the religious idea of America as a moral leader. Power, it is argued, is the energizing force of interstate relationships, especially in the particular area of relationships with the Soviet Union; hence the growing temptation of American administrations in the post-1945 period, both Republican and Democrat, to favor military solutions to political problems. It is in that sense that American imperialism finally relinquishes its claim to be different from all of the other imperialisms that have preceded it.

Nothing better illustrates how America, losing grip on its earlier claim to be the voice of the New World which seeks to redress the Old, has taken on the thought patterns of all empires in history than the more "philosophical" arguments that were presented by the representatives of the Reagan administration in defense of the Grenada action. These rationalizations show, more than anything else, how the exercise of geopolitical power lessens the moral sense and breeds arguments which, in the last analysis, rest upon the root thesis that "might is right."

Perhaps the best example of that temper of mind is the interview conducted by the right-wing historian George Urban with U.S. Ambassador to the United Nations Jeane Kirkpatrick, just days after the Grenada invasion. Her leading idea, in her words, is that

> the projection of our own morality on to the Soviet leaders has certainly no justification in history. But we keep doing it. We project the aspirations, hopes and behavior of "Benthamite Man"—of reasonable, prudent, democratic people—on the Politburo, and then are surprised to find that they don't behave like Anglo-Saxon Utilitarians. . . . But we have to compete with the Soviet Union—and compete effectively—in domains other than war, and that includes economic relations, not as a

form of purely economic activity, but as one of political power. It also includes information, communications, and technology. This approach is familiar to the Russians. They are deploying it against us; it is remiss if we fail to use it against them.[32]

There are certain attitudes inherent here. There is the notion that Soviet "man" is different from American "man," not only in an ideological sense but also as somehow being a different variant of the human species. This, of course, if accepted as truth, justifies the abandonment of a politics of détente. There is the attitude that the United States and Soviet Russia are enemies engaged in mortal combat, and not contestants in a power game that is really not much different from the power games that have engaged other protagonists in, say, the last 400 years. There is, most alarming of all, the attitude that the United States must adopt the same methods against the Russians that the Russians use against the United States, which really amounts to saying that America must adopt a behavior pattern determined by the nature of its antagonist and not by the democratic values that have always been regarded as intrinsically American. It means, in effect, a surrender of those values. This view can only be justified on the assumption that a nation can afford to separate its foreign policy from its domestic policy. It assumes that you can be "democratic" at home and "tough" abroad. Yet it is a grievously mistaken assumption. Foreign policy, in any nation, whatever its official ideology, is never an outlook capable of being separated from its internal position. Each enters into the other and influences it. It is well known how, in the case of the British Empire, the white racist attitudes spawned in the colonies were brought back to the homeland to become the basis of English feelings of contempt and disdain for the nonwhite peoples. A similar process could take place with an American empire which adopts force as the main pillar of its international geopolitical conduct.

As these justificatory arguments take hold, it becomes clear that they approximate more and more the arguments advanced by the Soviet leadership itself, as the embodiment of the rival empire. There is really not much difference between the Russian Brezhnev Doctrine proclaimed after the crushing of the "Prague spring" of 1968 and what might be called the Reagan-Kirkpatrick Doctrine proclaimed after the Grenada invasion. The Brezhnev Doctrine declared that "the sovereignty of individual socialist countries cannot be counterposed to the interests of world socialism and the world revolutionary movement"; in almost identical terms, the Reagan-Kirkpatrick doctrine determines that the U.S. capitalist system of world production, with its unfettered access to world markets, must be kept intact for its affluence and security. In both cases, keeping the system intact is seen as vital to the national security and prosperity. Although the ideological statements differ, both systems offer identical responses when they are seen to be challenged.

It is important to emphasize, once again, that in the American case, this is not just simply a matter of a particular national administration or government. Both "doves" and "hawks," as they are called, share the basic assumption that there is a national interest, of global dimensions, to be protected and advanced. There are differences about tactics and strategy. There are also differences of temperament; obviously such a difference, speaking of the office of the secretary of state, exists between a Cyrus Vance and an Alexander Haig, and, speaking of the office of the national security adviser, between a Zbigniew Brzezinski and a Henry Kissinger. But they are all united in their view of America as the "moral leader" of the West, almost as if there were no other candidates for that role. And it is of interest to note that the more "liberal" foundations and "think tanks"— which abound in America—hark back, in their innumerable symposia and publications, to what they perceive as the more "responsible" presidencies of Harry Truman and Eisenhower, notwithstanding the fact that the seeds of the present crusade against world Communism are there in the Truman Doctrine of 1947. The same sources, also interestingly, promulgate the theme that politics should "stop at the water's edge" in the cause of a foreign policy consensus, almost, again, as if the foreign policy of a democratic society could be artificially divorced from its internal domestic policies. The American "liberal," as much as his "conservative" antagonist, is thus trapped within a series of assumptions in which the American "way of life" is regarded as almost the sole custodian of "Western civilization."

As in the case, then, of the British Empire before it, the American empire is divided, in its directorate, between the "liberal imperialists" and the "conservative imperialists." Inevitably, as the crisis of the empire becomes more acute, the more intransigent element takes over the control and direction of policy. The others are seen as "weak" or "soft" or even "unpatriotic." A whole new imperialist philosophy emerges. It is argued that if a great nation possesses power then it must use it or die: that is the clear message, for example, of the Kissinger memoirs. Or it is argued, again this time by Kirkpatrick, that friends and foes must be identified in terms of the difference between "authoritarian" and "totalitarian" governments and regimes, a distinction that Kirkpatrick probably learned from earlier Harvard geopolitical evangelists like William Elliot and Karl Friedrich. To this argument, the only answer is that from the viewpoint of a political prisoner in a state prison—which is surely the only relevant viewpoint—it hardly makes any difference whether the regime that ill-treats the prisoner is termed "authoritarian" or "totalitarian": the argument is totally casuistical. To argue that a political prisoner in Cuba suffers from a "totalitarian" regime, whereas a political prisoner in Haiti suffers only from an "authoritarian" regime is to indulge in a cynical usage of words that is truly Orwellian.[33]

It is at this point that we enter into the curious world of the *realpolitiker*. In that world, the enemy is an empire of evil. Dialogue is useless, for you cannot trust his goodwill. Because he only understands force, you yourself must use force as the only measure of ensuring his compliance. So, the end justifies every means at your disposal; hence the proliferation of espionage, counterespionage, destabilizing activities, covert and sometimes overt actions against established governments seen as hostile, massive propaganda campaigns, and the general refusal of dialogue because you cannot make deals with the Devil. It is almost as if the old Puritan world of Cotton Mather were being resuscitated; although for the Kissinger type the more proper analogy may be with the period of post-1815 Europe when Metternich was organizing the alliance of reactionary Europe against the forces of revolution arising out of 1789. This, altogether, is the mentality of the faceless Cold War bureaucrats and war planners of the Washington government agencies, who consider it wholly respectable political discourse to congratulate themselves on the fact that civilian defense measures can reduce the American casualties of a nuclear exchange between the superpowers to "only" 92 million people. In brief, it is a mentality of a glib arithmetic of controlled annihilation, perceiving room for a cynical optimism in a future nuclear wasteland. Like Churchillian imperialism before it, it almost sees war as a grand experience in which the noble virtues of the nation receive their finest expression, without any appreciation of the fact that with the invention of nuclear power the age of Churchillian wars is over. It is not the least irony of this mentality that it has been the American soldier, from Sherman to Eisenhower, rather than the civilian politician or planner, who has seen, from his own grim experience, that, in Sherman's phrase, "war is hell." It remains to be seen whether the very future of civilization itself will rise or fall on the sharp razor edge of that mentality.

14

The Dependent Colonial Ideology and Mentality

It is the record of history that in every empire there are dependent colonial peoples, the "barbarians" as Greece and Rome saw them, who are sometimes more imperialist than the empire itself. They have accepted the role of being local provincial governing elites maintaining law and order in their provincial jurisdictions and always beholden to the imperial center. Whatever the particular imperial system—Assyrian, Persian, Roman, Ottoman, Alexandrian, and, in the more modern period, British, Dutch, French, Spanish, and American—they have seen their task as serving the interests of the imperial metropolis. Each empire, of course, has been different; there is a world of difference, for example, between the ancient theocratic-monarchical Babylonian Empire against which the Jewish minor prophets railed and the nineteenth-century Pax Britannica between 1815 and 1914. But all of them have had in common the capacity, in varying degree, to capture and hold the allegiance of their subordinate peoples, sometimes by force only, sometimes also by persuasion, as each succeeding one has put forward its claims to be the protagonist of a superior civilization in its own particular historical time and place. Colonial loyalty is thus the response to imperial domination.

The expression of this general phenomenon in the case of the modern English-speaking Commonwealth Caribbean is well known and amply documented. It is true, of course, that the postwar advent of national independence has put an end to colonial tutelage, so that it is no longer necessary for West Indian leaders to run continuously to London for aid, approval, and advice. London now belongs to a half-forgotten colonial past. But it is easier to change politico-constitutional status than it is to change frames of thought and feeling. Habits of cultural and psychological dependency continue into the postcolonial period; it would be almost unnatural to assume otherwise.

The details of that general dependency syndrome are again well known. It is there in the continuing policy of economic development strategies adopted by the postindependence governments based on the so-called Puerto Rican model using outside capital investment, despite the fact that official investigative reports coming out of Washington itself have shown that the model has failed to solve the crucial problems of mass unemployment, rural depopulation, and income inequity in Puerto Rico itself.[1] It is there in the continuing uncritical acceptance of the British cabinet-parliamentary model as the proper model for government, despite the fact that it may be inappropriate for ethnically pluralist societies like Guyana or Trinidad, where there exist racial-ethnic differences which the model never encountered in its original homeland; or despite the fact that British-type political party confrontations may actually tear apart the social fabric of small societies like St. Lucia or St. Vincent or St. Kitts, where small size makes such confrontations too heavy for such societies to carry. Or again, finally, it is there in the eager willingness to accept all of the cultural paraphernalia of the "advanced" Western societies—in food tastes, dress habits, entertainment media, consumption patterns, even manners of speech and behavior—which seem to their neocolonial imitators to be the proper thing, thus encouraging and fomenting a general habit of imported cultural imperialism.[2]

It is important to recognize the psychological roots of these general values and attitudes. They are related to the systemized interaction between the colonizer and the colonized generated everywhere by colonialism. The colonizer brings with him ingrained prejudices of racial superiority rooted, variously, in cultural arrogance, religious intolerance, and social status. The colonized responds by assimilating these prejudices himself, so that he comes to accept the low status of racial-cultural inferiority assigned to him by the colonizer's ideological system. The whole system of colonial government and education has persuaded him that success in life depends upon his acceptance, not only in mind but also in deeper, innermost spirit, of the metropolitan standards by which success is defined. This leads in turn to the psychopathology of rejection, which includes not only the rejection of native roots in culture and religion but, even more, the rejection of self; the colonized person learns to live a life of self-denigration and even at times self-hatred. Two additional sociohistorical factors, and especially in the colonial Caribbean, accentuated this traumatic process. The first was that since social class was identified with color in a rigid class-color code, nonwhite colonized people came to regard their origins, whether African or Asian, with disdain and even shame. The second was that as the colonial powers trained the local educated elites into their way of thought and life, the educated colonial became the willing carrier of that thought and life. So, in the Caribbean, it produced the well-known colonial "mimic men": the "black Englishman" more English than the English, the Antillean aping the *boulevardier parisien,* more French than the French, the Puerto Rican *piti-yanqui,* more American than the Americans. Shakespeare had dramatized the problem in his Prospero-Caliban encounter in the *Tempest,* and it has been a favorite theme of Caribbean literature since.[3]

It is, of course, possible to exaggerate all of this. The writings of both Albert Memmi and Frantz Fanon have portrayed it, in Freudian or neo-Freudian terms, as a clinical disease whereby the colonized person, suffering from social ostracism and cultural amnesia, seeks refuge in a self-hatred which destroys him or, according to Fanon, engages in a war of "holy violence" against the colonizer in which the very act of killing becomes a sort of therapy for the disease he suffers from. Yet both Memmi and Fanon were really generalizing from the grim, bitter experience of the Tunisian and Algerian anticolonial revolutionary wars. In the Caribbean, by contrast (Haiti and Cuba excepted) there has never taken place such a war of violent national liberation; certainly in the English Caribbean, there has never taken place the sort of barbarous civil war that tears the whole social fabric apart and from which Memmi and Fanon were generalizing. The pathological state of the colonized person, therefore, which both of those writers describe has hardly been typical of even the most anglophile of British West Indian colonial persons.

What has taken place, rather, is that, short of the acute and almost terminal traumatization that Memmi and Fanon talk about, the English-speaking Caribbean person has been subjected to a series of seductive temptations he has found it difficult to resist. Being black or brown, he has been asked to see himself, or has been persuaded to see himself, as white, so that in that sense at least he has been forced into the schizophrenic trauma of being two persons at the same time, as described in Fanon's *Peau noire, masque blanc.* Since the influence has not only been colonial but also that of a deeply class-conscious society, he has accepted class stratification as a natural law, so that in his own local society he repeats that sentiment of class snobbishness which remains, even today, the hallmark of the "mother" country. In cultural matters he has been taught that to speak creole is "bad English"; that in theater, Shakespeare and Shaw are still the models; that formal dress should still be the proper thing in all ceremonial matters, from the courts of justice to the university; and that in higher education the Oxbridge model should still be accepted as the admired norm. In the smaller island societies, especially—all the way from Bermuda and the British Virgin Islands to the Leewards and the Windwards, Grenada included—the "pomp and circumstance" of traditional British colonial rule still prevail to a surprising degree, notwithstanding the fact that, ironically, much of it has disappeared in Britain itself.[4] It only remains to be added that in much of this the colonial woman has suffered as much as the colonial man, perhaps sometimes even more.

Yet things, everywhere, change. A whole series of profound transformations over the last three decades or so—independence, industrialization, urbanization, modernization—have eroded much of the old anglophilism. Even more, the impact of new ideologies such as Black Power and *négritude* has helped the new and younger generation to slough off the old feelings of ethnocultural inferiority. There is a new sense of felt pride in the local West Indian tradition, whether it is expressed in the *reggae* music of Bob Marley; the Trinidadian calypso; the poetry of Edward Brathwaite, Derek Walcott, Martin Carter, Eric Roach, Mervyn Morris, and others; the "new history" of the younger historians; the explosive cosmology of religious cults like the Rastafarians; and much else. All of these diverse currents have fed a general stream of a new historical sense and a new cultural pride. It has not been so much virulently anti-English as simply seeking in the other ancestral roots—Asian, African, American—the wellsprings of a new nationhood.[5]

Yet it would be possible to read too much into this search for roots. It is arguable that it has touched only certain sectors of the regional population: the artists, the intellectuals, the radicalized youth, the more progressive elements of the middle class, the more nationalist of the political groupings, the more discontented elements of the petit-bourgeois class. It is only by concentrating attention on these elements that so many outside observers have been enabled to portray the region as "unstable" or "volatile," as so many recent book titles show. The vast majority of the regional peoples, as the political map reveals, are basically a conservative element contented enough not to "rock the boat." The history of elections, for example, in the Eastern Caribbean islands—which is the immediate environment of the Grenada Revolution—shows conclusively that winning parties have been the middle or right-of-center parties, whatever their nomenclature. The sociological base of that fact is that the processes of modernization and industrialization, while eroding the old anglophilism, have only generated a sort of *embourgeoisement* whereby, in absolute terms, a real improvement in living standards for practically every class has occurred, despite the fact that, in relative terms, the indices of inequality remain, have indeed become more acute. Despite, then, the real widespread poverty that remains, from Bermuda to Trinidad, a hard core of stubborn conservatism, at times openly reactionary, lingers in the regional society. Its representative center is the new middle class, but it is also evident in the peasantry and certain elements of the industrial working class.

Evidential data abounds for example, in the affluent consumerism of the new wealth and income generated, variously, by the industrializing boom in

Puerto Rico and the oil boom in Trinidad, marked by frenzied buying habits and the frantic search for material possessions as status marks. This is, in large part, the expression of the *nouveau riche* mentality. In the phrase of former Montserrat Prime Minister William Bramble, it breeds, especially in the smaller islands, bicycle economies with Cadillac tastes. In the phrase of Barbadian Prime Minister Errol Barrow, the real problem is not the high cost of living but the cost of high living. All of it is summed up in the Trinidad calypso hit "Capitalism Gone Mad." This materialism in turn, at once reflects and shapes a temper of antisocial aggressive individualism, no better illustrated than in the flight of many sectors of the Jamaican middle class from the mild social-reform program of the Manley government between 1972 and 1980, which they perceived as a dangerous communism; their mood of panic showed how this middle-class West Indian sector will readily resort to any measures—including in the Jamaican case a prolonged and vicious mass media campaign of hate and slander against a constitutionally elected government—once it feels its sense of property threatened.

This capitalistic individualism has had its original inspiration in the so-called Puerto Rican model of developmental strategy. It is therefore worth citing what a Puerto Rican observer has written about the social and political attitudes of the Puerto Rican representative sector. Those attitudes, he points out, are shaped by a vulgar quantitative measurement system in which the sole concept is that of money as commodity, with every crucial question—what is Puerto Rican "culture," for example, or what is the solution to the "status" question—determined by the monetary costs-benefits system of analysis. "A qualitative concept," he concludes, "like that put forward by Rousseau when he created his idea of the general will have no place in this system of thought, any more than does the Weberian enquiry into the nature of legitimacy, or the investigation of Durkheim into the concept of 'social morality' as an object or an entity. Everything social becomes completely quantified."[6]

It is that pervasive temper of mind that in one way or another characterizes the large, expanded middle-class groups and formations spawned by the processes of upward social mobility generated by the economic development strategies in the region since the 1950s. Its representative type can be met everywhere. He or she is the social snob. Their life style is one of conspicuous consumption, so that they are in a state of perennial private indebtedness. They are less interested in the social contract than in the social contact. They send their children to socially segregated private schools. They have the colonial taste for everything imported, since it comes from the admired metropolitan world. So, in Trinidad, for example, the East Indian will favor the popular movies from the Bombay studios while the Negro creole will favor those from Hollywood, both specializing in lurid sex and uninhibited physical violence. On the whole, they are cultural philistines, with their reading restricted to literature relating to their particular profession. Because their own self-image, in an ethnically mixed society, is based on both class and color prejudices, their image of others will be similarly based, producing the racial stereotypes which inhibit genuine social community and the growth of community consciousness. Their economic ideas will be those usually associated with the idea of "free enterprise" capitalism, so that, for them, poverty and unemployment are the result of individual human failings and not of the economic system itself.

Another observer, this time writing specifically on the English-speaking West Indian scene, has noted those prejudices:

It is an article of faith that luck and pluck alone, regardless of colour, parentage, intelligence, or aptitude, can push anyone up the narrow ladder to elite status. The flavour of Samuel Smiles exhortations or rags-to-riches Frank Merriwell tales suffuses the West Indian air, making colour as malleable a barrier to ultimate triumph as lower-class origins seemed to nineteenth-century British or American social utopians. Although social structures have changed little since slavery, a dynamic sense of individual mobility animates West Indian life. Myth outruns fact, but in the process makes its own reality.[7]

The political ideas of this type are equally conventional. They are the mainstay of the "establishment" parties in the political game. They are for "law and order" and support the party and the politicians who promise the most of it. They have an almost paranoid fear of anything that smacks of "socialism," seeing everything of that character, indeed, as being "communistic." They are more or less satisfied with the imported British style of government, with its honorary governors, nominated second chambers, and honors lists, since it appeals to their innate snobbishness; one day, after all, they may themselves become the recipient of a title in the Royal Birthday Honors list. They have accepted political independence only reluctantly, never with enthusiasm, in part because they mistrust their own ability to govern their own country and in part because they fear that independence will pave the way to dangerous social policies. In everything dealing with regional and foreign affairs, then, they value more than anything else metropolitan ties as safeguards against revolution, especially through contamination by way of Haiti or Cuba. It is in this area, more than any other, that their dependency complex is most pronounced.

That last point is vital. The West Indian middle-class groups, when in power as ruling elites, unequivocally identify their local class-national interests with what they perceive as the most friendly and powerful metropolitan power available. That power, of course, used to be Britain. But with the disappearance of the British Empire the colonial loyalty has shifted to the United States. The old anglophilism is still there. But it is now more and more replaced by a new pro-Americanism. The new postindependence elites identify American interests with their own. They regard American goodwill as crucial and basic, and accept for granted the permanency of American concerns in the region. They accept uncritically the Caribbean role in the global power struggle as it is assigned to them by the Washington planners. When an American spokesman declares that the Caribbean, strategically speaking, "is *mare nostrum*. . . . The United States is not under any circumstances going to permit these states to align themselves with elements openly hostile to this country in the cold war, it is not going to allow situations . . . in which there is a realistic possibility of Communist domination. It simply is not,"[8] they do not read that as a declaration of an assumed American right to intervene at any time in Caribbean domestic affairs but, rather, as a legitimate doctrine and, even more, as a guarantee of their own safety. They remain, of course, loyal members of the Commonwealth, and Britain is still regarded with affection. But British governments are seen as being too weak or unwilling to play the old protective role. It is in that sense that the old British colonial loyalty is replaced by the new American neocolonial loyalty.

Just as after 1898, then, the Cuban and the Puerto Rican oligarchies switched from Spain to the United States, so, sometime after the 1970s, the English-speaking Caribbean ruling elites have switched from Britain to America. The Grenada action is thus important because, in geopolitical terms, it is the leading example of that switch. It placed the final seal of approval upon the transference of loyalty.

The Grenada invasion thus deserves further attention insofar as it illustrated in its various moves and permutations the character of that transference. There was, of course, to begin with, the initial OECS-Jamaica-Barbados decision to invite the United States to lead the invasion, and from which everything else flowed. Apparently there was no serious consideration of the alternative policy of appealing to Britain, although the Anguilla affair of 1969 had set a recent precedent, with the West Indian governments of that time inviting Britain to intercede, as well as demonstrating that Britain could undertake such a military maneuver with ease. Some commentators have suggested that the reluctance to talk to London was due to a general West Indian feeling that Britain had evacuated its colonies without providing adequate postcolonial aid (as the Dutch had done with Suriname after 1975) and that, more than that, the readiness to aid white "kith and kin" in the Falklands in 1982 when compared with the unreadiness to help black "kith and kin" in the Windwards a year later seemed to suggest an element of racial prejudice. Whatever the case, Prime Minister Adams's disparaging remarks about the British government, coming from a Barbados which has generally been regarded as the most ultra-English of all the West Indian countries, underlined, as nothing else could have done, how regional leadership had passed, irrevocably, from London to Washington.[9]

But there is more than this. There is always something comic and absurd in the metropole-colony relationship, as the history of colonialism shows. The Grenada affair provided rich evidence of the absurdity. There was, from the very beginning, the absurdity of the unopened letters. In the first month after the 1979 coup d'état Prime Minister Bishop wrote a letter to Prime Minister Williams of Trinidad, which the latter, with characteristic disdain when confronted with matters he did not like, left unopened on his desk. Williams, perhaps, remembering that his own government had almost been toppled by an army mutiny in 1970, did not care to lend legitimacy to any similar event in neighboring Grenada. In a sort of countermeasure, Trinidadian Archbishop Anthony Pantin has recorded how he wrote a friendly letter to Bishop in November 1979, expressing his continuing friendship but hoping that the new regime would see validation through free elections, and how he received no answer.[10] There followed the idiocy of the matter of Bishop's letters of 1981 to President Reagan inspired by the desire to normalize relationships, the first being unanswered and the second being answered by a short, curt reply from an obscure low-level officer in the Barbados U.S. embassy, a calculated snub followed in 1983 by Bishop's failure to obtain a meeting with the president, explained away by an administration official with the comment that "people do not just walk into the White House and say they want to see the President."[11] All this was finally followed, in October and after, by the controversy surrounding the OECS letter of invitation to Washington, the alleged letter of invitation from Governor-General Scoon to the OECS itself, and the story of General Austin's invitation to the British government to intercede, which was received at a Scandinavian plastic-bag company in London that had an out-of-date Foreign Office telex number.[12] It is astonishing that in an age of rapid and sophisticated communications systems, heads of state should refuse to answer letters, misplace them, ignore them, let alone be unable to talk with each other.

As if this comedy of errors was not enough in itself to make the Commonwealth Caribbean the laughing stock of the world for a short time, it also made the region a theater of the bizarre. There was the crucial meeting of the weekend of October 22–23, in which presumably responsible heads of government could not agree on what was said or agreed to. There was the spectacle, which many West Indians found almost indecent, of Prime Minister Charles fielding questions for President Reagan asked by inquisitive liberal American reporters during their joint television appearance. Lesser West Indian figures joined in the charade. Dean Harold Critchlow of the Barbados Anglican Church pointed to biblical proof of Jesus' support for the U.S.-led invasion, adding that "there is no doubt that our destiny lies with America . . . we shall have to stop looking to Europe whence we have derived most of our former culture and develop meaningful ties with America."[13] At the same time the former secretary-general of CARICOM, Dr. Kurleigh King, was traveling through the islands as a newborn religious zealot, with the message that the answer to the West Indian crisis lay in acceptance of his newly discovered Oriental guru and his vision of transcendental meditation.[14] To these must be added two additional categories of neocolonial "mimic men." First, there were the hundreds of West Indians, from Jamaica to Trinidad, who wrote their fulsome "God bless America" letters to their local newspapers and for whom there is no excuse; at least the Grenadians who did the same thing had the excuse that they had been subjected to intolerable traumatic shock. As the American Friends Service Committee visiting team later pointed out, some kind of psychological mechanism seems to have been at work so that the Grenadians' perception of the events of October 19 and the events of the invasion was collapsed into a single whole, with the fear and terror perceived to be in the earlier revolutionary period and release flowing from the invasion.[15]

Second, there were those members of the West Indian elite who allowed themselves to be recruited as members of the post-October interim administration under the governor-general, notwithstanding the fact that the only legitimacy enjoyed by the advisory council was in fact that of force, that is to say, of the U.S. occupying elements. That all of them eagerly responded to that collaborative role says much, again, about the dependent colonial mentality. It is apparent that only illness prevented Dr. Alistair McIntyre, deputy secretary-general of the U.N. Conference on Trade and Development, and a well-known Grenadian, from joining the group. The same reason may have deterred journalist Alistair Hughes from joining; his story again has an element of the bizarre about it, for much of the outside reporting of the invasion almost seems to have suggested at times that the whole massive force of the American empire had been unleashed for the sole purpose of rescuing Hughes from his revolutionary tormentors.

But of all the dramatis personae in this scenario of Caribbean absurdity, the one that tells us most about the colonial dependent mentality is the figure of Governor-General Paul Scoon. He belongs to a type well-known in the West Indies, that of the obedient and deferential colonial public servant who has served his masters well, and received the appropriate rewards. Educated during the British colonial period at local Grenada schools, followed by brief periods of further education in Toronto and London, he taught for fourteen years at the Grenada Boys' Secondary School, as well as being hostel master, the equivalent of a teacher in a minor British public school. During that period, and later, he became a leading member of the

Grenadian colonial establishment, becoming, variously, chairman of the Board of Education, chairman of the governing body of the Grenada Teachers' College, president of the Association of Masters and Mistresses in secondary schools, and vice-president of the Grenada Civil Service Association. For all of this conventional public service he was rewarded with the honor of the Knight Grand Cross of the Most Distinguished Order of St. Michael and St. George (G.C.M.G.) and Officer of the Most Excellent Order of the British Empire (O.B.E.); thus he was initiated into the general policy of honorific titles whereby the British ruling class has traditionally taught lesser mortals how to become at once social snobs and loyal members of the ruling-class cause. It is said that his great gift was that of elocution, being able to recite long Shakespearean passages at will; in that sense he was the "black Englishman" incarnate, knowing more about English history and literature than West Indian history and literature. It is hardly surprising that, with that background, Scoon developed a finely honed instinct for survival, so that he was able to serve, without any evident qualms of conscience, four different governmental regimes of different ideological character: the Gairy regime (when he was first appointed governor-general in 1978), the PRG regime, the brief Revolutionary Military Council regime, and after that the U.S.-appointed regime. It is a record that compels a reluctant admiration. This is the kind of colonized person who is used by everybody and respected by none. It is the story of the little man who is pushed onto the big stage by the perverse accidents of history. He will be forever remembered as the Uriah Heep of Grenada history between the 1950s and the 1980s.[16]

But history, including Caribbean history, is never just absurd or bizarre. There is always an inner, inherent logic of vested interest and class ideology which gives it ultimate meaning. All of the quixotic elements of the Grenada story, therefore, fit into an understandable pattern once that interest and ideology are fully comprehended. They are, of course, the interest and the ideology of the reactionary Caribbean bourgeoisie. They lie behind—in their consistency and continuity—all of the bizarre episodes and comedic personalities of the event. It is the underlying rationale, and not the incidental characters, which unravels the mystery of the play.

The essence of the underlying rationale is contained in the phobic fears of the Caribbean neocolonial ruling elites. They resisted, and feared, the Grenada Revolution, not for what it actually achieved, but because it represented, in its ideology, a new departure in West Indian developmental politics. It constituted an attractive alternative model of planning; it put forward a creditable performance in providing housing, health, education, and land for the people; and, inspite of the centralized discipline involved, it managed to incorporate the masses into the state decision-making processes. Its example could have been contagious in neighboring small-island economies, where the ordinary people still remained a silent majority in between election times and where tiny petit-bourgeois "brown" elites continued the old, tired game of what Adam Smith called "the paltry raffle of colony faction." The Grenada model of consultative democracy struck a new note of institutional experimentation and collective self-help which, quite frankly, from the bourgeois viewpoint could not be allowed to continue.

But the matter, of course, could not be presented in such frank terms. It had to be disguised as something else. That was done by taking over the grandiose global anti-Communist rhetoric of the U.S. leaders. In the various pronouncements, then, of the West Indian politicians—Adams, Seaga, Charles—the borrowed rhetoric became their main justification. Adams told his Parliament that the Eastern Caribbean had its feet set on a battleground between the ideologies that rent the world, and that there was evidence of Cuban intelligence agents using Barbados as a central point to launch the development of radical political movements in the region to the advantage of Eastern Europe, but he offered no hard evidence to substantiate the charge. He added, in words that can only be construed as gross ignorance of Caribbean history, that "the English-speaking Caribbean has never been threatened by the military power of the United States. . . . There has never been any occasion where the Yankees have had a military occupation against our will in an English-speaking island. The Americans are to us, I believe, part of the English-speaking family of the world."[17] Not even Mr. Churchill, in his most imperialist moment, could have matched the ethnocentrism of those remarks. Adams, in fact, here speaks as a sort of Anglo-American colonial black who blithely ignores the record of U.S. imperial intervention in the Caribbean region and who can only do so because he is not really interested in what has happened to Haiti or Cuba or the Dominican Republic as part of that record. His is the voice of the colonial subject-person who believes that he has a "special relationship" with the American imperial power. He is his master's voice. It is little wonder that to many of his critics he was known, until his untimely death in 1985, as the West Indian "Uncle Tom."

Jamaican Prime Minister Seaga, as everybody knows, is a much more prudent man. He is, in part, a trained cultural anthropologist out of Harvard, whereas his Barbadian counterpart was a not-too-brilliant lawyer out of London. He does not succumb to the temptation of the legal mind to overstate the evidence when he knows that he has a weak case to defend. So, to begin with he told his own Parliament that Jamaica could not accept the Grenada mode of revolution because it made no allowance to institutionalize opposition and to change governments peacefully, nor could it accept brutal military takeovers or the use of gunpower to liquidate political opponents. With these principles none of his critics could disagree. But he went on, less convincingly, to speak about a "perceived threat" from Grenada which contemplated "acts of hostility against neighboring states" without supporting the charge with any hard evidence. Even less convincingly, Seaga went on to argue that Bishop had been a "moderate" in comparison with the military and political leaders who overthrew him; an argument almost hypocritical when it is remembered that during the four years of the PRG regime Seaga himself had insisted as seeing Bishop as a Communist enemy of West Indian democracy. No less significant is what Seaga did not say: he said nothing of the Trinidad charges that deception had been practiced at the crucial CARICOM meeting in October when, as is now known, the OECS-Jamaica-Barbados triumvirate had already decided upon invasion, in collaboration with the United States, as the answer to the problem.[18] When all is said in his favor, Seaga remains marked as the West Indian colonial *collaborateur,* the self-proclaimed financial "whiz-kid" who still believes, against all the evidence, that the Puerto Rican model of economic development by way of invited outside capital investment is the answer to poverty and mass unemployment. That kind of economic dependency leads, inevitably, to political dependency.

But of all the West Indian neocolonial triumvirate, Dominica's Prime Minister Eugenia Charles was, by any standard, the most intransigent, the most intractable, the most *incondicionalista* of the pro-American leaders. Coming from a "less developed economy" rather than a "more developed economy" like Barbados or Jamaica, she needed U.S. patronage more than the others. There is no doubt about her remarkable political gifts. Merely to outplay other contenders and become prime minister is no mean feat in small West Indian societies that are deeply macho and in which a woman, not to mention an unmarried woman, has to encounter a host of strong cultural prejudices. It is not surprising that her partisan troops, all over the region, see her in terms of the West Indian Margaret Thatcher or Indira Ghandi. Like them, she is rough, tough, abrasive. Not surprisingly, then, she has turned out to be the darling of the Washington crowd. Her apology for the invasion almost outdid that of the U.S. State Department. It amounted to a theory of international Communist conspiracy. The Grenada Revolution, according to her, was part of that conspiracy, with its links to Cuba, Soviet Russia, Libya, and North Korea. North Korea had been paying a Dominican citizen some $1,500 a month to foment discontent in the island; Libya had been offering scholarships to Dominican students for study, but in reality for terrorist training; the brief-lived military regime in Grenada itself had been manipulated by all of those Communist countries; and the OECS countries believed that Grenada was undertaking plans to invade them.[19] Very little concrete evidence has ever been offered to substantiate these charges. The evidence available, indeed, seriously questions the idea of a grand, worldwide Communist plot. If, for example, Cuba was behind the October events, why then did Castro sternly refuse to send military help to the Revolutionary Military Council, as the Havana official statements show? And if the Soviet Union was behind Grenada then why—as we now know from other published documentation—did Grenadian emissaries often receive, to their chagrin, cool treatment from their Russian comrades? The real world of international politics, even among friends, is not as simplistic as the conspiracy theory assumes.

The mind-set that believes the conspiracy theory, in fact, is at once defective and dangerous. It is less interested in fact than in plot. It sees everything in Manichean terms of the children of light and the children of darkness. Because it already knows the answers, it makes its decisions on instinct rather than reflection; Prime Minister Charles seems almost to take pride, in an interview elsewhere, that she and her colleagues only took five minutes to make up their minds after receiving the alleged request from Governor-General Scoon for aid. "I have never seen Caribbean leaders come to a decision so promptly," she remembers. "Everybody there knew what we had to do. There were no arguments. It just came instantaneously out of our mouths. This is what we have to do. Then we sat down and said, but how? You know?"[20] This is hardly the stuff out of which thoughtful and painstaking diplomacy is made. Indeed it seems to indicate the spirit of frantic haste, in which many of the decisions of the moment were made. The conspiracy theory justifies this by its circular reasoning: the opponents are evil; being evil, they cannot be trusted; and because they cannot be trusted they are not entitled to the normal courtesies that govern the relationships between states.

Once the courtesies, and the conventions that accompany them, are thus put aside, there grows up, quite naturally, a politics of hypocrisy. Both colonizer and colonized practice it. The Soviets ignore the world condemnation of the Afghanistan invasion; the Americans do likewise when world opinion condemns the Grenada invasion. Washington deplores what it sees as Cuban-Russian efforts to destabilize the Caribbean-Central America region, while at the same time its own CIA forces act to destabilize the Nicaragua revolutionary regime. In the Grenada matter, the Eastern Caribbean states lectured the revolutionary government because of its unwillingness to hold free and fair elections, while at the same time turning a blind eye to the comparable failure of the Burnham regime in Guyana. It is, of course, only fair to add that this was matched by the hypocrisy of the Burnham government itself, which denounced the Grenada invasion as an act of imperialist intervention even though that government itself had originally come into power as the result, in the 1960s, of similar intervention on the part of Britain and the United States. President Burnham had no moral ground to stand on, as his domestic radical critics pointed out; and his position simply had the consequence of confusing Guyanese public opinion on the whole Grenada matter.[21] All in all, as one regards the total end-result of the affair, with all of its lies, half-lies, deceit, and postures of self-righteousness, it is difficult to resist the conclusion that it has led to a serious decline in the moral quality of interstate relationships within the Caribbean which may take a whole generation to remedy and heal.

There is one final aspect of this general portrait of the colonial and neocolonial dependent mentality that merits notice. The colonized persons always crave recognition. They want to be rewarded for loyalty. In the West Indian case, the Grenada affair made the recognition and the reward possible. Almost overnight, the West Indian political leaders became front-page news. Prime Minister Charles appeared on American television with President Reagan, just as earlier Prime Minister Seaga had had the honor of being the first foreign head of state to be received by the president after Reagan's 1980 electoral victory. Used to British colonial neglect they now basked in the Washington limelight, with all of the media publicity this means in America. Human nature being what it is, they made the most of it. For the moment at least the West Indies became the center of world attention; as Prime Minister Adams rather coyly put it, for the first time since independence in 1966, Barbados had occupied a position on the center of the world stage, one that it had neither sought nor welcomed, since it arose out of tragic circumstances that affected all West Indians.[22] The invasion brought immediate material rewards, of course; almost overnight Dominica received a U.S. grant-in-aid of $15 million to complete its badly needed road program. But the psychological reward was perhaps even greater, for the West Indian leaders were made to believe that they had become valued allies of the metropolitan empire in its crusade against world Communism.

This was part cause, part consequence, of the switch from British colonial loyalty to American neocolonial loyalty already noted. In politics as in nature there is a law of gravity. As the center of world power shifts, the colonials respond. Power calls, compels, commands. More than anything else, the significance of Grenada is that it embodied at once the call and the response. For the previous West Indian generation the final accolade of recognition was an invitation to a Buckingham Palace garden party; for the post-Grenada generation it will be an invitation to a social event at the White House. President Reagan spends a vacation in Barbados; American warships make friendly calls to West Indian ports; Prime Minister Seaga makes a sentimental trip back to his alma mater of Harvard. At the same time, many of the new West Indian generation are beginning to lose something of the old anglophilism. They perceive a visible decline from the old high standards, for example, of the royal family, with Princess Margaret

disporting with her commoner boyfriends on Union Island in the Grenadines, and Prince Andrew exhibiting himself with his commoner girl-
friends in Miami. There are even some West Indians, many of them supporters of the Grenada invasion, who see Governor-General Scoon as a
colonial buffoon.

The British imperial presence, in brief, has lost much of its old mystery
and glamor. Americans are seen as more serious, more down to earth, more
practical, more generous. It is the well-known history of empire: Athens
replaces Persia, Rome replaces Greece. Even Paul of Tarsus, for all of his
subversive Christian message, was proud to be a Roman citizen. It would
be surprising if West Indians did not begin to feel the same way about their
new, possible American citizenship; the popular surge of pro-American
feeling after October in Grenada itself, with many wanting to become a
permanent part of the Union, possibly in the form of associated status after
the Puerto Rican model, is symptomatic. Many of them, too, remember
that something at least of the Grenada tragedy was set in motion from the
very beginning by the fact that, as the British Liberal party leader David
Steel has pointed out, the British government withdrew aid and support
from Grenada after the 1979 coup, and failed to respond to the Foreign
Affairs Committee's calls to renew the British presence, while by contrast
both Canada and the European Economic Community maintained friendly
ties with the new regime.[23] In the face of such hostility the old affections
slowly die.

In a way, all this is very logical. For over the last quarter of a century or
so the whole Caribbean region and society have been changed by the
sociocultural impact of American cultural imperialism, in the mass media
of newspapers, movies, and television, in the tourist industry, in commercial advertising, in the invading American popular cults and religions, and
even in educational patterns. The region's bourgeois elites, in their general
life styles, live more and more like their counterparts in Miami and New
York and Houston. Their children, even more, develop life patterns shaped
by the U.S. technologies of fast food, video cassettes, and hard rock music,
all of them reflecting the pleasure-seeking drives of a pervasive American
materialistic hedonism. It is perhaps no accident that in almost the last
piece he wrote, Prime Minister Williams of Trinidad and Tobago pointed
out to his audience how, in that changing American society, the old capitalist work ethic was increasingly being replaced with a new play ethic of
leisure.[24] It could, then, only have been a matter of time before cultural
Americanism engendered in its Caribbean followers a political Americanism, persuading many of them that their political destiny now lies with
the American empire. Grenada, in a manner of speaking, turns out to be
the earthquake that records on the seismic graph the moment of that
transition.

The general phenomenon of dependency in the modern world, relating the "developed" societies to the "underdeveloped" societies, is of course complex and multifaceted. Dependency is, at one and the same time, political, economic, and psychological. Earlier passages in this book have discussed the political and economic aspects of the case as it applies to the Grenadian story. But it is perhaps not too much to say that the psychological aspect is the most important for the simple reason that it is the most intractable. It is easier to change economic structures or political attitudes than it is to change mental habits, the ways in which people think. Popular conceptualizations of the world may survive long after the economic and political conditions that first generated them have disappeared. Two examples will suffice to show this. The Civil War changed the old American South economically almost overnight, yet it took a century or more for the ingrained mental habits of white racial prejudice to begin to disappear. Post-1945 Britain went through important economic changes under the guidance of socialist governments, yet those changes have done little to undermine in any serious way the mental habits of class snobbishness that continue to infect all social levels of the national life. Most men and women, under pressure, will change their jobs or join another political party, but most of them find it more difficult to modify the concepts of the world that they carry in their heads for the reason that those concepts rest on psychological elements in human nature much more immune to the ability to change.

It is hardly surprising, then, that the mental habit of psychological dependency on the part of former colonial peoples, as in the Caribbean, should turn out to be an even more stubborn problem. Economic and political dependency patterns have been easier to deal with. Again, two examples will suffice to illustrate the point. Alain Blérald's recent book on the economic history of the French Antilles seeks to show that the historic dependency on the French market system, going back to its origins in Colbert's seventeenth-century France, can be changed under new circumstances and that it does not have to warrant a theory of economic fatalism, as if things cannot change.[25] Thus again, the work of the young Puerto Rican scholar Benjamin Torres on the life and work of the Puerto Rican patriot and Nationalist party leader Pedro Albizu Campos shows how the habit of political dependency can be offset by a party program and leadership that openly defies the occupying colonial power and challenges its claim to legitimacy in the occupied territory. It is a sad blow to the cause of Caribbean political and cultural sovereignty that Torres died at the age of thirty-nine before completing his life work on Albizu.[26] Both of these examples show how it is, in a way, comparatively easy to challenge and change situations of economic and political dependency, compared with the problem of changing the habit of mental and psychological dependency.

This, in a nutshell, is the problem of Caribbean dependency. It is doubtful whether the controlling sector of West Indian society, those who are termed "decision makers" in the communications jargon—the upper crust, the town smart sets, the middle strata, the political and business elites— have really learned anything from the Grenada experience. They will continue to dismiss it as just some sort of Communism gone wrong, something that must never happen again. As is evident enough to anyone who has talked with these groups since 1983, they are anxious to forget all about it, almost to pretend to themselves that it never happened. They almost seem at times ready to embrace some odd theory of an evil alien intruder seeking to destroy them. Accordingly, Grenada in 1983 was the outcome of some malign Russian-Cuban conspiracy, just as Jonestown in 1978 was the outcome of some alien force entering from lower-class American society. As one listens to all this, it almost seems that whatever happens to Caribbean economic and political structures, the Caribbean habit of psychological dependency will never end.

15

The Lessons for the Caribbean State System

It is hardly necessary, at this point, to further underline the lesson that the Grenada affair at once reflected and precipitated a crisis of incalculable dimensions to the postindependent Caribbean state system. Involving as it did a state of armed conflict between member states of a common regional organization, it immediately raised, as does all such conflict, a gamut of fundamental questions. Can the regional organization, and regionalism itself as a principle, survive the experience? Is a regional system of collective security possible between states that differ on questions of economic strategy and foreign policy options, not to speak of ideology? Is the typical West Indian ministate viable? What is the future of the theory and practice of traditional sovereignty itself in the modern world, and its pressing realities? These questions go to the root of the authority of the nation-state itself. There can be little doubt that 1983 in the Caribbean raised, in agonizing form, all of these questions in much the same way as 1861 raised them for the American Federal Union, and as 1914 raised them for the old European state system. If, as so many people have said, the Commonwealth Caribbean will never be the same since Grenada, it is precisely because these questions have been raised and cannot be avoided.

In seeking to answer these questions it is vital to remember that the single, basic, fundamental fact from which all else flows, is that Grenada, like all of the Caribbean territories, has from the beginning been forcibly incorporated into the world economic system, and particularly that system in the form of the Western capitalist core economies. That has meant a system of structural dependency in which, by means of mechanisms of "enforced bilateralism," the colonial economies have become suppliers of tropical raw products for export to the outside industrial and commercial markets, with the terms of trade and exchange determined unilaterally by the metropolitan vendor forces, and to the disadvantage of the dependent sellers. That, of course, was the history of Caribbean sugar. Today, it is the history of Caribbean bauxite in Jamaica, Suriname, and Guyana; of Caribbean secondary industry as in Puerto Rico and the Dominican Republic; and of Caribbean tropical fruits and spices as in Grenada itself. The metropolitan control thus flows from the dual fact that the advanced industrial economies remain as the major source of investment capital and the dominant export market. The dependent economies, consequently, export their staple commodities and import their sophisticated necessities, notably food items, from the industrial centers in an exchange system over which they exercise little effective control; they sell cheap and buy dear. At the same time, it leads to a serious structural imbalance in their own domestic systems: they produce what they do not consume and consume what they do not produce.[1]

The economic dependency, almost by a law of nature, generates a political dependency. The whole developmental strategy—the drive for export markets, the lobbying for metropolitan preferential quotas, the competition to attract the big investment company or the offshore bank or medical school—places a premium on political "stability," which means a "safe" investment climate, a pliable labor force, a "sound" fiscal and taxation policy on the part of the host government, and a continuing guarantee against any possible confiscatory policies on the part of the local political leaderships. In turn, direct economic aid in this patron-client relationship is accompanied by political conditions by which the recipient of aid is expected to adopt a foreign policy favorable to the donor nation. The two most noticeable Caribbean examples of this process are, of course, Puerto Rico and Cuba. Recent statistical reports show that Cuba receives more than half of the total $6 billion of aid that the Soviet Union dispenses to its client states, while Puerto Rico receives an annual aid program from the United States, by means of the transfer of federal funds, of some $4.5 billion. So it is not surprising that Cuba generally supports Soviet foreign policy, with occasional exceptions such as its abstaining vote in the United Nations on the Afghanistan matter, while Puerto Rican governments without exception are ardent pro-U.S. supporters, as exemplified in the fact that only one sole member of the Puerto Rican legislature had the courage to cast his vote against the 1965 U.S. invasion of the Dominican Republic. With the independent regional states, of course, the pressures are perhaps not so crude. But they are there. They are there in the U.S. embargo against Cuba, to begin with, followed by the moves to isolate Grenada by excluding her from the 1981 U.S. Caribbean Basin Initiative program and by the hostile diplomatic attitudes adopted toward the socialist regimes of Burnham's Guyana and Manley's Jamaica. Even when such regimes, as in the case of Manley's Jamaica, attempted to adopt a middle way between the superpower rivalry they were rebuffed by the United States as a virtual ally of Cuba and thus themselves to be isolated, with the consequence that the weakness and disorder of the domestic Jamaican system could not withstand such isolation. It is in this sense that the dependent economy becomes the client state.[2]

The consequences of this general condition are far-reaching. The globalization of the superpower rivalry, extending to the Caribbean, presents the small nation-state with a heart-breaking dilemma. Since neither Moscow nor Washington are sentimental patrons, they demand from their Third World clients an absolute allegiance which permits no ambiguity or maneuverability. The Americans, earlier on, were only prepared to evacuate the Chaguaramas naval base in Trinidad in 1961 once they had been assured that Prime Minister Eric Williams was in the pro-Western camp; correspondingly, the Russians support Cuba unconditionally while their support of Bishop's Grenada was throughout lukewarm because of their general suspicion that national liberation movements can never be relied upon to become openly pro-Soviet Marxist-Leninist regimes. The basic weakness and vulnerability of the Caribbean states only serve to play into the hands of the more powerful external players in the ongoing game of the international anarchy. Their dilemma has been aptly assesed by one West Indian observer. Anthony Gonzales writes:

> Unable to pay their way, and in some cases even to defend themselves against a Ku Klux gang, the majority of the nation states in the region have been relegated to geopolitical pawns and havens for all types of adventurers, either in the form of states such as South Africa, etc., or private transnational agents who perceive the weakness of these islands and move in to secure some advantage. In a very real sense, the islands of the archipelago are up for grabs by external forces. One of the unfortunate consequences of this situation is that Caribbean leaders, especially those with meagre resources, tend to think that their interests are best served by playing all their international cards to secure some additional economic advantage with little awareness of the negative repercussions of some of this kind of action.[3]

So, it becomes a game of mutual exploitation. On the one hand the superpower patron uses its power, both economic and political, to seduce the small client state, on the other hand the client hopes that by compliance it will receive the aid that it needs. As the saying goes, it takes two to tango.

The Grenada affair brought to a head all of these complex considerations. All of the ingredients of the Caribbean menu were present: the bitter Soviet-American imperialist rivalry; the ambiguity of the Grenadian foreign policy as it sought to placate one side, then the other; the search for aid by small ministates plagued by internal economic crisis and external debt problems; the paranoid fear of the more conservative Caribbean states that they were threatened by a general Soviet-Cuban-Grenada conspiracy to overturn them; the exacerbation of the internal Grenada party crisis by intervening forces, the extent of which has yet to be determined; and the final decision on the part of the U.S. imperialist power to resolve it all by an act of naked aggressive military power. It is true that the Grenada affair contributed its own peculiar ingredient of an internal fratricidal struggle, whereby both factions destroyed each other, something hitherto unknown to the English-speaking Caribbean. Nevertheless, the affair exemplified the general character of the Caribbean colonial condition, a condition—to give it a final definition—in which the internal and domestic problems and processes of the Caribbean are utilized and exploited, and thereby diminished, by intervening extraregional forces. It all adds up to a general scenario of what another West Indian observer has properly called a "creeping cancer of off-shore sovereignty."[4]

If this line of argument is correct—that the economic and political weakness of the Caribbean states makes them dangerously vulnerable to outside forces, and especially the Cold War postures of the superpowers—it follows that future Grenadas can only be avoided by a thorough overhaul of the regional state system, with a view to establishing structures of regional power and authority that will be better able to cope with the problems of regional security and defense, as well as social and economic development. The majority of those states are Lilliputian ministates: the latest being St. Kitts-Nevis, formally independent as of 1983, with a total population of some 42,000, no more than that of a small American Midwestern township. Grenada showed that, first, no one single island-state of that size can undertake unilaterally a social revolution and, second, that if it is seen as a threat to others in the regional neighborhood no one of those others by itself can effectively organize a viable defense. The point was well stated by the opposition member of the Trinidad and Tobago House of Representatives, Nizam Mohammed, in that body's debate of October 1983 on the Grenada issue. "The crisis that has descended upon us," he declared, "has brought into sharp focus the limitations of sovereignty in the context of CARICOM nation states and the ineffectiveness of our existing institutions in the CARICOM region to protect and preserve the political integrity of the region and the sovereignty of individual nation states."[5]

It is painfully evident that the region, at the moment, does not provide the institutional mechanisms to meet that issue. The few bodies of a regional character which exist are weak and ineffective. The regional University of the West Indies, under a new "restructuring" plan, looks as if it will break up into separate national campuses. The Organisation of Eastern Caribbean States (OECS), founded in 1981, lacks a strong security defense force, which helps explain the invitation to the United States to lead the Grenada invasion. The Caribbean Economic Community (CARICOM), founded in 1973, even according to the findings of a friendly official report, has largely failed to fulfill its early expectations. That report, penned in 1980, noted, among other things, the inadequate progress made in the area of production integration, only modest gains in the area of functional cooperation and of intraregional trade, and a poor showing in the capacity of CARICOM to bring nongovernmental organizations, such as trade unions, into its work, as well as failing to generate any real support in the regional public opinion. The report's guarded optimism about the future has not been borne out by subsequent events, notably the minitrade war of 1983 with member governments restoring unilaterally to protectionist economic and fiscal policies in defiance of the spirit of regional cooperation. Certainly the Grenada events themselves dramatized the further failure to build up in any way the coordinated foreign policy between member states as set out in Article 17 of the original Chaguaramas Treaty. It is almost not too much to say that those events have put the entire integration movement into serious disarray, even possibly imminent collapse.[6]

Grenada, in sum, demonstrated the consequences of the fatal absence of any effective federal or regional authority. That absence sprang from the collapse of the West Indies Federation of 1958–62. Patrick Solomon has pointed out how things might have been different had the federation survived. A federal government would have possessed not only the legal right but the moral duty to take whatever steps were necessary to curb civil disturbances within its borders. If its own forces were inadequate, it would have had unquestionable authority to invoke assistance from friendly states, whether hemispheric, Commonwealth, or otherwise. External affairs, as in all federal systems, would have been the exclusive prerogative of the central government, so that there would have been no question of individual member states conducting foreign policies of their own. In such a system, indeed, the whole Grenada matter might never have occurred in the first place, since the federal government would have had authority to intervene in Gairy's Grenada in order to assure federal civil rights. Looked at in this way, Grenada 1983 is the aborted child of the dying federation of 1962. With a terrible inexorability, the one led to the other.[7]

As other West Indian commentators in their turn have pointed out, the ultimate responsibility for this situation is West Indian. It is an indictment of the failure of West Indian political will. The same spirit of insular nationalism that destroyed the federation, writes one of them, is today as powerful as ever, threatening this time the regional integration movement.[8] The root of the crisis, writes another, is not just the corruption of the political elites, but, even more, because West Indians as a whole seem to have no capacity for distilling the truth of their own condition, it is a crisis of the failure of moral and intellectual insight.[9] For yet another observer, Grenada presents the ultimate challenge to all West Indians: their response will determine whether they are prepared to be comfortable with the satellite status of yet another imperial power or whether they are still capable of founding a federal union of regional states, distinguished by its ideological independence, and thus establish a new basis for regional freedom.[10]

Yet the victim has not been the integration movement alone. Another casualty is the principled basis of that movement, the concept of "ideological pluralism." The Ocho Rios Declaration of the CARICOM summit conference of 1982 accepted the principle in the statement that while "the emergence of ideological pluralism responds to internal processes and is an irreversible trend within the international system, we are committed to ensuring that it will not inhibit the processes of integration." This echoed the observation of the 1980 experts' report that "ideological pluralism may be a shield against enforced sameness; but should not be a sword against solidarity."[11] The Caribbean states which at once invited and supported the U.S. invasion of Grenada by that very act compromised the spirit of ideological give-and-take. Their acquiescence gave notice that they embraced the U.S. spirit of ideological intolerance in which there can be no room for conciliation and compromise, so that even the mildest form of socialist domestic experiment is perceived as "antidemocratic" and "anti-American." Ideological pluralism will inevitably give way to ideological polarization.

===

All this, it is almost elementary to say, is sad and depressing. The willingness and capacity of West Indian leaders to act in a responsible and united manner in the face of the Grenada crisis was sorely tested, and found wanting. The rule of unanimity of the OECS Treaty was violated. Equally, the commitment of the CARICOM Treaty to full and open consultation was also violated. Both of those treaties, either explicitly or by inference, accepted the principle that dialogue, and not force, should be used as the instrument for the resolving of differences between their member states, a position reiterated by the Trinidad and Tobago minister of external affairs in his address to the 1983 session of the General Assembly of the Organization of American States.[12] Most crucial of all, perhaps, the concept of "ideological pluralism" was sacrificed to Cold War doctrinal rigidity, rooted in the conviction that the region "belongs" to the United States, expressed in the 1982 statement of Assistant Secretary of State Thomas Enders that the United States "will not accept the future of the region being manipulated by Havana," and earlier in the 1927 statement of Undersecretary of State Robert Olds that "we do control the destinies of

Central America, and we do so for the simple reason that the national interest absolutely dictates such a course. . . . Until now, Central America has always understood that governments which we recognise and support stay in power, while those that we do not recognise and support fail.''[13] The end result is that the Caribbean state treaties have been more honored in the breach than in the observance. As has well been said, a treaty does not a community make. Grenada may well turn out to have been the last nail in the coffin.

It is this general concatenation of elements—both internal weakness and external—that has led to the deterioration of the Caribbean state system. It now faces a period of needed reconstruction. It must at once strengthen existing regional institutions and invent new ones as it becomes, along with Central America, the focus for the intensified conflict between the superpowers, lest it be drawn more and more into that conflict to the point of no return. More than any time before it confronts the basic issue of war or peace. The drift toward polarization has to be stemmed, or at least contained; otherwise, it will lead assuredly to other Grenadas. That, surely, is one of the lessons of the Grenada events, summed up in the words of the 1984 Trinidad calypso:

> From the frying pan into the fire
> Six of one and half a dozen of the other
> From Caesar to Caesar

The three cardinal desiderata of that reconstructive effort were set out plainly in the 1981 resolution of the Caribbean Conference of Churches: (1) the establishment of a zone of peace in the region, (2) a final structure for the peaceful settlement of disputes, and (3) the effective containment of the militarization process, whether used by external forces to "destabilize" governments perceived as enemies or by internal domestic forces to curb dissent. It is a trinity of ends; no single one being feasible without the fulfillment of the other two.[14]

As one contemplates these ends, certain considerations come to mind. To begin with, no one who looks at the practical realities of the Caribbean world is likely to believe that some sort of Kantian "perpetual peace" is around the corner. Neither the Soviets nor the Americans are likely to relinquish their interests in the region in a hurry. Nor is anybody entitled to believe that some sort of regional federal or confederal organization is going to appear overnight, following the dream of nineteenth-century Antillean thinkers like Marti, Hostos, and Betances. For some such organization presupposes a certain commonality of interest and ideology on the part of all members, and it is obvious that in the contemporary Caribbean such a commonality does not exist between, for example, socialist Cuba and capitalist Puerto Rico, or even for that matter between CARICOM members such as socialist Guyana and capitalist Jamaica. Nor is this sort of cooperative organization made any more possible by the decision of the CARICOM heads of state, in their meeting of July 1984, to enlarge the membership by granting observer status to Haiti, the Dominican Republic, and Suriname, for it challenges common sense to believe that there was anything much in common between, say, democratic Trinidad and dictatorial Haiti, not to mention the fact that Haiti and the Dominican Republic have themselves been separated from each other for more than 150 years by suspicions and hatreds rooted in profound cultural-ethnic differences.

Yet another factor is the temptation, natural enough in the circumstances, for many of the regional states, desperate in their conviction that they cannot make it alone, to establish a patron-client relationship with the protective "big brother," whether it is the United States or the Soviet Union. And if, finally, added to all this is the endemic fever of personal dislike and animosity between individual Caribbean leaders—so evident in the Grenada affair—then it becomes palpably clear that no miraculous event is going to make the Caribbean, in any foreseeable future, a zone of peace, a demilitarized region, or a functioning cooperative system of member states agreeing to settle their differences by the time-honored processes of negotiation and diplomacy. That, looking at the regional scene in dispassionate terms, looks like a hope beyond the shadow of a dream.

What, then, is the answer to this general impasse? It lies, most probably, in the urgent necessity for all of the regionalist-minded groups in the area— in the trade unions, the churches, the universities, the political parties—to organize a united front based on the frank recognition that to a long-term problem there are no short-term answers. It must go back to the original intent of the Nonaligned Movement to keep apart from both of the great power expansionist systems and yet to maintain, as far as possible, civilized linkages with both. It must recognize, however, that in the Western hemisphere at least the more pressing danger to regionalism comes from the North American power, which is geographically nearer; and in any case the Cuban missile crisis of 1962 proved that with their long and vulnerable lines of communication the Soviet Union may not sustain a credible offensive against the United States in the Caribbean. Nor, in nonmilitary terms, can they match the power of the United States to use economic influence in the area, most notably the use of schemes like the Caribbean Basin Initiative as an alternative to regional integration.

The Caribbean regionalists must also ceaselessly insist upon the right of all ideologies to coexist in the region for, as Neville Linton has shown, the economic integration basis of the European Economic Community has not been negatively affected by the fact that in one member state, Italy, the Communist party is the largest, electorally speaking, and that in another member state, France, the Communist party is actually a participating part of the current Mitterand government.[15] That is also the lesson of groupings as diverse as the group of 77 in the UN Conference on Trade and Development and the Commonwealth of Nations, in which a wide variety of ideological opinion can go hand in hand with common effort based on overriding common interests. It is not inconsequential to note that this accommodating temper, in its Caribbean form, predated the Grenada Revolution, with the 1972 decision of the leading West Indian states, in defiance of Washington, to give diplomatic recognition to Cuba.

More than this, the region must consolidate and expand its extraregional linkages. Most regional states are already members not only of the United Nations but also of the Organization of American States, the Inter-American Development Bank, the Latin-American Economic System, and the United Nations Economic Commission for Latin America. Some of them, like the Dominican Republic, are members of the Socialist International. Others, like Jamaica, are members of the International Bauxite Association. Many of them—and this was not just Bishop's Grenada—have trading relations with the Eastern European Communist countries and with some of the Arab countries. These expanding networks are rooted in the perceived necessity to replace bilateralism with multilateralism. Moreover, as the 1980 report on CARICOM put it, the area is not just a trading club but a community of states and peoples in the Caribbean.[16] According to the well-known law of international relations, the more friends you have the safer you are. There is safety in numbers. The CARICOM members themselves have already had some success, acting jointly, in helping to resolve such issues as the independence of Belize, Venezuela's claim to the Essequibo district of Guyana, and the Law of the Sea. That sort of cooperation must now become global, to the end of terminating the old assumption that certain regions, like the Caribbean, are preempted by the great powers as their exclusive "spheres of influence." For in a unified world, the world itself is ultimately the only viable political unit. The age of "spheres of influence" is over as surely as the great age of European exploration, starting with the voyages of Columbus, is over. Caribbean statesmanship must rise to that challenge.

In that global search for friends and allies, it is vital that the United States itself should not be forgotten. The fact that much of modern America is imperialist and that, further—as already noted—much of liberal America supported the Grenada invasion, does not mean that the America of Jeffersonian liberalism is dead. The Jeffersonian spirit still lives, as the civil rights movements and the anti-Vietnam War movement of the 1960s and 1970s show. There are even glimmers of that spirit in the more "liberal" elements of the U.S. establishment, notwithstanding the fact that many of them betrayed the spirit in their reaction to the Grenada invasion.

(It is interesting to note that the Democratic party 1984 election campaign did not mention Grenada, sensing that on that issue President Reagan was invulnerable.) Yet, America, in its larger sense, is a democratic, volatile, and multiple society, with its old liberal spirit still very potent; it is far from being the monolithic imperialist giant caricatured by its Third World critics. So if on the one hand there is the voice of imperialist America in the Kissinger Commission report of 1984 (which advocates escalation of the military assault against the Central American enemies) there is, on the other hand, the 1983 report, issued by the Woodrow Wilson International Center for Scholars in Washington, and representing in its signatories the world of American business, academia, the military, and diplomatic circles, which argues, first, that the basic roots of hemispheric insecurity are primarily economic, social, and political, and not military, and second that the sources of instability are mainly internal to each nation and, accordingly, that external influences are secondary. The 1986 report of the Inter-America Dialogue group reiterated the same sensible liberal message.[17]

Nor should the voice of academic liberalism be overlooked, for the universities play a not unimportant role in the shaping of American public opinion. Even when it is a typically cautious voice, it can insist that of all the options open to U.S. foreign policymakers the most reasonable is a collaborative option which, while accepting that the United States has legitimate interests in the Caribbean, demands that there must be restraints upon direct and independent U.S. action. Multilateral rather than bilateral avenues are seen as the proper ones to explore, since the countries of the region themselves have a major stake in the issues involved and can themselves make a major contribution to their resolution.[18] Even the right-wing Rand Corporation can publish a position paper which, while still accepting the conspiracy picture of "subversive" enemies undermining the U.S. hegemony in the Caribbean, warns of the dangers of "quick-fix military solutions" and advocates an "economy of force" policy that does not neglect the social, economic, and political dimensions of "unrest" in the region. Caribbean leadership should make the most of these differences of emphasis which the different groups of the American ruling elites display.[19]

Yet leadership, like charity, begins at home. The existing machinery of regional government must be improved. Both the Council of Ministers of CARICOM and the Standing Committee of Ministers for Foreign Affairs must be given new life and energy; both were bypassed in the Grenada matter. There must be regular meetings of the CARICOM heads of state; there was not a single meeting in the entire seven years between 1974 and 1981. The CARICOM secretariat, located in Georgetown, Guyana, must somehow emerge from its obscurity; most West Indians would not be able to identify its secretary-general by name, any more than most Americans would know who are the official chairpersons of the major political parties. The secretariat, indeed, has seemed to be a body of faceless and unknown civil service bureaucrats; even worse, there has been no secretary-general since William Demas who has been able to match his stature as a well-known Caribbean thinker and economist and who resigned in 1979. It is imperative that the secretary-general be able to speak openly and boldly for CARICOM, just as the secretary-general of the United Nations speaks for that body and what it stands for.

Beyond this, and among other things, the region must begin also to improve its diplomatic image. It was the traditional practice in the old British colonial West Indies for governors and administrators to be selected from the type of the Oxford "passman." It has equally been the traditional practice, up to the present day, for U.S. ambassadors in the region to be party "hacks" or wealthy party donors given their appointments as reward for their services. The postindependence regional governments have followed suit by filling too many of their new consular and ambassadorial posts with the type of the cautious civil servant. What is needed is the kind of imaginative appointment such as Manley's designation of Lucille Mair, an articulate university lecturer, as ambassador to the United Nations; or Bishop's designation of Richard Jacobs, another articulate university lecturer, as ambassador to Cuba and later to Moscow; or, to take another example, Venezuela's appointment of an intelligent and bright woman like Maria Clemencia Lopez Jimenez as ambassador to Trinidad and Tobago.

The practical and immediate problems presented by the demands of regionalism are thus obvious enough. But the Grenada matter presents an even larger problem, since it dramatically spotlights the whole question of state sovereignty in the modern world. It is not just a local Caribbean matter of small microstates being too weak in natural resources or territorial size to make their own way in that world. It is, even more, the larger truth that quite simply there is no place in a unified world for the nation-state, anywhere, to hope to survive by policies of economic autarchy or even of regional economic "blocs." The historical period of the independent nation-state, which began in the sixteenth century, is patently over. All of the problems facing the modern world, including the ultimate problem of planetary survival, can only be solved by international planning, which will probably commence with regional planning. That is why, in the French Antilles, the majority electorate prefers to remain an overseas department rather than "go it alone" as an independent state in an uncharted sea. That is why, too, the Puerto Rican minority forces which presently fight, and quite properly, for national independence will find that, as soon as Puerto Rico becomes a separate republic, it will have to begin thinking of surrendering some of its new sovereignty to some sort of federated regional organization so that political independence does not lead to economic disaster. No small country can now seriously hope to defend itself by its own efforts alone; that is why both Suriname and Guyana, faced with boundary disputes, turn either to a more powerful neighbor like Brazil or to larger bodies like the Organization of American States. That is why, finally, the Grenada revolution collapsed, because it became a pawn on the superpower chessboard.

The conclusion, surely, is inescapable. The world has gone beyond the stage, which was essentially a part of the age of bourgeois supremacy, of national self-determination in both the spheres of economic and political life. Internationalism, as well as the intermediate stage of regionalism, means cooperation for purposes that go beyond the nation-state. This does not necessarily mean the end of nationalism or the nationalist spirit, which is, after all, deeply embedded in the human psyche, and it is worth remembering that the Grenada Revolution was as much about that spirit as it was about Marxism-Leninism. It means, rather, that as the separaton of nation and state takes place, the spirit of national pride will seek its fulfillment more and more on the cultural plane, less and less on the economic and the political. Nor is this pure idealism, for countries as politically diverse as Haiti, Cuba, Puerto Rico, Barbados, and the Dominican Republic already participate and compete in events such as the Caribbean Festival of Arts and the Central American and Pan-Caribbean games without any of the acrimony and violence that has marked the world of Olympic Games in recent years. That kind of friendly regional intercourse at the cultural level can, in the long run, pave the way for cooperation on the economic and political level. It can improve the chances that that cooperation will take place peacefully, and not through the way of life imposed by every empire from Rome to America upon its tributary provinces.

16

The Lessons for the Caribbean Left

Naturally and quite properly, the most bitter and principled denunciation of the destruction of the Grenada Revolution came from the forces of the left, both regional and international. It was virtually unanimous, bringing together for once, at least, all of the competing groups and sectarian doctrines, coming, literally, from all parts of the world where the socialist philosophy in one way or another is sustained. They recognized that their primary responsibility was to understand what lessons the episode held for the left movement, in terms of policy, tactics and strategy, ideological content, and, in general, the theory and praxis of revolution. They saw, without difficulty, that there was no problem in understanding the behavior of both the West Indian bourgeoisie and the North American imperialist, since both of them acted in logical accord with their respective class interests. The real post-mortem had to deal with the fact that October 1983 was in large part a self-inflicted wound of the revolution itself. It thus became necessary, and is still necessary, for the progressive movement, in the best spirit of democratic self-criticism, without nostalgia or evasive apologetics or scapegoating, to ask, and seek to answer, the crucial questions: what went wrong in the internal dynamics of the revolution, why did things go wrong, and what are the long-term implications for the Caribbean revolutionary cause in the future? Murder, after all, is one thing. Suicide is quite another.[1]

The first lesson, and perhaps the most important, comes from the fact that the revolution in St. George's, for reasons both internal and external, became early on an armed revolution. In the form of both the army and the popular militia, the visible symbol of the revolution became the gun and the rifle, along with the army fatigues after the Cuban fashion, and along, too, with the public rhetoric of the revolution that became increasingly militaristic in its tone. The scale of weaponry was too big if meant to control internal dissent, and too little, as events turned out, to resist external attack. It is not clear whether Bishop and his colleagues realized, until the very last moment, the grim implications of that situation, for in the last resort it is the man with the gun who becomes the final arbiter of doctrinal differences in the revolutionary situation, whether it is Cromwell or Bonaparte or Stalin or Hitler. In such a situation the revolution is not child's play or a gentlemanly game but, as October 19 showed, a matter of what particular faction is in control of the armed power of that state. If Bishop had read his Machiavelli or his Hobbes he would have known that this fact is the Achilles heel of all revolutionary processes.

For it is urgent to remember, speaking of the socialist movement in more general terms, that that movement began in the nineteenth century, with Marx and Engels and others, as an antiwar, antimilitaristic movement which saw the armed state such as Prussia or Czarist Russia as the enemies of the popular revolution. It was not pacifist, but it was decidedly antimilitarist. It was revolutionary, but it was suspicious of the Bonaparte tradition. Grenada 1983 reinforces the lessons of that tradition: first, that the military force must always be under the firm control of the civilian power, and, second, that the civilian power holders must never be tempted to use a military solution to the internal problems of the revolutionary process. Unless those conditions are met the process enters a self-destructive phase in which the gun will ultimately speak and in which the local Cromwell or Bonaparte will use the gun to consolidate his own bid for power.

The mixture of revolution and armed force is thus a heady mix, with clear danger. The militarization of the Grenada Revolution, which is part of the enveloping militarization of the Third World countries as a whole, runs counter to the older socialist tradition. It certainly led to many of the tactical mistakes made by both sides in the Grenada affair. Speaking in general terms, it is a process that leads to a sort of revolutionary romanticism, which tempts people to think in terms of the "revolutionary moment," of the quick overthrow of bourgeois governments, even of what one writer has called the concept of "holy violence" in the political thought of Frantz Fanon.[2] Such a process thinks in terms of sabotage, underground activities, and secret plotting and almost becomes a form of left-wing terrorism. One becomes enamored of schemes, plots, clandestine organizations; and even a Marxist as authentic as C.L.R. James has taken Walter Rodney to task for playing around irresponsibly with arms, which led to Rodney's planned death, in June 1980 at the hand, allegedly, of agents of the Burnham government. The emergence of Rodney as a revolutionary hero, it is worth adding, went back to the Jamaica government's withdrawal of his work permit at the local university, University of West Indies.

More and more reliance on the gun leads to the appearance of the revolutionary struggle of the military chieftain. The doctrines are used as slogans rather than as serious theories. It all usually ends up in a new form of military socialism. Such a process obviously took place in Grenada with the emergence of such military men as Austin, Liam James, Cornwall, and Layne, although we await further evidence before we can determine whether any one of them had been able to establish his supremacy over the others by the time the revolution ended. Nor can any Caribbean socialist who knows the history of the great modern revolutions plead ignorance on this matter. The famous passage of Burke, already noted, clearly warned how the internal power struggles lead, almost inexorably, to the appearance of the military adventurer ambitious and determined enough to take advantage of them. We neglect the lessons of history at our peril.

It follows from this that the Caribbean democratic left must be on the alert as to what friends they make in the revolutionary struggle. This is not just a matter of the army sergeant or major who dreams of being the Bonaparte of the revolution. There are others who jump on the revolutionary bandwagon, and anybody who visited St. George's during the revolution will have recognized them, for they all made the honorary pilgrimage, wined and dined by the revolutionary government: the hard-line Communists, the Marxist academics, as well as, plain and simply, the opportunists, the glib orators, the sloganeers. There were, of course, better friends of the revolution, in the best sense of that term: the journalist like Rickey Singh, the writer like Merle Hodge, the poet like Martin Carter, the novelist like George Lamming, all of whom supported and worked for the revolution with dedication, and not all of whom, by any means, hesitated to voice from time to time their misgivings about certain aspects of the revolution. The left movement must remember Cheddi Jagan's warning in his "critical support" speech in the Guyana of the 1970s: "not everyone who cries 'Comrade, Comrade' shall enter into the kingdom of Socialism."

But if the type of the opportunist and the self-serving adventurer had been the only type to emerge in the Grenada experience there would have been little problem. For all well-organized political parties and movements learn very soon how to deal with them. The matter is more serious because there also appears the much more complex type of the hard-line Marxist-Leninist, perhaps even Stalinist, who, by ability, talent, and command of the revolutionary literature, stake out for themselves, quite legitimately and indeed almost naturally, leadership roles in the revolutionary process. They are dedicated, earnest, hard-working, almost puritanical in their private lives, trained in the schools of both the Black Power Movement and the revolutionary Communist tradition. They are, beyond doubt, dedicated to a degree. But it is that very dedication that makes them also dangerous. For we are here in the presence of the professional revolutionists, so well

known in both the history of the old European left and the new Third
World left, who along with that dedication are also, too often, possessed of
a temper of moral unscrupulosity. They are prepared to accept any measures, even the most extreme, if they believe, as they often do with real
sincerity and conviction, that the measures are necessary for the preserva-
tion and furtherance of the cause. It is almost a religious type, which is why
the frequently used comparison with the leadership types of the old European wars of religion is apposite. They are incorruptible in private habits,
except that they are capable of being corrupted by power. The type was
well summed up by Lord Acton in his observation on the brilliant Jesuit
theologians of the seventeenth century who wrote in favor of the doctrine
of tyrannicide just as their modern counterparts are willing to use the
weapon of political assassination. "It is," wrote Acton, "this combination
of an eager sense of duty, zeal for sacrifice, and love of virtue, with the
deadly taint of a conscience perverted by authority, that makes them so
odious to touch and so curious to study."[3]

The favorite candidate of most observers of the Grenada struggle for
this habit of mind seems to be Bernard Coard. They are probably right. But
yet another lesson which the regional left ought to learn is to avoid the
temptation to make one particular person the arch-villain of the play, almost as if this were a Victorian melodrama. For the Central Committee
1983 minutes demonstrate that the habit of mind and ideology here discussed was widespread, touching almost certainly the majority of the committee. Because that is so, the left must not allow itself to become bogged
down in the sort of useless and nasty speculation that has characterized the
Caribbean rumor mill since October 1983: whether Bishop or Coard or
Coard's wife or General Austin, or somebody else, was the person who
started the rot. All this is fruitless and counterproductive guesswork unless
and until we have more detailed and reliable evidence than we now possess. It is not for the left to go down into that gutter.

Admitted that the role of personality is always important, it is the business of the serious analyst to seek to identify the more general institutional
and philosophical factors that entered into the total equation of events.
Otherwise, the left will commit the sort of mistake that Engels warned
against (with the approval of Marx) toward the end of his life:

> When you enquire into the cause of the counter-revolutionary suc-
> cesses, there you are met on every hand with the ready reply that it was
> Mr. This, or Citizen That, who "betrayed" the people. Which reply
> may be very true or not, according to circumstances; but under no cir-
> cumstances does it explain anything, or even show how it came to pass
> that the "people" allowed themselves thus to be betrayed. And what a
> poor chance a political party stands whose entire stock-in-trade consists

in the knowledge of the solitary fact that Citizen So-and-So is not to be trusted.[4]

The available evidence points to the fact that this temptation to blame individuals for general problems led to serious distortions in the Grenada revolution. The anti-Bishop forces succumbed to this temptation by casting Bishop in the role of the "one-man" leader; now, many are tempted, in equal fashion, to find another individual scapegoat. Yet the problem is much more complex. For in the passage just quoted, Engels did not mean to deny the importance of the factor of human individuality in the revolutionary process; a recognition of that factor has always been present in Marxist theory, as is evident enough in Georgi Plekhanov's brilliant 1886 essay "The Role of the Individual in History." What Engels was warning against was the temptation to place primary blame on individuals for failures rooted in more general causes. The personal and the general go together; they are not mutually exclusive. Everything we know about human nature in politics tells us that personal rivalries can be disguised as doctrinal differences and that, conversely, debates about such differences can be rooted in, and influenced by, the same rivalries.

Once this is understood, it becomes easier to understand the very special role that personality and the charisma of individual leaders play in Caribbean society and politics. These are not continental societies, nor is it a continental politics. This fact leads to two things: first, the political struggle becomes intensely personalized, resulting in an almost cannibalistic savagery of tone, as can be seen, to take one example only, in Da Breo's account of the power struggle in the St. Lucia Labour party over the last few years;[5] second, it leads to what Singham, in his study of pre-1979 Gairyite Grenada, called the "hero and the crowd" syndrome.[6] Hence the well-known brand of Caribbean messianic leadership: Butler and Williams in Trinidad, Bustamante and the two Manleys, father and son, in Jamaica, Mūnoz-Marin in Puerto Rico, and Castro in Cuba. All of them have possessed the magnetic force of character, which is something different from the glamorized personality of television politics. The general truth behind this tendency was summed up magisterially by Cardinal Newman, speaking generally of this type of leadership in human affairs, when he wrote that "the heart is commonly reached not through the reason, but through the imagination by means of direct impressions, by the testimony of facts and events, by history and by description. Persons influence us, voices melt us, looks subdue us, deeds inflame us. Many a man will live and die upon a dogma; no man will be a martyr for a conclusion."[7] The West Indian "man of words" is the regional expression of that truth.

There are two lessons in all of this for the regional progressive forces. The first is that charismatic leadership is a given variable, not likely soon to disappear, because it is rooted in the Caribbean civil culture and the Caribbean human psychology. It is proof of its resilience that the Grenada revolution, which conceived of itself as an objective historical process, could not escape its touch. The second lesson is that precisely because charisma is so omnipresent in the region and because, too, it is a heavy burden for any one person to carry—for it can lead to delusions of grandeur if the person does not have the inner reserves of moral strength to resist it—it is all the more imperative that the progressive movement, in its different parties and groups, construct institutional mechanisms to control and contain it. It is in that sense, of course (whatever might have been the motives behind it) that the Central Committee's proposal, in the Grenada discussions, of the joint leadership plan had a point: in pushing for collective leadership and collective responsibility they were making a stand against the habit of "one-Manism" which has been the bane of Caribbean politics. As Cudjoe succinctly puts it, "one-Manism" on the right cannot be replaced by "one-Manism" on the left.[8] The difficulty was, of course, that such a genuine system of collective decision making ran counter to the exigencies of Leninist party organization. Yet, despite that, the regional progressive movements must find some appropriate institutional forms which will at least in some way curb the trend to individualism and hero worship.

Once the role of the individual is thus placed in its proper perspective, the ground is cleared for some critical discussion of the role of theory in the Grenada experience. It has already been shown how, certainly by 1982, the PRG had fully adopted the Marxist-Leninist doctrines of revolutionary process and party organization, with the party structure, indeed, including categories of membership, being modeled slavishly on the pattern of the Russian Communist party rather than on that of the Cuban Communist party. It thus becomes appropriate to ask whether the Leninist body of thought and analysis was the proper one for the Grenada ideologues to embrace and relevant to the special problems that they confronted.

That discussion must surely begin by questioning the assumption—implicit in the widely used term "Marxism-Leninism"—that Lenin's political thought is an integral part of Marxism and indeed can be claimed as its doctrinal successor. It is true, of course, that there is much to support the claim, for Lenin absorbs all of the cardinal Marxist themes—the economic determinism, the class struggle, the nature of capitalism, the dialectic of thought and action, the predestined role of the proletariat as the agent of the passage to the communist society. But as in all doctrinal systems, master and disciple are never quite the same; glosses are added as the literature grows. Different sociohistorical differences also lead to new and different theses.

Lenin's version of classic Marxism arose out of conditions in a Czarist Russia which were different from the conditions of Western Europe out of which Marx and Engels shaped their doctrines. The former was an autocratic society which had experienced neither the Renaissance nor the Reformation, the latter a basically bourgeois liberal society shaped by the European liberal tradition. Oppression and injustice were endemic in Russia right up to 1917. That forced all opposition into a conspiratorial mold, so that the conspiratorial atmosphere was already prepared for the Bolsheviks long before the famous split with the Mensheviks in 1903. Marx and Engels lived and worked in the open society of mid-Victorian England, while Lenin and others lived and worked in the closed Byzantine society of the Czars. In the Russan situation, then, the revolutionary struggle perforce had to become one of underground activity, intrigue, schemes, plots, all conducted in the dark, pessimistic worlds described in the novels of Gogol and Dostoevsky. Lenin's response to these conditions was to formulate his idea of the Communist party as an elite vanguard party, so that the dictatorship of the proletariat became transformed into something more akin to the Jacobin idea of a Committee of Public Safety, than to any content that Marx and Engels had given to the term. For there is hardly anything in the work of Marx and Engels which suggests that the Communist parties they had in mind should become tightly knit, iron-disciplined advance troops, imposing their ideas upon the general working-class movement, so that, in the Russian case, as Alexander Herzen put it, Communism became "Tsarism turned upside down." The Leninist position argued, rather, that the revolution must be placed into the guiding hands of an experienced party elite which, because its members possessed the theoretical understanding denied to others, would then be able to guide the masses in the struggle.

This view became, as is well known, the major bone of contention in the debate between Lenin and Rosa Luxemburg, who espoused the different theory of revolutionary "spontaneity." In Luxemburg's view, organization, enlightenment, and struggle could not be separated from each other. From the dialectical point of view they are all necessary ingredients of a total process whereby the working class learns, by trial and error, to become the agent of fundamental social transformation. In 1904 she wrote:

On the one hand, apart from the general principle of the struggle, there is no ready-made, pre-established, detailed set of tactics which a central committee can teach its Social Democratic membership as if they were army recruits. On the other hand, the process of the struggle, which creates the organisation, leads to a continual fluctuation of the sphere of influence of Social Democracy. It follows that the Social Democratic centralisation cannot be based on blind obedience, nor on the mechanical subordination of the party militants to a central power. Yet again on the other hand, it follows that an absolute dividing wall cannot be erected between the class-conscious kernel of the proletariat, already organised as party cadre, and the immediate popular environment which is gripped by the class struggle and finds itself in the process of class enlightenment. For this reason, the construction of centralism in Social Democracy, as Lenin desires, on the basis of these two principles: (1) On the blind subordination of all party organisations in the smallest detail of their activity to a central power which alone thinks, plans, and decides for all, and (2) The sharp separation of the organisation kernel of the party from the surrounding revolutionary milieu, seems to us to be a mechanistic transfer of the organisational principles of the Blanquistic movement of conspiratorial groups to the Social Democratic movement of the working masses.[9]

But there was even more to it than this for Rosa Luxemburg, "Without general elections," she wrote later in 1918, "without freedom of the press, freedom of assembly, and freedom of speech, life in every public institution slows down, and becomes a caricature of itself, and bureaucracy emerges as the one deciding factor." Then, "Public life gradually dies, and a few score party leaders, with inexhaustible energy and limitless idealism, direct and rule. Amongst them the leadership is, in reality, in the hands of a dozen men of first-class brains, even though, from time to time, an elite of the working class is called together in Congress to applaud the speeches of their leaders, and to vote unanimously for the resolutions they put forward."[10]

Luxemburg's critique helps to explain the general trajectory of the world Communist movement after 1917. Because Lenin was the brilliant architect of a successful revolution and Rosa Luxemburg the architect, and indeed victim, of an unsuccessful revolution, it was Lenin's theory of party that dominated the movement until at least the period of World War II. A Muscovite orthodoxy grew up in which all other national Communist parties were obliged to accept the party line established by the Comintern, or be denounced as traitors to the cause. Their ethical behavior echoed that of Moscow: the passion for conspiracy, the need for deception, the centralized and autocratic dictates, the contempt for fair play, the ruthless discrediting of all other socialist groups and persons, the ready identification of intellectual dissent with moral criminality, and the rest. The road to Moscow, like the road to Rome for the loyal Catholic, became the only permissible route; everything else was "social fascism" or "right-wing deviationism" or "petit-bourgeois opportunism." It is true that not all of this can be laid at the door of Lenin himself, for all the evidence about him shows that he was wholly selfless, devoid of any trace of personal ambition, full of personal kindness, a sense of humor, and an essentially humble nature. We also know, from his famous piece on the dangers of "left-wing infantilism," that he was fully aware of the dangers involved when Communist parties isolated themselves from the main struggle by adopting a purblind attitude of doctrinal purity and refusing to participate in trade unions, cooperatives, and parliaments. It is in this sense that the worst excesses of the new Russian system were committed in the Stalinist period. It is nonetheless true that it was the very centralized party structure created by Lenin himself that made Stalin's rise to power so easy and rapid. After the expulsion of Trotsky, the system became a combinaton of the Leninist structure and the Stalinist spirit.

It has been necessary to look briefly at this historical background because it explains so much about the Grenada Revolution and its demise. It is obvious enough that the PRG bodies, for example the Political Bureau and the Central Committee, as well as Coard's OEAR group, became themselves expressions of that same combination of Leninist structure and Stalinist spirit. This is all the more surprising, even astonishing, when it is remembered that after 1945 the combinaton was challenged by the rise, first in Tito's Yugoslavia and then in France and Italy, of Euro-Communism, with the refusal of the national Communist parties to accept any longer uncritically orders from Moscow. Oddly enough, however, as Soviet influence thus waned in Europe it received new life in many of the new Third World countries. A number of factors facilitated that resurgence: the emergence of a revivified U.S. imperialism, the willingness of Moscow to give aid to the new national liberation struggles, and, not least of all, the fact that many of the popular mass movements in Asia and Africa had had no direct experience of how Communist parties worked. In the particular case of the Caribbean, it is worth adding that the latter point was especially important since, with the exception of pre-Castro Cuba, Communist parties, if they existed at all, were weak and ineffective, and generally regarded as unimportant. All of this, in turn, was immeasurably aided by the Cuban Revolution after 1959; Havana, like Moscow, became the source of new revolutionary enthusiam.

The stage was thus set for the Stalinization of the Grenada Revolution. No one can read Rosa Luxemburg's words of 1918 without seeing how they came true in St. George's after 1979, with a small group of able and dedicated men establishing and maintaining power by means of a new party-state apparatus. There was the same denial of civil liberties, conveniently dismissed as 'bourgeois' and thereby becoming dispensable. There was the same transformation of the doctrine of "collective leadership," mentioned as early as the 1973 NJM manifesto, into a secret inner group accountable to no body of public opinion. There was the same insistence, made by Lenin and reiterated by Stalin, that the party is the weapon of the dictatorship of the proletariat.

The Grenada party, indeed, was selective to a degree: at the very end it was composed of only 94 full members, 51 candidates, and some 150 associates.[11] The system of popular democracy, in the form of the parish zonal councils, village coordinating bureaus, and mass organizations, was certainly innovative and a step in the right direction. But real policy was made from the top and then transmitted to the bottom, with those popular bodies playing a merely approbatory role. Many of their meetings, as well as the study groups, became instruments of ideological indoctrination; one observer has remembered being present at a class where the organizer did little more than read five and a half pages of Stalin's turgid prose.[12] The sole real link, indeed, between the party and the general public was the figure of Prime Minister Bishop, a link thus dependent upon the hazardous mechanism of a single individual. There was no other mechanism whereby public criticism could be brought to bear upon the leadership, for it alone determined the lengths to which criticism would be allowed to go. The result, in the end, was that in the final critical period, the Grenadian people had no institutions of any kind through which they could have expressed their feelings. As Thorndike puts it, summing it all up, the Grenada revolutionaries, by taking over the Russian party model as their own, fell into the precise trap that they had been so anxious to avoid—that of a psychological dependence upon external modes of government and assumptions developed for quite different societies and problems.[13] If the test of any politico-constitutional model is how well it works out in practice, then the Moscow model turned out to be no more appropriate to the local needs than the Westminster model.

All this, of course, was the question of structure. But there was also the question of spirit. Here it is important to note that there existed in the Grenada Revolution, in reality, two spirits. On the one hand, there was the popular spirit of the people as a whole. That the revolution was a popular revolution there can be little doubt. Grenadians, men, women, and young people, responded with enthusiasm to a government, and especially Bishop and other ministers, which tried to explain to them what they were doing, and why they were doing it. They instinctively realized that "popular democracy" meant something more than casting a vote every few years; and whether it was repairing a village road or building a school or helping an elderly citizen to read or discussing the details of the national budget, they responded with real enthusiasm. They went through a new political education which, for all its doctrinaire character, made them think about concepts such as socialism, nationalism, and imperialism. It was not until the last year of the revolution that this spirit began to sag.

On the other hand, there was the spirit of the official party-state leadership which, over the ten years between 1973 and 1983, moved from democratic reformism to national-liberationist anti-imperialism to Marxism-Leninism, and ending with the Stalinist purge of October. During that period, it is now clear, the regime became one of government by secret committee, isolating itself more and more from the popular base. That was clearly perceived by Richard Hart, the former PRG attorney-general, in his own contribution to the post-mortem. Hart avoids taking sides on the Bishop-Coard matter—for he blames both of them equally, Coard for his secret resignation from the Central Committee in 1982 and Bishop for reneging on his acceptance of the joint-leadership agreement—but Hart concludes that the Central Committee membership as a whole was the real offender. In Hart's words, they decided to deceive everybody, including fraternal parties outside, as to what was going on; they took the simplistic approach of assuming that "all you had to do to solve the problem was to bring the most efficient man in the party (Coard) back into joint leadership and then the Central Committee would be solving all its problems." As a result, state functions went on but the internal party situation was hidden.[14] In this way—although Hart himself does not draw that conclusion—the leadership forgot the lesson, which Lenin ceaselessly preached, that the revolution must always be where the masses are, and separates itself from the masses at the risk of degenerating into bourgeois democracy.

The dominant spirit thus became one of apocalyptic dogmatism, of what the Webbs, in their book of 1935 on Soviet Russia, called the "disease of orthodoxy." Once again, the lengthy and turbulent minutes of the Central Committee and party plenary meetings of July–October bear testimony to that truth. The "science" becomes the only truth. It must be followed slavishly. Those who resist it are yielding to their "petit-bourgeois" weaknesses. How absurd that charge was is apparent when we remember, as Don Rojas has said, that all of the leadership, the Coards as much as the Bishops, were themselves, sociologically speaking, petit-bourgeois: "Even the class composition of the party itself was petit-bourgeois basically—radical petty bourgeois people who had evolved beyond their own class and become proletarianised."[15] The French Antillean socialist Jean Girard has commented sadly on the doctrinaire temper. "I find," he writes, speaking of his reading of the documents, "the blindness of dogmatism which transforms reality in the name of the 'scientific approach.' I find the intolerance which eliminates commonsense in the name of so-called 'ideological level.' I find, under a new disguise, the same old contempt of the people, their knowledge and emotions, their talents and their profound aspirations."[16] It is not too much to say that a sort of schizophrenic malady led, finally, to a terminal condition in which the party spirit killed the popular spirit.

There is one last illustration of that schizophrenic character of the revolution that merits attention. It concerns the revolution's foreign policy. That its policy was in many ways remarkably successful has already been noted. As Gill has shown, Gairy's uninspired foreign policy was replaced after 1979 with a spirited and activist policy characterized by forceful position statements on a broad range of regional and international issues, giving the new Grenada a positive international image in the general struggle against colonialism, imperialism, and racism. Multilateralism was served by a strong diplomatic policy which gave Grenada friends and allies from all over—the Caribbean countries themselves, the Latin American countries, the Commonwealth, the Arab and African worlds, and the European countries, both capitalist and communist, all of them exemplifying a total range of ideological positions. The measure of at once international political recognition and international economic aid that the new government was able to muster was indeed spectacular.[17]

Yet, at the same time, much of that achievement was tarnished by the fact that at some point the Grenada Revolution decided to throw in its lot with the Soviet camp, as early, perhaps, as the 1980 Afghanistan vote, which some Grenada officials later conceded to have been a tactical error. The anti-British vote on the Falklands-Malvinas issue was more correct, for it gained Latin American friends who were near neighbors, whereas, by contrast, trying to buy goodwill from a Soviet Union that was located on the other side of the world was far more problematic. There is some reason to believe that Bishop chose the Afghanistan vote in order to placate his more ultraleft faction.[18] If that is so, it shows how the Stalinist temper began to influence foreign policy. It is at least certain that the growing hostility of the United States fed that temper. The result was a foreign policy which sounded less and less genuinely nonaligned as it criticized South Africa for holding political prisoners and remained silent about political prisoners in Cuba, or attacked Israel for Zionist imperialism and said nothing about Russian imperialism in Poland.

It is at this point that the schizophrenic condition reasserted itself. At home, the revolution was essentially reformist. Abroad, it adopted a foreign policy of a spirited anti-imperialism and world revolution, which by necessity became a vigorous criticism of the United States. It thus entered into the difficulties engendered by such a contradiction, which a little earlier had engulfed the Manley regime in Jamaica. Indeed, the Jamaican comparison is instructive. As Paul Ashley describes it, Manley's socialist experiment in Jamaica involved itself in a "yawning disjuncture" between its domestic and foreign policies. As local domestic problems became intractable, the Manely government sought compensation by adopting a militant posture on the international revolutionary stage, without considering whether a small underdeveloped state could really afford such a posture. Ashley summarizes:

The Manley regime became a victim of its own verbal excesses—policies being announced, schemes being conceptualized, ideas and hunches being publicly aired—with little or no appreciation of public sensitivity, the inadequacy of the bureaucratic mechanisms involved, the interaction between various policy alternatives, and the intricacies and ramifications of any attempt to confront the traditional order. With the emphasis being on the feats, and neglect of the failures, the regime eventually succumbed largely because of the disenchantment of the intended beneficiaries. In sum, the foreign initiatives undertaken by the Manley regime failed to deliver the material betterment that was promised.[19]

To be a failure on the domestic front and a glamorous hero on the international front invites disaster, for at some point reality overtakes rhetoric.

It is clear that Bishop repeated Manley's mistakes. As the revolutionary momentum sagged at home, compensation was sought by brave, defiant speeches on the international revolutionary circuit. The orator in Bishop, just as in Manley before him, succumbed to that easy temptation. It is one matter to deliver a magnificent, denunciatory oration in Budapest or Managua or even Toronto or New York, quite another to persuade the electorate back home that the oratory does anything to help them in their daily problems of poverty and unemployment. In one way, it is just another expression of the personality cult. In another way, it is an expression of what a friendly observer has called the David-Goliath syndrome, which may be psychologically satisfying to the leadership of the small country but does not necessarily redound to its advantage.[20] And, in yet another way, it places too much sentimental trust in the spirit of international revolutionary solidarity. For the final irony is that, in the Grenadian case, the pro-Cuban-Soviet foreign policy did not yield the dividends expected of it. That is painfully clear from the reports that Ambassador Richard Jacobs made from Moscow to his Grenadian superiors, full of complaints about his Soviet hosts. He was only permitted access to low-level Soviet party officials; Grenada was regarded as a small, distant county in a low-priority area; and Grenada was assigned, as an English-speaking country, to the United States and Canada Department; to all of which may be added the fact that Bishop was refused an audience with President Yuri Andropov during his last visit to Moscow in April 1983.[21] And, of course, at the very end, neither Havana or Moscow were prepared, for prudent reasons, to send armed help to Grenada as the Americans prepared to invade. To argue, as Trevor Munroe has, that the Cubans were remiss not to send such aid is to indulge in quixotic revolutionary sentimentality, for so to argue is asking a living revolution to sacrifice itself on the altar of a dead one; not to mention that the argument assumes, contrary to all known fact, that the Grenadian people as a whole were prepared to undertake armed resistance.[22]

What this all means was summed up by Perry Mars, writing from Guyana before October 1983.

> In terms of foreign policy orientation it is necessary, firstly, to start from the concrete reality of the situation rather than from premises or principles called from the air, so to speak. The immediate environment within which Caribbean states oriented toward socialist development operate is defined by a predominance of hostility or potential hostility with a capacity to actually nullify or negate particular instances of progressive developments in the region. Given this unfavourable predominating influence, perhaps the best foreign policy approach is to assume in a figurative sense the tactic of the guerilla and capitalise on the weakness while avoiding the strength of the powerful enemy which in this case are the forces of imperialism . . . in the sense of capitalising on the weakness while skilfully avoiding the destructive wrath of imperialist intervention.[23]

It is obvious that the foreign policies adopted by both the Manley and Bishop regimes failed to learn that prudent lesson. They elected to adopt a foreign policy of open defiance against the United States while failing to realize that in the game of global *realpolitik* they could not necessarily rely upon the traditional spirit of international socialist solidarity for support, not to speak of the support of the Soviet Union. As much in the international socialist camp as in the international capitalist camp, the nationalist urge to protect "national interests" is more powerful than the spirit of international fraternity. Both Manley and Bishop thus failed to understand that in the history of international socialism over the last one hundred years or so, most national socialist movements, including that of the Soviet Union, have given priority to their own national interests rather than to the interest of a great global socialist cause. That is why in 1914, all of the European socialist parties supported their respective national governments in the war; why in 1939 Stalin signed the Nazi-Soviet pact; why, earlier on, Rosa Luxemburg herself lost to Jozef Pilsudski when she argued for socialist internationalism against Polish nationalism; and why, in our own day, no socialist internationalist movement came to the rescue of Grenada in October 1983. In summary, both Manley and Bishop neglected the lesson that revolution, like charity, begins at home.

====

The Caribbean left must learn from all of this. It must decline to accept the Leninist concept of party structure, which in its ultracentralism neglects the problem of accountability to the larger working-class movement, for in that structure the party becomes a law unto itself. It must certainly have nothing to do with the Stalinist corruption of Leninism, for although Lenin himself never behaved as a dictator, Stalin certainly did. It must be always suspicious of extraregional friends, however much those friends may speak the appropriate revolutionary language. The guide to follow there is Aimé Césaire's fine *Lettre à Maurice Thorez* of 1956 in which the Antillean poet-leader announced his resignation from the French Communist party on the ground that, as he put it, the anticolonialism of the Parisian commissars carries within itself the stigmata of the very colonialism against which it fights. It bears the same assimilationist bias, the same unconscious chauvinism, the same conviction of Western superiority, the same assumption, which runs from the European right to the European left, that Europe must do the thinking and the acting for the colonials, which thus robs the colonials of that right of initiative which is the ultimate right of personality.[24]

Most urgent of all, perhaps, the left must hold firmly, in the future, to the principle—which should never even be debatable—that socialism must go hand in hand with democracy. The ongoing debate within the Caribbean intelligentsia, it is true, demonstrates that it is no easy matter to establish satisfactory criteria for what constitutes "democracy," and not the least contribution of Grenada was that it sharpened that debate. It made people throughout the region reexamine assumptions that they had taken for granted. Yet at the same time Grenada has shown us that there are certain principles involving "democracy" that are, as it were, immutable. There is the principle that in a democracy worthy of the name, decisions are arrived at by the process of discussion, and not by the method of coercion. There is the principle that the rulers are ultimately dependent upon the free choice of the citizen-body, and that this body can, at reasonably frequent intervals, change their government peaceably, if they are so minded. From this follows the principle that in the making of that choice the electorate has full and free access to all of the information and all of the differing viewpoints which allow an informed choice. The secret ballot, of course, is indispensable. But secrecy should not be carried so far that public policy decisions are made by secret bodies which are not in some way accountable to public opinion.

These principles apply as much to nongovernmental bodies as they do to governmental institutions. No progressive political party, in particular, should follow the road of the New Jewel Movement which ultimately led to secrecy, intrigue, and murder. The point was underscored by the statement of the Guyana Working People's Alliance that "the tragic events of October 19 in Grenada raise a question that all serious parties will have to face: whether or not differences which develop inside the party should be put for public discussion before they get out of hand."[25] The statement was accompanied by the report of Working People's Alliance member Rupert Roopnarine, who had also visited Grenada during the crisis. The "compartmentalization of knowledge" within the PRG Central Committee, he noted, was a fundamental error which extended to keeping regional fraternal parties in the dark about the internal struggles until it was too late.[26]

Roopnarine added to this observation a warning about sectarianism. "We must conduct our differences," he observed, "with maximum generosity." It is a needed warning. Left-wing factionalism can only lead to weakness. That is why Lenin himself, at the end of World War I, urged all of the small warring groups in Britain to forget their differences and organize a single Communist party, and, after that, to seek to participate in the activities of the Labour party, however bourgeois that party might be. Otherwise, they would remain isolated doctrinal groups, just talking to themselves. That lesson still holds in the Caribbean, even more so after Grenada. Sectarianism, as Roopnarine saw, must give way to a united front based on tolerance, not on ideological purity. If a West Indian comparison is needed, that can be seen in the case of Trinidad, the West Indian society nearest in spirit to Grenada. All of the four leading opposition groups—the Tapia Movement, the Democratic Action Congress, the Organisation for National Reconstruction, and the United Labour Front—have merged into an Alliance in preparation for elections against the People's National Movement government led by Prime Minister George Chambers. Yet, notwithstanding the general carnival character of Trinidad politics, Trinidadians would think that Chambers had gone mad if he suddenly told a poet like Derek Walcott or a novelist like Earl Lovelace that they must alter their literary ways, or instructed a newspaper editor like Ken Gordon that he could only publish news favorable to the government. Likewise, they would begin to doubt their own sanity if, in the leadership ranks of the Alliance, Basdeo Panday of the Oil Workers Trade Union were to publicly lecture A.N.R. Robinson of the Democratic Action Congress or Karl Hudson-Phillips of the Organisation for National Reconstruction about their evil petit-bourgeois habits and ask that they recant. They would be even more amazed if, the Alliance coming into power, the new government would indicate to the leading calypsonian, the Mighty Sparrow, that he should only compose calypsos in praise of the new regime. Yet all of this, in one way or another, happened in revolutionary Grenada. Even when the high and benevolent intentions of the PRG leadership are accepted, no socialist in his or her right mind would call any of this democracy, at least in the sense that democracy has evolved, historically, since its beginnings in the Greek city-state.

If, then, Grenada teaches the Caribbean left anything at all, it is that Caribbean socialism must go back to the more humane tradition of Marx and Engels as they laid the foundations of the modern revolutionary philosophy. Both Marx and Engels saw the emptiness of the bourgeois democracy of their time, but they did not reject it out of hand, seeing that under certain circumstances, for example those of liberal Victorian England, it could become an aid and proper channel for the advance of the working-class struggle. As Marx's correspondence in particular shows, they had their own share of the habit of fierce controversialism. But they never pretended that they were entitled to some sort of infallibility so absolute that it would tempt them to establish what is virtually an inquisition to enforce their dogmas. They believed that the revolution they worked for must become a universal, world revolution. They could not have ever condoned the later Russian historiography, much of it possibly written by Stalin himself, which in our own day has replaced the idea of the solidarity of the international proletariat with a new, narrow and xenophobic Russian nationalism; as Klaus Mehnert puts it in his brilliant essay on the subject, the all-encompassing humanism of Marx has given way to a messianic doctrine of Russian salvation, calling for the conversion of the whole world to its demands, and which inevitably leads to isolation, intolerance, and loneliness.[27]

It is to the credit of both the Cuban and Grenadian revolutions that they did not readily follow that new line, for their foreign policies adhered more faithfully to the original Marxist idealism about international fraternity. Only one caveat, however, must be entered: both revolutions attempted something of their own in rewriting their national histories, invoking, for example, José Marti and T. A. Marryshow as honorary heroes, respectively, of their revolutions, thus running counter to the fact that it is highly unlikely, to say the least, that either of them would have approved of the growth of a new centralized state power in the lands of their birth. It might also be added that the temptation of certain West Indian writers to speak, in quasi-psychological terms, of a "new Caribbean man" has a faint echo in it of the revisionist dogma of the "new Soviet man."

All in all, the supreme lesson of the Grenada Revolution, when all its achievements and faults are put together, is that the Caribbean progressive movements must hold fast, more than ever, to the three vital conceptions of liberty, equality, and rationalism which have marked those movements in their historical development, starting with the pre-Marxist groups of the early English and French socialists. Liberty means that citizens must be able to live and move freely without unnecessary constraint on the part of the state. This principle was certainly compromised in Grenada as the government began to copy the Cuban method of local committees for the defense of the revolution, placing citizens under constant surveillance, which in any society must lead sooner or later to a police state. Equality means that no person or group is entitled to special privilege on the basis of wealth or education or social position, since that leads to the acquisitive society. Not the least achievement of Grenada was to vigorously insist, both in word and in deed, upon that principle, not least of all in a new public language in which everybody was "comrade," just as in Cuba everybody is *compañero*. Rationalism, finally, means two things. It means, first, that all problems in life are susceptible to rational explanation and not to some obscurantist concept, for example, the will of God. Undoubtedly, one of the most intractable problems for the Grenada leadership was the religious obscurantism of the popular, pentecostal churches which, by that very reason, constituted one of the enemies of the revolution. Rationalism means, second, that all differences, in society, government, and politics, must be resolved by persuasion and not by force. It is in that area, of course, that the revolution committed its gravest mistake.

≣

There is one final point, not very optimistic. True believers, whether in religion or politics, rarely manage to escape their dogmatism. So it can hardly be expected that the hard-line factions in the Caribbean left will learn these lessons. That is painfully evident from a reading of the document written by Leon Cornwall, presumably in 1985, and smuggled out of the St. George's prison. It is an unrelenting apology for the Coard faction, to which Cornwall belonged. He interprets the results of the election of December 1984 as a rejection of the Grenada people of Gairy, and not as a mandate for the newly emerged parties. He chastizes the Maurice Bishop Patriotic Movement, which emerged as one of the many parties seeking electoral support during 1984, as "a party of opportunist breakaway elements from the New Jewel Movement." Contrary to all known facts, Cornwall asserts that "large sections of the masses, but particularly the workers and youth, talk among themselves about 'when the next revolution comes.' " He claims Bishop was "a genuine revolutionary democrat and anti-imperialist fighter," almost as if his murder had never occurred. What is now needed, he concludes, is a new anti-imperialist front "applying Leninist principles and standards." The final irony is that Cornwall claims that the Coard faction now favors elections, overlooking the fact that while in power the PRG had throughout dismissed elections as bourgeois trickery. It is rumored that Coard himself is preparing his own account of the story. It will be interesting to see if his version differs in any way from the Cornwall piece.[28]

17

1984: The Orwellian Aftermath

The immediate consequence of the U.S.-led invasion, of course, was the establishment of an indefinite American occupation of the island. Again, of course, it was an occupation welcomed enthusiastically by the Grenadians, for after the trauma they had gone through they might even have welcomed the Nazi panzer divisions as savior. The public opinion surveys made by the University of the West Indies following the invasion testify to that enthusiastic welcome.[1] The establishment of an Interim Governing Council (the Advisory Council), appointed by Governor-General Scoon, set up a semblance of legitimacy for the restoration of "law and order." Most of its members, with the exception of the university lecturer Patrick Emmanuel, were nondescript bureaucrats whose only legitimacy, in truth, rested on the American military presence, making them, as it were, a sort of West Indian Vichy regime. As the Bahamas foreign minister told the General Assembly of the Organization of American States: "the occupying forces in Grenada have made possible and are presently enforcing, by the authority of their arms, a one-man proxy executive authority, based on unprecedented constitutional convolutions."[2] The former PRG Attorney-General Lloyd Noel has pointed out that the governor-general, in various proclamations, has brought back into force of law only those parts of the prerevolutionary Constitution of 1973 which he sees fit, while arbitrarily revoking certain elements of the PRG public legislation and retaining others. The only proper constitutional course, Noel argues, should have been the reenactment, in its entirety, of the 1973 Constitution.[3]

What has actually happened, speaking of the constitutional situation, is that the governor-general and the Advisory Council—until the latter was replaced by the elected government and legislature after the 1984 election—became the "mimic men" of the U.S. occupying force. But at the same time they pretended in typically West Indian mimic form, that they were their own masters. Governor-General Scoon insisted that he took no orders from the newly appointed U.S. embassy; the chairman of the Advisory Council insisted that he took no orders from the governor-general; both of them were playing out a comic charade almost as if they were governor-general and prime minister in Jamaica or Trinidad. They thus perpetuated, perhaps to feed their sense of importance, what Bentham would have termed constitutional "fictions." They issued proclamations, orders-in-council, and statutory decrees, with all of the appropriate protocol, as if they were in charge of a sovereign nation state, whereas, in grim fact, they were a new U.S. neocolonial dependency.

For no empire in history conquers a new territory and then evacuates. It sets up a machinery of governance to guarantee its continuing control of the newly conquered province. So, in Grenada, Americans moved in with typical American efficiency to ensure the dividends of their new conquest-investment. The military invasion was followed by a second invasion of diplomats, economic advisers, disaster-relief experts, journalists, U.S. Agency for International Development (USAID) officials, police training specialists, and perhaps most ominous of all, an Army Psychological Operations team whose function, as everywhere, is openly propagandist. Throughout 1984 all of these forces undertook the consolidation, political, economic, and psychological, of the counterrevolution.[4]

How, in detail, the Americans did that in 1984 would constitute a truly Orwellian story. George Orwell himself, who was more of a traditional Edwardian individualistic liberal than any kind of socialist, would have appreciated its piquant irony: an American state-power behaving in authoritarian style under the guise of proclaimed democracy. Former PRG members, such as Kendrick Radix, were held by the U.S. security forces in small wooden packing crates, Vietnam-style, before interrogation by political officers. Radio Free Grenada was taken over by media experts to broadcast pro-American and anti-Cuban propaganda, so that it became, in the words of one reporter, the only show in town.[5] Coard and Austin were exhibited to the press, as blindfolded and half-naked prisoners, again in Vietnam style. Security forces swept throughout the island, arresting without benefit of warrant suspected PRG sympathizers and PRA members. At road blocks everywhere soldiers searched and seized innocent passengers. Pope Paul's Ecumenical Center at Gouyave was raided and closed down as a suspected center for Communist propaganda, when the U.S. squad simply found a map of Puerto Rico, books on Honduras and El Salvador, and some Cuban literature. Hundreds of foreigners who had worked for the PRG were expelled or "invited" to leave as "potential security risks" on the basis of a list prepared by Governor-General Scoon's office. Some U.S.

journalists were expelled, including Donald Foster, whose earlier radio documentary on Grenada was felt by Scoon to have "defamed" the country.[6] All in all, the U.S. presence evolved from conquering army to a regime of thought police.

Not the least disturbing aspect of all this was the treatment meted out to the captured PRG prisoners, including Austin and the Coards, both husband and wife, originally some forty-eight in number and coming down to nineteen at the time of their scheduled trial in the fall of 1984. The accuracy of the information contained in smuggled letters from jail by some of the prisoners, including a long letter by Coard, could perhaps be questioned. But since the allegations were repeated by the defense counsel, the account of their imprisonment may almost certainly be accepted as substantially true. They relay a sad litany of prisoners held in solitary confinement twenty-three hours a day, denied adequate writing materials to communicate with relatives and friends, denied medical attention except for the more urgent cases, permitted only brief periods to receive visits from relatives and to consult with defense attorneys—both Coard and Selwyn Strachan report that they had been permitted to see their lawyers for less than forty minutes over a six-month period. Even worse, prisoners were subjected to continuous harassment by guards, including sustained torture periods by police, resulting in forced signatures to confessions. There were also widespread threats of detention made by U.S. personnel against individuals likely to be witnesses for the defense, along with promises of visas to the United States to other possible witnesses so that they would be absent from proceedings. The defense lawyers Ramsey Clark and Jacqueline Samuels-Brown corroborated much of this, which constituted, in their view, denial of rights to counsel, denial of prompt arraignment and habeas corpus, unlawful investigation and interrogation, jeopardizing the possibility of a fair trial. Finally, there was the fact that the physical maltreatment had been undertaken by Barbadian police personnel, brought in by the Americans two days after the invasion, and the further fact that the prisoners were throughout treated as prisoners of war and not citizens charged with probable cause of criminal offenses.[7]

These events were only the short-term aftermath. The long-term aftermath, it is already becoming evident, will be more serious, perhaps even more sinister. It goes without saying that the naïve expectation of some Grenadians, in the immediate postinvasion euphoria, that the Americans would take them in as the fifty-first state of the Union will not be so; if Puerto Ricans have been fruitlessly begging the U.S. Congress for that favor for some eighty years it is hardly likely that Grenada would gain it overnight. What is much more likely to happen is that Grenada will be treated like the Dominican Republic after the U.S. invasion of 1965. Military occupation will end, to be followed by a combination of secretive political interference and massive economic aid to ensure long-term continuing imperialist control of the country. The modern imperialist uses such indirect measures to safeguard his rule. He knows that the older measures of political incorporation and permanent military occupation can only produce for him the colonial headache of a Northern Ireland situation. So, in the case of the Dominican Republic after 1965, the Washington politico-military planners masterminded two main strategies, the one political, the other economic. The political strategy included "free" elections marked by fraud, coercion of police terror, CIA machinations, opposition party members shipped off to the United States by the thousands, presidential candidates handpicked by Americans, all the way from Antonio Imbert and Reid Cabral to Hector Garcia-Godoy and Joaquín Balaguer, with the end result that although Trujillo was dead, as the consequence of a CIA-engineered assassination plot, *trujillismo* reemerged in the form of *balaguerismo*. The CIA with its various "fronts," was in the vanguard of this scenario of plot, counterplot, and intrigue, its agents including the sinister figure of Sacha Volman who for years had been able to penetrate Latin American progressive movements under the guise of a "labor expert," supported by the AFL-CIO and U.S. Socialist party leader Norman Thomas.[8]

The U.S. economic strategy reinforced this political manipulation with injections of massive financial aid to the Dominican Republic. That included a total of some $500–600 million from the USAID between 1962 and 1967; funds to build a renovated infrastructure—roads, lights, water—needed by foreign investors; new public legislation to encourage U.S. capital investment, including incentives such as low wages, generous tax holidays, easy repatriation of corporate profits, and acquisition of lands. The best-known recipient of all this was the U.S. agribusiness conglomerate Gulf and Western, set up in 1967 as a direct beneficiary of the 1965 invasion, and which since then, has become, with its luxurious Central Romana headquarters, the dominant economic force and a potent political influence in the republic, including a cultural role as seen in the Hollywood-style concerts occasionally given by Frank Sinatra and his Mafia-style entourage in the Romana Las Vegas-style hotel, stridently pushing the American image.[9] Another beneficiary has been the other multinational corporation Club Mediterranéen, which specializes—as in its Punta Cana operation on the east coast of the republic—in expensive, highly segregated tourist enclaves featuring private airstrips, lavish food and liquor services, water sports, and a general atmosphere of vulgar hedonism including public nudity (the last insult to a deeply Catholic society).[10] Not the least dangerous aspect of this new mode of exploitative transnational capitalism is that, by paying higher wages than the local national level, and also by providing generous welfare and housing services for its local employees, it weakens and bypasses the local trade union movement, replacing it with compliant company unions. That insidious goal has been pursued by Gulf and Western in the Dominican Republic and by the reshaped United Fruit Company in Honduras.

The postinvasion period in Grenada closely followed the Dominican Republic pattern. Financial support earlier denied to the PRG regime now poured in, with an initial U.S. grant of $15 million to repair and rehabilitate roads, utilities, and communications, followed by additional funds to complete the international airport, denounced as overambitious during the revolution and now accepted as essential to an expanded tourist trade (which in the long run can only lead to the ecological damage and cultural pollution already evident in Barbados). Two factors were noticeable about that policy. First, its major architects were the Americans. The American Friends Service Committee which visited in December 1983—January 1984 reported that the local interim government had no coherent, overall approach to the USAID officials, that its members dealt individually with the U.S. people, and that no member of the Advisory Council had even seen a copy of an economic study prepared by the U.S. Government Inter-Agency Team, outlining U.S. economic plans for Grenada, which had been prepared in November 1983 and was distributed to the Friends Service Committee before their tour.[11] Second, as that same economic report made clear, the philosophy of the reconstruction effort was one of unbridled free enterprise capitalism: revise investment and tax codes to favor private enterprise; develop a labor code to ensure a compliant labor force and to qualify Grenada for inclusion in the U.S. Caribbean Basin Initiative; sell off public sector enterprises to private interests; lift price controls on basic foodstuffs; reduce import duties; and eliminate the role of the state in marketing imports.[12]

All of this, in effect, amounted to a determined assault upon the social and economic gains of the revolution. The shutting down of many state enterprises—the asphalt plant, the prefabricated-housing plant, as well as work on the final touches on the airport—has resulted in a spiraling rate of unemployment. Social programs such as the free milk distribution program, the medical care program, and the national transportation system, have been abandoned or sharply curtailed. The Land Development and Utilisation Act, which sought to enlarge land use by compulsory government leases on idle or underutilized estates, has been waived, with much acreage being returned to the big landowners. Likewise, the cooperative development scheme, set up to provide easy loans, training, and technical assistance to agricultural, fishing, and handicrafts cooperatives, has been dissolved, while the state-run Agro Industries plant, which processed locally grown vegetable and fruit crops, has also been abandoned. Perhaps even more ominous is the concerted move against the trade unions, especially those perceived as having been pro-PRG, with the local business elements now feeling free to hire and fire as they please and with the offensive being led by agents of the CIA-related American Institute for Free Labor Development. The purpose is to reshape the union movement into the mold of the American style of pro-business, jobs-oriented, apolitical unionism, which runs counter to the tradition of Caribbean unionism where the unions in all of the major territories have long ago abandoned that archaic concept of the separation between unionism and politics.[13]

What all this has meant is a general plan which seeks to make the new Grenada safe for capitalism. Reports coming in from St. George's add detail to that development. Real estate agents and tourism officials congratulate themselves as they anticipate not only a rise in the tourist traffic but also a rise in local property values, which will undoubtedly encourage real estate speculation.[14] Community health services begin to decline as local doctors revert to lucrative private practice, becoming in effect medical accountants who pay more attention to their bank book than to low-paid voluntary public service.[15] Many of the social ills that proliferated in the old Gairy period are beginning to resurface, such as high unemployment, prostitution, crime, and the use of drugs.[16] Nor can matters improve as the plans of U.S. business groups, already under way, to build new tourist hotels in the island result in an unbridled tourism which, as in Barbados and the Bahamas, will inevitably play havoc with traditional social mores. All in all, it is not too much to say that the real loss in the destruction of the revolution is the disappearance of the revolutionary appeal to Grenadians, and especially the younger people, to forget the pursuit of private hedonistic satisfactions in the service of a larger public good that called for sacrifice, dedication, and social spirit.

The political game plan has followed suit. No doubt most of the members of the Advisory Council, and possibly even some of the American advisers, wanted a return to free elections in the best of the democratic tradition. But it soon became clear that Washington, along with its West Indian allies, was determined that such a process should be arranged in such a way that would bar the return to power of any groups even remotely related to progressive, left-wing ideologies. Elections, as everybody agreed, would have to be held. But measures would have to be taken so that they should not get out of hand. So, surviving PRG ministers like Radix and Louison were harassed lest the NJM stage a successful revival. The old British electoral "winner take all" system, in which there is sometimes a serious discrepancy between votes polled and seats obtained, was retained. The country saw another invasion of what one writer called "the ambitious exiles," political aspirants from abroad organizing new political parties overnight without any known mass base, and all of them prudently pro-American in their announced programs, thus promising a return to the old discredited political system and its style.[17]

There can be little doubt that, as in the Dominican Republic, the Americans had their favored candidates, and subsidized them in the CIA style; although, as always, those operations would not be known until some congressional committee exposed them later on, after the damage had been done. But it is known that Washington did not want a return to power of Gairy, who returned to the island proclaiming that he would revive his party but would not run as candidate, and who in his public pronouncements was megalomaniac as ever, seeing himself as the great prophetic leader blessed by both God and the United States to lead Grenada back to sanity.[18] But it is clear enough that the Washington planners did not want Gairy, not necessarily because they could not accept him as an authoritarian politician but because they felt that, once back in power, he would probably provoke another left-wing rebellion. What they wanted, obviously, was Gairyism without Gairy, just as in the Dominican Republic they had wanted *trujillismo* without Trujillo. For it is the nature of the imperialist power everywhere that it will have no compunction in jettisoning its bought clients once the clients have served their purpose. It remains to be seen whether that policy will succeed against a political player as shrewd and sinister as Gairy.

It remains to look at the regional dimensions of the aftermath. The July summit meeting of the CARICOM heads of state agreed not to bring up the Grenada issue, although Prime Minister Chambers's speech there showed that the wound was by no means healed. At the individual territorial level, Prime Minister Seaga, playing the Grenada trump card, called a snap general election in Jamaica which was boycotted by the opposition, leading to a one-party Parliament and thus imposing further strain upon an already weakened parliamentary system. On the other hand, the two general elections in St. Kitts-Nevis and St. Vincent, with the ruling party winning in the former and losing in the latter, seem to indicate that Grenada was not an issue since both campaigns were typical mud-slinging, gossip-ridden small-island battles revolving around personalities. Reasonable voices like those of Trinidad and Tobago's Minister of External Affairs Basil Ince and Guyana's Foreign Minister Rashleigh Jackson spoke out to pour oil on troubled waters, while even Prime Minister John Compton of St. Lucia and Prime Minister Eugenia Charles of Dominica, the regional "hawks" in the invasion, now spoke in conciliatory tones, as if they had begun to comprehend the damage done to the regional movement.

Even so, it still remained true that after Grenada, as Foreign Minister Jackson emphasized, ideological pluralism would give way to ideological conformity.[19] That was manifested in a number of ways. There was the case of *Caribbean Contact* editor Rickey Singh, whose work permit was withdrawn by the Barbadian government supposedly because of his articles critical of that government's role in the invasion, and constituting a truly vindictive act on the part of Prime Minister Adams, forcing Singh to uproot home and family and find hazardous employment as a professional journalist elsewhere.[20] There was Prime Minister Seaga's public threat to launch a "shattering offensive" against all "saboteurs and traitors" who would seek to destroy the country. He accused some twenty-five Jamaicans, mostly from the centrist opposition party, of having recently traveled to Cuba, Grenada, and the Soviet Union, and announced an unproved claim that a Russian plot existed to assassinate members of his government.[21] Not to be outdone, Prime Minister Charles introduced a series of bills into the Dominica Parliament entitled the Treason Act and the State Security Act. The first made hanging a penalty for treason, treason being defined as applying to any citizen who "forms an intention to levy war against the state or to overthrow the government or constitution by force of arms." The second makes it an indictable offense if any citizen "from the circumstances of the case or from his conduct it appears that his purpose was a purpose intended to be prejudicial to the safety or defense of the state"; it also includes a clause giving citizens the legal right to arrest one another without a warrant if the citizen thinks "there is immediate danger that that other person will commit or attempt to commit an offense against this act."[22] This is lèse majesté with a vengeance. It establishes the dangerous doctrines of intent and tendency to incite, both of them inimical to traditional civil liberties, and both of them, interestingly, invoked earlier on in 1965 in the report of the Subversive Activities Commission set up by Prime Minister Williams of Trinidad and Tobago at that time.

It is painfully apparent that the post-Grenada Caribbean is entering into a period of creole McCarthyism. All left-wing, progressive, even mildly liberal groups and movements will be subject to sustained harassment by governments taking advantage of the apparent popularity of their actions in the Grenada event. Prime Minister Adams's attack on the Caribbean Conference of Churches, an ecumenical but hardly revolutionary organization, is typical. So also is Prime Minister Seaga's attack on the Jamaica Workers party, in an attempt to unleash thereby a "Red Scare" for partisan purposes. This is all the more misguided because although that party is admittedly Communist it was hardly likely that its leader, Trevor Munroe, whose only violence is verbal, was about to launch a coup d'état from his university office. Whole articles and columns are written in the mass media to persuade their readers that socialism, everywhere, means state terrorism and deprivation of liberties. Mediocre plays are written to teach the lesson that revolution, like crime, does not pay.[23] Movies will probably follow suit, just as they did after Jonestown in 1978. It is not inconceivable that attempted purges of "subversive" faculty members will take place as the regional university campuses come more and more under the control of the local national governments. For it is not irrelevant to remember that the transition from Black Power nationalism to Marxism-Leninism within the new left-wing groups of the region in the 1970s and the 1980s really commenced with the so-called Rodney riots of 1968, set off by the Jamaican government's decision at that time to revoke the work permit of Walter Rodney at the university.

This climate of opinion is not likely to abate with the newly established U.S. presence in the region. To the contrary, that presence is likely to make it worse. The American propaganda machine has already set itself up; radio stations, including the U.S.-operated Radio Antilles based in Antigua, purvey daily the American message. American travel writers visit Grenada to boost it as another jewel in the mass tourist industry.[24] Propaganda units, under the guise of being centers of academic study, like the Army War College in Washington, send down "professors" to defend the American imperialist position, only to be sometimes confronted, to their surprise, by hostile audiences.[25] The American ambassador to Paris makes a surprise visit to Martinique (the first ever) to warn French Antilleans about the Cuban "menace," to cast disparaging remarks on the Antillean independence movement, and to support the French government in its utilization of French Guiana as a guided missile site.[26] In Grenada itself, the ubiquitous American "advisers" interfere in local political matters in order to encourage an electoral alliance between the three or four emerging centrist parties, with a view to preventing either a Gairy victory or a victory for the rejuvenated NJM. A new and enlarged U.S. diplomatic presence makes itself felt as Americans perceive that any residual British responsibility no longer exists in the region.[27] That began, of course, with the setting up of a full-blown embassy in Grenada itself, replete with USAID and U.S. Information Agency officers. It expanded as plans were discussed for similar missions, with or without embassy status, in the other Eastern Caribbean islands. It would seem astonishing to the student of modern international protocol that a small island like, say, Montserrat or St. Vincent would warrant the expense of a resident U.S. ambassador, until one realizes that it makes sense once one understands that Washington is determined that there shall be "no more Grenadas."

But the most unwanted consequence of the new American presence is that it will immeasurably accelerate the ongoing militarization of the region. Militarization, of course, has had its own internal causes within the Caribbean since the 1960s: the buildup of the Cuban state defense forces, in part to protect the revolution against another Bay of Pigs invasion, in part to provide military aid to fraternal groups and parties in Africa and Central America; a similar buildup in Guyana, in part to curb internal dissent, in part to meet any unfriendly act from Venezuela; and the surreptitious recruitment of hired gunmen by the Jamaican political parties, which has caused so much mayhem in the Kingston slum districts.

These local factors are now compounded by the external factor of American militarism. It comes with an experience finely honed in the particular case of Puerto Rico, in which the colonial status of that territory has permitted its virtually unrestricted military use by the Pentagon forces for nearly a century since 1898. The record includes military bases; the vast Roosevelt Roads naval complex; the Army Reserve Forces; a militarized National Guard, some of it trained in counterinsurgency warfare at the U.S. training school in Panama; the use of the islands of Vieques and Culebra as weapons testing and maneuver sites; the introduction of the Reserve Officers Training Corps into the state university; the imposition of obligatory military service; and, not least of all, the introduction of the American practice of armed civilian police into the local life, so different from the British tradition.[28] Not the least disturbing of these patterns and forms of institutionalized violence is that they also foster in the civilian populations at large a psychology of compliance, even approbation, as the widespread popular resistance to gun control legislation in the United States itself shows.

The translation of these patterns, in however modified a form, to the traditionally placid island societies of the Eastern Caribbean can only work havoc, in the long run, with social and political mores. With only small police forces, no armies, and occasionally small defense forces, those societies must now come to terms with the pressing need for some system of adequate regional defense, implicit in the 1982 regional security agreement signed by Barbados, St. Lucia, Antigua, St. Vincent, and Dominica. Nobody except an outright pacifist could disagree with the need for such a system. The dangers lie elsewhere. In the first place, a regional military force could grow up without the equivalent of a regional political force (in the form of a regional federal government), thus creating not only the practical problems of financing, command structure, and coordination, but also the distinct possibility of a military corps not fully accountable to proper civilian control. A bifurcated sovereignty, half-military, half-civilian, would ensue, sowing seeds of potential conflict. Second, such a defense structure, of necessity, would require falling back on the United States for weapons and training, which in fact is now already under way, with U.S. military training teams instructing local police and defense members on five of the islands since December 1983. This leads in turn to a new bone of contention in the local politics, as the continuing acrimonious debate on the Barbados Defence Force exemplifies.[29] These are momentous changes in societies where, traditionally, armed personnel have only been seen and heard on state ceremonial occasions. They are even more momentous when placed within the framework of the larger debate as to whether the Caribbean can ever become a "zone of peace."

=====

The aftermath, all in all, has turned out to be truly Orwellian. It has about it all of the "double speak," the twisting of words to mean their opposite, which Orwell caricatured in his 1949 sermon-novel *Nineteen Eighty-Four.* There was the baggage of lies, half-truths, and self-righteous rationalizations to justify the act of invasion, including the mendacities about the "invitation" of the OECS countries, the nonexistent physical danger of the medical school student body, and the ludicrous claim that a tiny Caribbean island could be regarded as a serious threat to the national security of the American state power. World opinion was invited to believe that a power empire would occupy a small country in order to restore "democracy." The U.S. propaganda machine used the mass media to present the case that war was necessary in order to bring "peace." The U.S. State Department termed the invasion "a pre-dawn vertical insertion." At much the same time the department replaced the word "killing" in their handbooks with the phrase "unlawful or arbitrary deprivation of life." It would be difficult to imagine General Ulysses S. Grant or General George Patton using such language.

The hypocrisy, even more, included a systematic campaign, not merely to discredit the Grenada Revolution, but also to stain its memory by presenting Maurice Bishop as a "moderate" civil rights hero who had been betrayed by his Marxist comrades, after four years of ceaseless U.S. propaganda denouncing the same Bishop as a dangerous Marxist himself, as if to suggest that the real purpose of the invasion was to save Bishop's record and reputation. It was almost as if the Vatican were to canonize a heretic, or the Soviet Union confer the Order of Lenin on Kerensky. You murder Caesar; then you arrive at the funeral to praise him. It would be more true to say that the Americans tried to mythologize Bishop as a worthy adversary in order to glorify their own victory. The student of American society is tempted to conclude that the hypocrisy flows from the Puritan heritage, with its compulsion to find some moral excuse for even the most inexcusable of actions. It would have been far better, perhaps, and certainly more honest, if the U.S. imperialists in 1984 had spoken with the direct and brutal candor with which the Athenian ambassadors—as Thucydides tells us—addressed the defeated Melians in the Peloponnesian War. Orwell himself at least would have appreciated that.

18

Some General Observations

As one seeks to summarize the Grenada Revolution, both its events and their meaning, certain conclusions seem to be beyond dispute. In the first place, despite the name, it was not a revolution in the sense of the great modern bourgeois and proletarian revolutions of the modern post-Reformation period. Its life span was too short to establish a new political and social order of a permanent nature. In that sense, it was more like 1848 than 1789, not so much the harbinger of profound changes in social class structure and economic organization as a brief revolutionary interlude, destroyed by the counterrevolution. Second, and consequentially, its lasting importance will probably be symbolic. Just as the French left lived for a century or more on the romanticized memory of the great Commune of 1793, and just as the English Whig historians created their liberal myth out of the revolution of 1688, so the West Indian radical historians of the future will probably see Grenada in much the same way. Third, and finally, that very symbolism may in fact be perceived as contributing in itself to the betrayal and demise of the revolution. For if, as Castro put it, it was a big revolution in a small country, that aspect of the matter could possibly have imposed upon it a burden of symbolizing the world revolutionary movement, of being its heroic carrier in a hostile region, which perhaps it was not able, or could not even be expected to carry. No revolution can carry the entire world on its shoulders.

The political scientist, as distinct from the historian, will be more interested in the concerns about social and political theory which have inevitably been evoked by the Grenada experience. That experience at once reflected and reinforced the widespread debate, especially in the Third World, about the meaning of all of the conceptual modalities involved in the general world condition: imperialism, socialism, nationalism, Marxism-Leninism, capitalism, populism, and the rest. The developments in both the capitalist and Communist world camps since the 1960s have meant that those concepts no longer possess the pristine clarity that they once possessed. If the Grenada post-mortem helps to straighten out some of that doctrinal confusion the revolution will not have been entirely in vain.

To begin with, the Grenada action throws some light on the character of modern imperialism, at least in its American manifestation. Classic interpretations of the phenomenon, starting with the early Hobson-Lenin-Hilferding school and continuing in the later Baran-Sweezy-Magdoff writings, have rooted it in the need for monopolistic capital to penetrate and control the world market as supplier of raw material products and markets for finished goods, usually under the guise of free trade. But the economic factor was hardly present in the Grenada action; it would seem hardly credible that the invasion was undertaken in order to protect the nutmeg market for American business. Or even, for that matter, to guarantee the larger Caribbean purchasing market, whose consumption is miniscule within the total value of U.S. global exports. The noneconomic factors were far more evident: the psychological factor of religious anti-Communist fervor and the military factor. The psychological factor is important because it shows how states of mind, in groups and individuals who are more imperialist than others, play an independent role and explain otherwise incomprehensible and nonrational acts. The military factor is important because it shows how imperialism moves qualitatively into militarism, so that the need of the military to test their weapons in real combat, as well as the need of the arms industry to justify its role in the national economy, come to transcend purely political or economic considerations in the final policymaking process. Grenada showed, in almost pure form, how those factors have become primary, rather than secondary, in U.S. imperialism, just as, indeed, did the Vietnam War. It is only possible to discount them if one accepts, for example, the naïve argument of, say, Schumpeter in his early essay that because capitalism, as a historical form, is based on economic rationality, it is therefore anti-imperialist, so that imperialist habits are atavistic, seen as archaic survivals of the feudal, precapitalist past.[1] The argument—pure abstractionism at its worst—if applied to the Grenada action would require us to overlook a number of crucial facts that disprove it: namely, that no segment of the American business class opposed it, that it was acclaimed by the American people as a whole, and that the only few dissenting voices came from liberal elements in the churches and the universities. Grenada, in brief, brought out into the open the existence of a popular social imperialism in American life. The Caribbean forces fighting for change will have to come to terms with that fact.

Just as there is variety in the concept of imperialism, so there is also in the concept of socialism. There can be no doctrine of the "immaculate conception" of socialism for the simple reason that the multitude of socialist, neosocialist, populist and national-liberationist movements which have emerged since 1945 all over the world, from Afghanistan to Zimbabwe, have been shaped by, and have responded to, different sociohistorical conditions peculiar to each particular country. Variety is the spice of life, everywhere. The official language of the Grenada party leadership was Marxist-Leninist, although in reality it was more Leninist-Stalinist. But it was in large part a borrowed language. It accepted the sacred texts to the point of overlooking whether Grenadian realities fitted into them or not. Stalin's position on the question of the subnationalities did not fit, since Grenada is a small, homogeneous society with no such problems. Marx's position on the leading role of the industrial working class did not fit, since no such class of any real significance existed in the Grenada social structure. Marx's disdain for the "idiocy of rural life" also did not fit, since Marx had in mind the serf-peasantry of the Russia of Gogol and Dostoevsky. Rural village life in present-day India, with its religious superstition, its backward agricultural methods, and its continuing caste system, may resemble still that Marxist image, but certainly not the Grenadian small proprietorial landowning peasantry which is by no means isolated from the urban influence. There is, of course, peasant conservatism, which Leninist ideologues have always tended to overlook. But in Grenada it is a conservatism with a Caribbean character. Bishop seems to have understood it. But the ultraleft faction simply dismissed it as ideological "backwardness."

Because of these differentiating factors, the main driving force of the Grenada Revolution was what George Lichtheim, in his brilliant little essay of 1971, speaking in general terms, called "populist socialism."[2] As Bishop's speeches make clear, its message was based on the idea of the natural unity of the people as a whole, rallied around a truly selfless leadership, defending the national sovereignty of the country against its enemies. Unlike Stalinism, it did not rely solely on terror and intimidation, nor did it contemplate the liquidation of the peasantry as a class. It was ultranationalist, invoking the memory of the late-eighteenth-century struggle of the mulatto Fédon against the English colonial rule. It was also anti-imperialist, not so much for purely theoretical reasons as for the fact, known to all, that the U.S. administration was throughout actively engaged in destabilization exercises against the revolution. For as a French left-wing journal has put it, speaking specifically of Cuba but inferentially for the Caribbean as a whole, the Cuban people did not invent anti-imperialism: rather that sentiment was thrust upon them by imperialism itself, going back for more than a century.[3]

The Grenada Revolution, then, was essentially a peasant-based movement of *poder popular* led by a small urban intelligentsia. It thus accepted the Maoist emphasis upon the new role of the peasantry in the anti-imperialist struggle. But that emphasis was never fully articulated. Indeed, it is of interest to note that the teachings of Chairman Mao were rarely, if ever, included in the PRG lexicon. They were neglected in favor of the orthodox Leninist approach. The historic Sino-Soviet split had forced all of the world revolutionary parties to make a choice. For good or ill, the Grenada party chose Moscow rather than Peking. The revolution thus inevitably became a less popular worker-peasant movement and more the vehicle of an elitist avant-garde drawn from the local urban petit-bourgeois intelligentsia. It thus led, as already noted, to the antidemocratic ultracentralism of the Leninist model. It encouraged a certain revolutionary naïveté, as can be seen in Richard Jacobs's assertion, soon after 1979, that "the arming of the people guarantees the democratic nature of the revolution, for it ensures the effective end of cliqueism, minoritarianism, and personalism characteristic of the old regime."[4] It also encouraged a habit of doctrinal intolerance, so that the Grenada leadership forgot the admonition of the Chinese leader Chou En-lai that "we must not imagine that just because we are Communists we have some heaven-sent ability to lead intellectuals in the work of cultural construction, and that it is impossible for us to make any mistakes. Such a view is extremely dangerous."[5]

It is arguable that the Grenada leadership forgot that lesson because it was a young leadership; Bishop at the time of his death was only thirty-nine years old. Older revolutionaries are wiser heads; like Chou En-lai they have spent a whole lifetime in the revolutionary struggle and have acquired a wisdom about human nature that the younger people have yet to learn. That kind of wisdom was painfully absent in the Grenadian situation. Experience, and the wisdom that accrues from it, counts. There is a world of difference between the professional revolutionary and the amateur revolutionary, even if they speak the same doctrinal language. It is a pity, in a way, that the Grenada leaders did not have the opportunity, with the revolution firmly established, to think about their experience, to reflect over it, and write in retrospect about it, in the manner of the young Nicaraguan *sandinista* guerrilla fighter Omar Cabezas in his published memoir about his experiences. Much of the Grenada mystery would be clarified if we had in our hands a similar memoir by Maruice Bishop or Jacqueline Creft or Unison Whiteman.

There was, finally, the element of nationalism in the Grenada Revolution and what it teaches about the relationship between nationalism and socialism. The revolution was nationalist in the sense that it was proud to be Grenadian and, after that, West Indian. It sought to protect, more than anything else, the political and cultural sovereignty of the Caribbean region. It did not therefore degenerate into a kind of "my country right or wrong" nationalism nor into being a sort of Shangri-la utopia after the manner of the small communitarian experiments of nineteenth-century America. It was determinedly internationalist in its sympathies, as evident from its many foreign policy statements, noteworthy among them being the address made by Minister of Foreign Affairs Unison Whiteman to the second special session on disarmament at the United Nations in June 1982, with its spirited denunciation of the wasteful and unproductive global arms race that threatened ultimate nuclear holocaust.[6] No one nation, not even the biggest, can "go it alone" anymore. A socialist revolution may indeed come to power by itself, as Cuba and also Grenada itself have proved. But it is equally true that no such revolution can hope to survive for long unless it receives aid from other sources in the world movement. Whatever other lessons they may not have learned, the Grenada leadership did not allow itself to forget the lesson that socialism, ever since its beginnings, has been dedicated to the principle of internationalism.

=

In the final analysis the Grenada experiment was betrayed by the three forces of U.S. imperialism, the ultraright wing of the West Indian bourgeoisie, and the ultraleft faction of the New Jewel Movement. Once granted the character and necessity of their objective interests, each one of them could present a plausible case in their defense. Necessity creates interest; and interest creates policy. To see those forces simply as if they are evil is, then, grossly oversimplistic; that is the mistake of the torrent of revolutionary rage presented, for example, in the denunciatory poetry of a young Caribbean writer like Lasana Sekou in his *Maroon Lives,* in which the U.S. force becomes the "Babylonian whore" and the Caribbean force "baying jackals."[7] That manner of looking at the matter, however real the anguish behind it, only offers a simple answer to a complex problem and hardly advances meaningful analysis that might arrive at the truth. Historical forces rarely act simply in response to motives, whether good or bad. They act, rather, in response to concrete interests, whether of social class, military power, or economic structure.

Is it possible—in, say, the period between now and the end of the century—that any of the forces involved in the Grenada story will change their basic character; or will they remain the same? The answer, of course, depends upon whether they have the capacity to learn and change.

There is not much reason to be optimistic on that score. The characteristic traits of U.S. imperialism, culminating in the Grenada invasion, cannot be seen as aberrations but as continuing behavior patterns which, since World War II, have had as much in them of Kennedy liberalism as Eisenhower conservatism. The catalogue bears repeating: the felt need to build up the national military power, an emphasis on confrontation with the Soviet adversary, strategies of exploiting Soviet weaknesses, covert and overt destabilization practices against regimes and movements seen as threats, assertion of American power as the supreme arbiter of world affairs, and the conviction that most of the Third World problems are caused by evil Soviet interference and provocation. It is a general policy summed up by U.S. diplomat George Kennan in the 1950s:

> We cannot be too dogmatic about the methods by which local Communists can be dealt with. . . . Where the concepts and traditions of popular government are too weak to absorb successfully the intensity of Communist attack, then we must concede that harsh governmental measures of repression may be the only answer; that these measures may have to proceed from regimes whose origins and methods would not stand the test of American concepts of democratic procedure; and that such regimes and such methods may be preferable alternatives, and indeed the only alternatives, to further Communist successes.[8]

There is, of course, an alternative foreign policy inherent in the more liberal American tradition, summed up in the assertion of the late Senator Frank Church that "the American people were not prepared by their national experience for the role of either ideological crusader or practitioner of the old style 19th-century *Realpolitik*. We came to believe that we could set a democratic example to the world by the way we governed our own society, and we came to believe after each of the two world wars that it was worthwhile to try to build something new under the sun . . . to try to move forward in international relations from the rule of force toward the rule of law, from the unreliable balance-of-power to a world security community."[9] But there is little indication that the American public cares for that alternative. It is not a question of a "good" people against a "bad" ruling class, as some critics naïvely assume. It is, rather, that the majority of the American people, either by their own volition or because they have been persuaded by the vast propaganda machine of the mass media, have decided that the imperialist path is the correct one. Reagan's 1984 landslide victory reflected the mood.

Nor is there much hope for the conversion of the West Indian bourgeosie to any saner view of the matter. Grenada was a victory for its most reactionary elements. The bourgeosie's mind-set is one of dependency, for they have no history of independent struggle. Their anti-Communism is perhaps even more manic than that of the Americans, for they feel more threatened as vulnerable islands. Their moral bankruptcy is almost complete, as their devious behavior in the preinvasion activities showed. As a French radical group from Bordeaux points out, middle-class political parties in Grenada follow the lines set by their patron parties in the metropolis, following the Puerto Rican pattern, where the island parties are being assimilated into the U.S. mainland parties.[10] They do not really believe in the capacity of their people to raise themselves by self-help. They dismiss any such effort, as in Grenada, with ridicule and contempt, an attitude aptly expressed in the opinion of the novelist V. S. Naipaul—who is in the habit of promulgating pontifical judgments on the Caribbean from his London refuge—that revolutionary Grenada "was the story of a retarded island community hijacked by people with slightly more education into the forms of a grandiose revolution. The revolution blew away and what was left in Grenada was a murder story."[11] The sneer is typical of a mind itself retarded by its inability to comprehend anything of hope and compassion and endeavor in the Third World, forever the sardonic anglophile snob who, for all his talent, shows just how crippling the colonial mentality can be. Just, indeed, as Froude and Trollope mirror the prejudices of the old Victorian West Indian planter class so Naipaul mirrors the prejudices of its successor, the brown-black governing class of the modern independence period.

The only and last hope, then, is that the Caribbean left will learn from the mistakes of Grenada. For modern socialism, in the Caribbean as elsewhere, is historically the child of the European rationalist tradition, obligated to search for the universal laws that govern human behavior. As one reads the postrevolution commentaries, there can be no doubt that the left has been roughly shaken out of much of its revolutionary complacency and that it has—except for the most intransigent hard-liners—valiantly reexamined its major presuppositions in light of the Grenada events. Its members can now see that it was wrong to embrace uncritically the Moscow model of party organization; to assume that revolutionary rhetoric would explain all; and to close ranks behind the revolution lest any criticism, however mild, would give aid and comfort to the enemy.

This self-critical examination of the matter is remarkable, and encouraging, for its general consensus about what went wrong. Bill Riviere writes:

> The collapse of the Grenada process must be traced to a failure of the revolutionaries to resolve fundamental strategic, tactical, and organisational questions. The Coard group incorrectly decided it was time to take the process on to the socialist stage. It incorrectly resolved the problem of the Party's isolation from the broad masses. It incorrectly opted to make the Party the source of all power. In a nutshell, the Coard group applied Marxist-Leninist principles in a rigid and orthodox rather than, as it should have done, in a flexible and creative way.[12]

The Guyanese Working Peoples' Alliance (WPA) opines that

> The whole Grenada crisis has caused the WPA to be more sensitive to the question of a strict regime of human rights under any social system.

Our party serves notice that while fully honouring its commitment to the defense of the region against external aggression, it will exercise its right and duty to examine the actions even of friends who claim to be pursuing revolution, especially when those friends have state power. When the denial of basic rights takes place under cover of Left intent, it opens up the floodgates for rulers with other political intentions to suppress their opposition. Human rights standards cannot be imposed on governments of only one outlook. In most modern societies, taking into account economic and social development in the twentieth century, there should be no difficulty in harmonising the rule of law with revolutionary needs. Revolutionaries must not be seen as inconsistent in the defense of fundamental civil, political, cultural and economic rights."[13]

Clive Thomas has summed it up best of all. He writes:

I would like to sum up my position on this matter [of Grenada] by generalising it into a proposition, which is that after Grenada no social project carried out in the name of the masses of the Caribbean peoples, whether by government or opposition, will receive widespread support from the popular forces and their organizations if it does not clearly embrace political democracy as its norms of political conduct.[14]

Thomas adds a more particular warning to the West Indian intellectual class as it becomes involved in such projects. He continues:

Many of the progressive intellectuals, like their counterparts in Eastern Europe and North America, have been demonstrably uncritical of political processes initiated in the name of the "Left." The practice has been to operate as "cheerleaders," applauding actions by the Left, rather than as constructive and creative critics. While this is seen as "giving solidarity," in reality it indicates an important weakness of this social stratum. The weakness referred to stems from the failure of this group to grasp, intellectually and in practice, the distinction between recognising a process of social development which is objectively progressive, and giving direct, uncritical political support to the class or group which is in control of state power at the time this takes place . . . loyalty to the regime in power is substituted for a constructive critical attitude. In this substitution, intellectuals as a group negate what is to my mind their single most important social attribute, namely, the fact that by their high levels of education and training they develop, on the whole, a striking capacity for creativity and the exercise of independent critical power.[15]

===

Thomas is most certainly correct in his assessment of the role of the intelligentsia in the revolutionary process. Yet perhaps the real tragedy of the Grenada Revolution, apart from the betrayal of the intellectuals that Thomas mentions, is the fact that, quite simply, it was so short-lived. It never had the chance to develop, to grow, to fulfill its promise, to overcome its mistakes and move forward to something greater. As far as can be determined no one at the top kept a diary. There is no record of the revolution produced by a friendly outsider comparable, say, to Edgar Snow's *Red Star over China*. Nor is there any substantive interview material by a friend to match Lee Lockwood's *Castro's Cuba, Cuba's Fidel* (1967), or Graham Greene's reminiscences of General Torrijos, *Getting to Know the General* (1985), or the books written by Basil Davidson in the 1960s and 1970s on the modern black African revolutions. This lack, in turn, was made worse by the oriental-like secretiveness of the organs of the revolution—the party, the Central Committee, the Political Bureau. It all ended with the planning and execution of a counterrevolution which will be difficult to forget and impossible to forgive.

===

That, of course, is the dark side of the moon. But there is a brighter side, and any account of the Grenada Revolution must end by remembering it. For all that it did wrong, the PRG leadership was able to mobilize a mass enthusiasm for the revolution that no other Caribbean country save Cuba has managed to do. Certainly, there was very little such enthusiasm for either the West Indies Federation of 1958–62 or the advent of independence in the 1960s and 1970s; both of those movements in fact were monopolized by the elite politicians, the motorized middle-class salariat, and the educated professional "opinion makers." Somehow or another, in Grenada, a spark seems to have been touched that enabled a whole populace to engage itself in refurbishing its house. As Jay Mandle describes it in his book, the numerous discussion meetings on the budget, the parish and zonal council meetings, the mobilization of the population for the campaign to end illiteracy, all gave the Grenadian people, however imperfectly, a real sense of participating in the affairs of the country. Beyond that, the revolution helped Grenadians to see themselves in larger regional, even world terms, thus shedding some of the "small island" mentality.[16]

The revolutionary achievement can also be appreciated from a slightly different angle. Payne, Sutton, and Thorndike, in their book on the revolution, refer to the "exceptionability" of the revolution. In many ways, of course, it was exceptional.[17] But the exceptionability fades a little when it is remembered that the events of October 19, 1983 have much in common with the events of early 1986 in Haiti and the Philippines, for in all three cases a Third World populace showed itself capable of undertaking an act of spontaneous resistance and rebellion against a despised and corrupt regime. In all of those cases, furthermore, the resistance was undertaken without benefit of political party or vanguard elite, suggesting that the overthrow of other despotic regimes will be undertaken, not by armchair socialists or underground conspirators meeting in smoke-filled rooms, but by the people themselves taking to the street. In this sense, Grenada is not alone. It forms part of a pattern that is *sui generis* Third World. As Colin Henfrey has put it, Lenin's *Theses on the Colonial Question* set a norm of expecting the Third World to wait for the First to define and make a revolution, but in practice the Third World has done rather better.[18] Since 1983 a whole literature of pompous and meretricious books by self-appointed experts has been published, trying to establish the "lessons" of Grenada for the outside First World—the book by Sandford and Vigilante, *Grenada: The Untold Story,* announcing itself as an analysis that "illustrates the geopolitical challenge facing Western democracies in the Third World," is a case in point.[19] In truth and in fact, the story of Grenada, told or untold, does not refer to the outside, rich, privileged world, for whom its "lessons," if any, are almost irrelevant. It refers, rather, to Grenada itself, then to the Caribbean region, then to the Third World. As such, it is a record and an achievement that age shall not wither nor time condemn.

19

1986: Denouement

For every crime there is, or at least there should be, a punishment. The final verdict of the Grenada court trial was delivered by the jury of Grenadian citizens on December 4, 1986. Of the eighteen prisoners convicted, fourteen, including Hudson Austin and Bernard and Phyllis Coard, were sentenced to die by hanging, three were found guilty of manslaughter and sentenced to imprisonment for a total of 121 years, and one, the soldier Raeburn Nelson, was acquitted.[1]

The trial proper began on April 23, 1986, and was one of the most prolonged criminal court trials in West Indian history. But in truth it began in early 1984, when a six-week preliminary enquiry was conducted by Magistrate Lyle St. Paul (who later removed himself from the case after receiving death threats) to determine if a case had been made out for committal to a higher court (the Grenada Supreme Court).[2] After the Grenada Appeals Court rejected a motion by the prisoners challenging the legality of the High Court, the way was made clear for a transfer of the case to that court under Chief Justice Archibald Nedd. It is ironic that the alleged unconstitutionality of the court was answered by the argument that it had been set up by the People's Revolutionary Government operating under the well-known doctrine of necessity.[3] In the meantime Justice Nedd retired and was succeeded by Justice Dennis Bryon, who thereafter bore the brunt of the proceedings.

The team for the prosecution was led by the Trinidadian counsel Karl Hudson-Phillips, and the team for the defense by a group of Jamaican and Guyanese lawyers. The British lawyer Lord Gifford was refused permission to join the defense team on the grounds, upheld by the Court of Appeals, that Grenada law, like that of most of the other islands, does not permit lawyers practicing outside of the region to practice in the local courts or to be admitted to the local bars.[4]

From early 1984 until April 1986, when the High Court proceedings started in earnest, there were numerous delays as well as successive motions by the prisoners concerning, variously, their difficulties in obtaining services of counsel, the allegation that pretrial publicity had made a fair trial impossible, and charges that ill treatment at the prison had been permitted by the Barbadian commissioner of prisons, Lionel Maloney. With reference to that last motion it is worth remarking that some people thought it somewhat hypocritical of international human rights bodies to have intervened on the prisoners' behalf. "This is what annoys me," Anglican Archdeacon Hoskens remarked tartly. "Where was Amnesty International the last four years? Where were the Quakers? Why are they speaking out now?"[5]

From the first, the prisoners took the position that the trial was run as a kangaroo court masterminded by the American imperialists. They therefore refused to cross-examine prosecution witnesses, satisfying themselves instead with making prolonged speeches—sometimes lasting five or six days—in defense of the revolution (mostly absurdly irrelevant to the charges) in the midst of which they vociferously protested their innocence. This was accompanied by unruly behavior in court—chanting of slogans, stamping of feet, clapping of hands, and hurling of insults indiscriminately at judge, prosecutors, and jury—which frequently led to the forcible removal of the prisoners from the courtroom. Throughout, it was noisy, rowdy, and tumultuous. Many of the prisoners complained, sometimes with justification that their rights were violated, saying they were not allowed full access to their lawyers; they were not provided with sufficient time or writing materials to prepare their defense; they were deprived of the papers seized by the U.S. occupation forces which, they asserted, would prove their innocence; and that many of the statements introduced in court had been obtained from prisoners questioned by Barbadian police interrogators under duress or as a result of torture—an accusation never really proved.[6] Bernard Coard claimed in addition that a number of diaries kept by himself and others had disappeared from the prison and requested the court to order a thorough investigation by an independent body.[7] With regard to the U.S.-seized papers, Selwyn Strachan added the strange request that President Reagan himself should be subpoenaed and brought before the court for questioning.[8] It was, in sum, a long process in which everybody suffered some trauma.

This being the West Indies, there were, of course, some lighter moments. Bernard Coard, urging at one point that Chief Justice Byron withdraw from the case, told him that he should not allow himself to become an object of fun like the English cricket bowler who was humiliated when the great West Indian batsman, Gary Sobers, hit him for a perfect thirty-six runs in a single over, a record of six sixes, in Swansea.[9] At another point, the defense team leader, Jamaican Howard Hamilton, complained that he could not understand the broad brogue of a Barbadian policeman witness (West Indians make fun of Barbadian speech in much the same way that Americans might make fun of a Boston accent), to which Hudson-Phillips replied that he, in turn, had difficulty with Hamilton's own Jamaican accent. This prompted the magistrate to recall an earlier incident in which a St. Lucian, who spoke only French patois, stood before him as an accused. He asked if anyone in the court spoke patois and could interpret, and a Barbadian man volunteered to help. St. Paul described how the accused said repeatedly in patois *"culpable, compassion"* (I am guilty, have mercy), and when the judge asked the Barbadian interpreter what the accused meant he replied: "The man say he guilty, but he want compensation."[10]

===

Naturally enough, it was the substantive evidential material of the trial that was of uppermost importance. It consisted of the case presented by the prosecution and the extensive court speeches, not taken under oath nor supported by a final address to the jury—a right that the defendants declined—of the defendants. As the record unfolded day by day it became clear that two questions of crucial importance had to be answered: first, Who, individual members of the Central Committee or the Committee as a whole, ordered the armored expedition to Fort Rupert and the killing of the Bishop group? and, secondly, What series of events took place at the fort to justify the killing?

Responding to the first question, most of the accused disavowed a Central Committee decision. Practically every one of them denied responsibility while claiming to feel grief at the death of Bishop, a man with whom all had close relationships, they alleged, going back in some cases to childhood and adolescence in the closely knit Grenadian society. As to their movements on the fateful day of October 19, all had alibis that sounded suspicious. Coard himself claimed that he was taken to Fort Frederick for security reasons (and once there was protected in a tunnel) since it was felt that following Bishop's release by the crowd his own life was in danger. He added that during this period he and his wife decided to leave the country and began packing, only to find that it was too difficult to make travel arrangements and get to Pearls Airport on the other side of the island (it's quite possible that he feared being intercepted in the trip by a hostile crowd, somewhat like Louis XVI at Varennes in 1791).[11] He went on to say that he was only informed of the killings later that afternoon and was stunned by the news. At another point he testified that his continuing concern throughout for Bishop was substantiated by the fact that, days before the final crisis, he had advised Bishop that he (Bishop) would "go somewhere else, maybe Cuba, and cool it for a few years."[12] One cannot but wonder about this advice of a true friend, inviting Bishop, as it were, to abandon the revolution.[13]

Others of the accused offered similar stories. Hudson Austin—who reminded the courtroom that he had been a Methodist preacher in his early days—claimed that at the time he was on sick leave and only learned of Bishop's death from a soldier who drove up to his house in an army jeep to deliver the news. He was incredulous, he said and went immediately to the Fort Frederick army headquarters where Lt.-Colonel Ewart Layne confirmed the information.[14] Layne himself, in turn, testified, again in an unsworn statement, that he actually knew nothing about Bishop's being placed under house arrest until a week later and denied the assertion of the prosecution witness George Louison that the arrest had been announced on October 13 at a general meeting of the party.[15] Selwyn Strachan, finally, testified that he went to his office on the morning of October 19 to begin his normal ministerial duties and that as the trouble began his personal security guards advised him to go to the army headquarters for his own safety, from which point he later heard gunfire and was then informed of Bishop's death.[16] All of these leading witnesses, following Coard, denied that any order had emanated from the Central Committee for the mass executions.

Similar ambiguous evidence was presented in relation to the actual events at Fort Rupert. Ewart Layne, second in command of the army at the time, asserted that the Central Committee had nothing to do with the decision to send troops to recapture the Fort Rupert headquarters. "I was the only person besides General Austin," he testified, "who was authorised to move forces at any time, place the army on the alert or for combat battle."[17] Calistus Bernard, in turn, maintained that on orders from Layne he led the armored group to Fort Rupert. "The orders," he said, "were for us to restore order to the Fort and get out the civilians, to organise a defense for the headquarters, to make an assessment of the damage and see what crisis measures could be used to get the situation under control." He added that the shooting was instigated by the Bishop people and, therefore, that the army had acted simply in self-defense. He went on to compare the situation to an imaginary scenario in which a group attempts a takeover of the Pentagon in Washington and then waits to see what will happen.[18] Layne, at another point in his testimony, corroborated that version. "I gave no instructions," he said, "to commit murder, but gave instructions for the military unit to recapture Fort Rupert and restore full order. When the unit arrived it was ambushed and soldiers killed including the commander, who was fatally shot. It became chaotic and under those conditions certain persons met their death."[19]

It was not surprising that the jury, even after such a prolonged trial, took only three hours to arrive at their verdict, for the prosecution had effectively demolished the case for the defense. Led by Hudson-Phillips and the local acting director of public prosecutions, Velma Hylton, the prosecution team examined and dissected the statements of all the defendants. It dismissed as irrelevant all of the lengthy statements defending the record of the revolution as not being pertinent to the questions at stake; they were not so much circumstantial evidence as exculpatory statements. It relied heavily, by contrast, on the statements presented by the prosecution witnesses, more than forty-five of them.

All of that evidence, of course, cannot be fully rehearsed at this point. One must await the final published verbatim record of the Grenada court to read it in full. But certain vital points emerge. According to the statement of Colville McBarnette, one of the accused, the executions were ordered by the Central Committee during a meeting at the Fort Frederick army headquarters, with Coard acting as chairman.[20] Joseph St. Bernard, who confirmed that account, said that he saw members of the Central Committee drive up to the army camp in five cars while the demonstration was heading up to Fort Rupert, minutes before the departure of the armored group to the fort. This evidence was made all the more believable by the fact that St. Bernard was an office attendant at the Richmond Hill mental institution adjoining Fort Frederick and so was within sight and hearing distance.[21] In turn, Cecil Buxo, a professional optometrist, stated how, minutes before the shooting, he observed—by means of a powerful telescope, which enlarged things some eighty times, used at a friend's house some five hundred yards from the Coard house—a meeting of most of the Central Committee members, including Coard and Austin, at the Coard house.[22] Those accounts, at the least, put into question Coard's own testimony of being in hiding at the fort headquarters during that period of time. To all that evidence was added the testimony of many witnesses, some of them wounded survivors, who added gruesome details, from first-hand observation, of the massacre of the prisoners in the Fort Rupert courtyard.[23]

Hudson-Phillips pinpointed the crucial questions in his long summing-up to the jury that lasted some twelve days or more. All of the evidence, he suggested, showed that there was a concerted decision by the Central Committee for the Bishop group to be killed in the operations at Fort Rupert; for if the purpose of the armored detail was simply to restore order and get the civilians out of Fort Rupert, then why the heavy bombardment? "If there was not some previous decision or instruction," he said, "why were they marched up to the top square? Do you think that an officer of the rank of Abdullah Bernard could have taken that decision by himself or on his own?"[24] He went on to point out that the manner in which the bodies of Bishop and his colleagues had been disposed of was enough in itself to convict the accused. None of them in their statements had said anything about what was done with the bodies. Referring to the evidence of one witness that the bodies were burned in a pit and looked like "fried eggs," he asked: "Is this the normal way of dealing with people when they pass on?"[25] Pressing the point, he reminded the jury that cremation was not normal in Grenada: "As ordinary men and women of the world, when you hear someone has died, you ask, when is the funeral? And you probably inquire whether you can bring some rum and coffee to the wake."[26] Nor, it seemed, had any of the accused made enquiries as to how Bishop, whom they claimed to have loved, had died. As a final point, Hudson-Phillips addressed himself to the excuse presented by three of the soldiers—Andy Mitchell, Vincent Joseph, and Cosmos Richardson—that they had fired their guns against the prisoners in the square under orders. Is not conscience, he asked, above obedience to orders. "If you are in the forest and you see a manicou (opossum) and an officer tells you to cock your weapon, that is alright, but if what you see is a line of defenseless people, aren't you going to ask the officer, 'What are you doing, Chief?' "[27] He concluded by charging that the Bishop group had been deliberately murdered and not just shot down under cross fire, as the defense had claimed. Stressing that the law regarding murder was the same before, during, and after the rule of the People's Revolutionary Government, he summed up by saying: "The Lord didn't give any person on any committee power to determine if any person should live or die. As far as the shooting on the top square of Maurice Bishop, Jacqueline Creft, Norris Bain and others, that shooting was totally unjustified. Those persons were defenseless."[28]

It is worth adding a final note on the sociology, so to speak, of Caribbean murder. West Indians, in particular, seem to have taken over the English morbid fascination with murder in all of its forms. But the Grenada murder was different from all previous forms. It was not, for example, a straightforward crime of passion, like the Luis Vigoreaux–Lydia Echevarria case of 1985 in Puerto Rico. Nor was it anything like the Boysie Singh murders in the Trinidad of the 1940s, which seem to have been concerned with smuggling operations. Neither was it similar to the Michael Malik murders of the 1960s, also in Trinidad, which were part of a radical black activist group and its internal personal jealousies. A case for similarity could be made with respect to the election violence that took place in Jamaica in 1980–81, when some 800 people were killed by rival gang warfare, old Chicago style, with the gangs being affiliated with the two major political parties. But the ideological factor was much more potent in the Grenada affair, with its Marxism-Leninism being more doctrinaire than the mild socialism of the People's National Party in Jamaica. A much more plausible analogy can perhaps be made with the 1982 killings in Surinam, when some fifteen opponents and critics of the new Bouterse government were murdered in cold blood. But again there was an important difference in that the Surinam bloodbath was mainly occasioned by the ethnic group fears and rivalries of Surinamese society, a factor quite absent in the Grenada case. Murder *aficionados* will also remember that Agatha Christie placed one of her crime stories, *A Caribbean Mystery,* in a small, English-speaking West Indian country (which sounds to the reader like Grenada itself). But that, of course, was simply an individual matter, with one tourist hotel guest, with a previous murder on his hands, fearing that a fellow guest would recognize him. It is intriguing to speculate as to what might have happened if a real Miss Marple had been present in Grenada in October 1983.

Yet murder it was in any case. It will certainly go down in the books as one of the celebrated murder trials. The West Indian calypsonians have already written their ballads on it. The Mighty Sparrow's calypso *Grenada* is a typical example:

> Gairy squander all the money,
> and the Mongoose treat people like beast.
> Then Bishop take over the country,
> through party traitors he's deceased.

> Bajan come, John Compton, Eugenia and Seaga,
> had to import Yankee soldiers
> to stop the Grenada massacre,
> Cuba, que pasa?

Clint Eastwood has made the first movie on the invasion, although the U.S. armed forces have objected to the way in which he portrays a typical U.S. Marine. The tourist industry, with typical bad taste, has already included Fort Rupert in its tours for the idle curiosity seekers.

But the best and most proper remembrance of the whole event, in its completeness, will be that of the Grenadian people themselves, who showed that they could rise to the challenge of an awful crisis with all of their pride and decency and compassion. It is perhaps not inappropriate to apply to them the moving language of President Lincoln's Gettysburg Address:

> The brave men, living and dead, who struggled here have consecrated it far above our poor power to add or detract. The world will little note nor long remember what we say here, but it cannot forget what they did

here. It is for us the living rather to be dedicated here to the unfinished work which they who fought here have thus far so nobly advanced. It is rather for us to be here dedicated to the great task remaining before us—that from these honored dead we take increased devotion to that cause for which they gave the last full measure of devotion. . . . [29]

As they remember 1983 that is the supreme and binding message for the Grenadian people, and, beyond them, for the West Indian people as a whole.

Notes

1 Introduction: A Caribbean Tragedy

1. For what the original encounter of the Old and the New World meant in moral and intellectual terms, see Beatriz Pastor, *Discurso narrativo de la conquista de América* (Havana: Ediciónes Casa de las Américas, 1983), passim.
2. Gordon K. Lewis, "Lessons from a Revolution Betrayed," *Caribbean Contract 2*, no. 8 (December 1983):2, 12.

2 The Caribbean Background

1. J. E. Cairnes, cited in Karl Marx, *Capital* (London: George Allen & Unwin, 1938), 1:251–52.
2. Juan Bosch, *De Cristobal Colón a Fidel Castro: El Caribe, frontera imperial* (Madrid: Ediciónes Alfaguara, 1970). See also Eric Williams, *From Columbus to Castro: The History of the Caribbean, 1492–1969* (London: André Deutsch, 1970); and Ralph Davis, *The Rise of the Atlantic Economies* (Ithaca: Cornell University Press, 1973).
3. Josefina Oliva de Coll, *La resistencia indigena ante la Conquista* (Mexico City: Ediciónes Siglo Veintiuno, 1974).
4. Michael Craton, *Testing the Chains: Resistance to Slavery in the British West Indies* (Ithaca: Cornell University Press, 1982).
5. Ken Post, *Arise, Ye Starvelings: The Jamaica Labour Rebellion of 1938 and Its Aftermath* (The Hague: Martinus Nijhoff, 1978); also see Ken Post, *Strike the Iron: A Colony at War, Jamaica, 1939–1945* (Atlantic Highlands, N.J.: Institute of Social Science, 1981).
6. For the Jonestown event see Gordon K. Lewis, *Gather with the Saints at the River: The Jonestown Guyana Holocaust, 1978* (Río Piedras, Puerto Rico: Institute of Caribbean Studies, University of Puerto Rico, 1979).

3 The Island Background

1. Patrick Emmanuel, *Crown Colony Politics in Grenada, 1917–1951* (Cave Hill, Barbados: Institute of Social and Economic Research, University of the West Indies).
2. M. G. Smith, "Structure and Crisis in Grenada, 1950–1954" in *The Plural Society in the British West Indies, 1950–1954* (Berkeley and Los Angeles: University of California Press, 1965), pp. 262–303.
3. "Report of the Agricultural Commission," *St. George's Chronicle and Grenada Gazette,* March 28; April 4, 11, 1896.
4. *West India Royal Commission Report* (London: Her Majesty's Stationery Office, 1945), Cmd. 6607, p. 201.
5. Simon Rottenberg, "Labor Relations in an Underdeveloped Economy," *Caribbean Quarterly* 4, no. 1 (January 1953):54.
6. "The Banana in St. Lucia," *Voice of St. Lucia* (Castries, St. Lucia), March 9, 1963.
7. See Gordon K. Lewis, *The Growth of the Modern West Indies* (New York: Monthly Review Press, 1968), pp. 157–58.
8. *Proceedings of the West Indian Conference Convened by the Dominica Taxpayers Reform Association, Dominica, British West Indies* (Castries, St. Lucia: Voice Printery, October–November, 1932), pp. 1–2.

4 1951: Gairy, Gairyism, and the Populist Revolt

1. W. Richard Jacobs and Ian Jacobs, *Grenada: The Route to Revolution* (Havana: Cuadernos de Casa de las Américas, 1980), ch. 3; see also W. Richard Jacobs, *The Grenada Revolution at Work* (Port-of-Spain, Trinidad: Unique Services, n.d.).
2. A. W. Singham, *The Hero and the Crowd in a Colonial Polity* (New Haven: Yale University Press, 1968).
3. *Report of the Commission of Enquiry into the Control of Public Expenditure in Grenada during 1961 and Subsequently* (St. George's, Grenada: Government Printery, May 8, 1962).
4. *Report of the Commission of Enquiry on Grenada,* under the chairmanship of Sir Herbert Duffus (St. George's, Grenada, 1975); see also Alistair Hughes, "A Breakdown of Law and Order," *Trinidad and Tobago Review* (January 1979); and also "Gairy's Overthrow: A Question of When and How," by a Correspondent in *Trinidad and Tobago Review* (Port-of-Spain, Trinidad) 3, no. 2 (May 1979): 14; and also "Papa Doc in Grenada," *Moko* (Port-of-Spain, Trinidad) 2, no. 12 (April 4, 1973).
5. Jacobs and Jacobs, *Grenada: The Route to Revolution,* ch. 5; see also Allan Harris, "The Road to Coup d'Etat," *Trinidad and Tobago Review* 3, no. 1 (March 1979):22.

5 1973: The Rise of the New Jewel Movement

1. Jacobs and Jacobs, *Grenada: The Route to Revolution;* and David E. Lewis, *Reform and Revolution in Grenada, 1950–1981* (Havana: Ediciónes Casa de las Américas, 1984).

2. Sir John Mordecai, *The West Indies: The Federal Negotiations* (London: Allen & Unwin, 1968); Sir Fred Phillips, *Freedom in the Caribbean: A Study in Constitutional Change* (Dobbs Ferry, N.Y.: Oceana Publications, 1977), chs. 6, 7.
3. *Report of the Economic Commission on Unitary State Proposals* (Port-of-Spain, Trinidad: Government Printery, January 1965).
4. Jacobs and Jacobs, *Grenada: The Route to Revolution,* pp. 60 and 69.
5. Ibid., chs. 4 and 5; and Fitzroy Ambursley, "Grenada: The New Jewel Revolution," in *Crisis in the Caribbean,* eds. Fitzroy Ambursley and Robin Cohen (London: Heinemann, 1983).
6. Jacobs and Jacobs, *Grenada: The Route to Revolution,* pp. 60, 69.
7. Eric Williams, *Inward Hunger: The Education of a Prime Minister* (London: André Deutsch, 1969).
8. Bernard Coard, *How the West Indian Child Is Made Educationally Sub-normal in the British School System* (London: New Beacon Books, 1971).
9. Jacobs and Jacobs, *Grenada: The Route to Revolution,* pp. 94–95.
10. Lewis, *The Growth of the Modern West Indies,* pp. 118–19.
11. Ibid., pp. 131–42.
12. Jacobs and Jacobs, *Grenada: The Route to Revolution,* p. 80.

6 March 13, 1979: The Coup d'État

1. Sir Shridath Ramphal, secretary-general of the Commonwealth, article in *Trinidad Express* (Port-of-Spain, Trinidad), November 29, 1983, pp. 13, 14.
2. Harris, "The Road to Coup d'Etat," p. 22.
3. Ibid.
4. Ibid., p. 23.
5. Justice Aubrey Fraser, article in *West Indian Law Journal* (May 1979), reprinted in *Trinidad Express,* December 16, 1983, p. 8.
6. Frantz Fanon, *Studies in a Dying Colonialism* (New York: Monthly Review Press, 1965), ch. 2.

7 1979–1983: The Revolutionary Achievement

1. Peter Gomes, *The Marxist Populism of C.L.R. James* (Mona, Jamaica: Institute of Social and Economic Research, University of the West Indies, 1979).
2. George Brizan, *The Education Reform Process in Grenada, 1979–1981* (Ottawa: International Development Research Centre, 1982); and Brizan, "Conspiracy or Genuine Critique: A Response to Monica Payne's Review Article," *Bulletin of Eastern Caribbean Affairs* (Cave Hill, Barbados) (May–June 1983):17–20.
3. *Maurice Bishop Speaks: The Grenada Revolution, 1979–1983* (New York: Pathfinder Press, 1983), p. 257.
4. "Three Years of the Grenada Revolution," ibid., see especially speech of March 13, 1982, pp. 255–72.
5. David E. Lewis, *Reform and Revolution in Grenada,* ch. 7.
6. "Education in Grenada, July 2, 1979," speech of July 2, 1979, in *Maurice Bishop Speaks,* pp. 42–47.

7. "Two Years of the Grenada Revolution, March 13, 1981," speech of March 13, 1981, ibid., pp. 128–42.
8. Sebastian Clark, *Grenada: A Workers' and Farmers' Government with Revolutionary Proletarian Leadership* (New York: Pathfinder Press, 1980). See also M. Martin, *Volcanoes and Hurricanes: Revolution in Central America and the Caribbean* (London: Socialist Challenge, 1982).
9. Ambursley, "Grenada: The New Jewel Revolution."
10. Jacobs and Jacobs, *Grenada: The Route to Revolution,* p. 123.
11. Ambursley, "Grenada: The New Jewel Revolution," p. 203.
12. David E. Lewis, *Reform and Revolution in Grenada,* pp. 206–7; see also *In the Mainstream of the Revolution* (St. George's, Grenada: Fédon Publishers, 1982).
13. Anthony P. Maingot, "Requiem for a Utopia," *Miami Herald,* October 30, 1983, pp. 10–60.
14. "In Nobody's Backyard, April 13, 1979," speech of April 13, 1979, in *Maurice Bishop Speaks,* pp. 26–31.
15. "Women Step Forward, June 13, 1979," speech of June 13, 1979, ibid., pp. 32–41. For further discussion of the economic track record of the revolution see Wallace Joefield-Napier, "Macroeconomic Growth During the PRG Regime: An Assessment," Conference on Grenada cosponsored by Caribbean Institute and Study Center for Latin America, Inter-American University, San Germán, Puerto Rico, October 17–19, 1985; and Jay Mandle, *Big Revolution, Small Country* (Lanham, Md.: North-South Publishing, 1985).

8   1983: The Road to October

1. Patrick Solomon, article in *Trinidad Express,* December 14, 1982, pp. 3, 4.
2. *Grenada Documents: An Overview and Selection* (Washington, D.C.: U.S. Department of State and Department of Defense, September 1984); and Paul Seaburg and Walter A. McDougall, *The Grenada Papers* (San Francisco: Institute of Contemporary Studies Press, 1984).
3. See among others: interview by Paul McIssac with Kendrick Radix, *Village Voice* (New York), November 23, 1983, pp. 13, 14, 15; see also interviews with Don Rojas in *Washington Post,* December 26, 1983; *Sunday Sun* (Barbados), October 30, 1983; and *Inter-Continental Press,* report published in *Sunday Guardian* (Port-of-Spain, Trinidad), November 6, 1983; see also portions of interviews with Louison and Radix in *Washington Post,* November 9, 1983, and *Wall Street Journal,* November 8, 1983.
4. See statement by Kendrick Radix presented at the Second Conference on Culture and Sovereignty in the Caribbean, Mount St. Benedict, St. Augustine, Trinidad, January 14, 1984.
5. Interview with Kendrick Radix, "Revolutionary Suicide," *Village Voice,* November 22, 1983, pp. 31, 32.
6. Tomas Borge, minister of the interior, Nicaragua, cited in the *Trinidad Express,* January 24, 1984, p. 17.
7. Steve Clarke, "Introduction," *Maurice Bishop Speaks,* pp. xxviii–xxix; also *Latin American Regional Reports: Caribbean* (London), November–4, 1983, p. 3.
8. Kendrick Radix and Merle Hodge, statements presented at the Second Conference on Culture and Sovereignty in the Caribbean.

9. "Central Committee Report on First Plenary Session, 13–19 July 1983," in *Grenada Documents: An Overview and Selection,* sec. III, pp. 110–23; and "Grenada Explodes," special issue *Caribbean Review* 12, no. 4 (Fall 1983):1–68.

10. George Louison, interview in *Wall Street Journal,* November 8, 1983.

11. Personal recollections of author, First Conference on Culture and Sovereignty in the Caribbean, St. George's, Grenada, November 1982.

12. H. Michael Erisman, ed., *The Caribbean Challenge: The United States Policy in a Volatile Region* (Boulder, Colo.: Westview Press, 1984).

13. Figures cited in *Everybody's Magazine* (New York) 7, no. 7 (November 1983):20.

14. Kendrick Radix, statement at Second Conference on Culture and Sovereignty in the Caribbean.

15. "Lessons in Marxism, 4," *Barbados Advocate* (Bridgetown, Barbados), November 16, 1983; Minutes of "Central Committee Report on First Plenary Session, 13–19 July 1983," in *Grenada Documents:* An Overview and Selection, sec. III, pp. 110–23; and Bary Levine, introduction, "The Alienation of Leninist Group Therapy: Extraordinary General Meeting of Full Members of the NJM: Minutes recorded by an unidentified notetaker," *Caribbean Review* 12, no. 4 (Fall 1983):14–15, 48–58.

16. "Grenada Explodes," passim; *Trinidad Express,* February 6, 1983, p. 8; *Grenada Documents: An Overview and Selection,* Document 112. See also report in *Boston Globe,* November 6, 1983.

17. "Grenada Explodes," passim; *Grenada Documents: An Overview and Selection,* Document 113; and "The Grenada Papers, Minutes of the NJM Central Committee," Part VIII, in ibid.

18. *Grenada Documents: An Overview and Selection,* Document 113.

19. "Lessons in Marxism, 4."

20. "Grenada Explodes," passim; *Grenada Documents: An Overview and Selection,* Document 113.

21. Selwyn Ryan, *Trinidad Express,* January 1, 1984, p. 6.

22. *Current Economic Position and Prospects of Grenada* (Washington, D.C.: World Bank, April 19, 1979), Report no. 2434-GRD; and World Bank, *Economic Memorandum on Grenada* (Washington, D.C.: May 12, 1980), Report no. 2949-GRD.

23. Cited in Alistair Hughes, *Grenada Newsletter* (St. George's, Grenada) 11, nos. 7, 9 (1983):2–3, 1–2.

24. Quoted in Michael Massing, "Grenada Before and After," *Atlantic Monthly* (February 1984):78.

25. Bernard Coard, *Report on the National Economy for 1982 and the Budget Plan for 1983 and Beyond,* presented to the National Conference of Mass Organisations, February 24, 1983 (St. George's, Grenada: Government Printing Office, 1983), p. 73.

26. "Central Committee Meeting of August 26, 1983," in *Grenada Documents: An Overview and Selection,* Document 111, passim.

27. For Guyana, see Clive Y. Thomas, "State Capitalism in Guyana: An Assessment of Burnham's Cooperative Socialist Republic," in Ambursley and Cohen, eds., *Crisis in the Caribbean;* and more generally by Clive Y. Thomas, *The Rise of the Authoritarian State in Peripheral Societies* (New York: Monthly Review Press, 1984).

28. *Grenada Documents: An Overview and Selection,* Document 113-13.

29. Ibid.

30. Fitzroy Bain, remarks in ibid., Document 113–25.
31. "Behind the Revolution's Overthrow," interview with New Jewel leader Don Rojas, in *Inter-Continental Press* 21, no. 25 (December 26, 1983):759.
32. Vincent Noel, letter to members of the Central Committee and Party, October 17, 1983, in "The Grenada Papers," in *Grenada Documents: An Overview and Selection*, Part VIII.

9   October 19, 1983: "Bloody Wednesday"—The Guns of October

1. *Boston Globe,* November 6, 1983, p. 24.
2. *Caribbean Review* (special issue) 12, no. 4 (1984).
3. *Trinidad Express,* October 18, 1983, p. 8.
4. Ibid., November 7, 1983, p. 17.
5. For the general outline of events, see "Grenade Assassine," *Antilla Special* (Fort-de-France, Martinique), December 1, 1983; "Focus on Grenada: Special Issue," *Friends for Jamaica Newsletter* (New York) 3, no. 2 (1983); *Latin American Regional Reports: Caribbean* (London), November 4, 1983; Hugh O'Shaughnessy, *Grenada: Revolution, Invasion and Aftermath* (London: Sphere Books, Hamish Hamilton, 1984); Cathy Sunshine and Philip Wheaton, *Death of a Revolution* (Washington, D.C.: EPICA, January 1984).
6. Bernard Diedrich, "Interviewing George Louison," *Caribbean Review* 12, no. 4 (1984):17–18.
7. Ibid. See in addition the even more revealing interview with Louison in *Indies Times* (St. George's, Grenada), April 7, 1984, pp. 4, 5.
8. Ibid.
9. Michael Als, *Trinidad Express,* November 4, 6, 1983, pp. 16, 17.
10. Don Rojas, interview, *Inter-Continental Press* 21, no. 25 (December 26, 1983):760.
11. "Statement Broadcast by General Hudson Austin on Radio Free Grenada, 16 October 1983," in *Documents on the Invasion of Grenada, October 1983,* comps. Sybil Farrell Lewis and Dale Matthews (Río Piedras, Puerto Rico: Institute of Caribbean Studies, University of Puerto Rico, 1984), pp. 5–10.
12. Sylvia Belmar, *Trinidad Guardian* (Port-of-Spain, Trinidad), November 12, 1983, pp. 7–8.
13. Alistair Hughes, *Grenada Newsletter,* p. 6.
14. Desmond Gilbert, *Daily Gleaner* (Kingston, Jamaica), November 14, 1983, pp. 17, 18.
15. Hughes, *Grenada Newsletter,* p. 8.
16. Gilbert, *Daily Gleaner.*
17. Ibid.
18. Peter Thomas, *Trinidad Express,* November 8, 1983, p. 2.
19. Belmar, *Trinidad Guardian.*
20. "Report by Anonymous Nurse," *Trinidad Guardian,* November 11, 1983, p. 4.
21. Thomas, *Trinidad Express,* p. 7.
22. Belmar, *Trinidad Guardian,* p. 8.
23. Don Rojas, interview, *Inter-Continental Press* 21, no. 25 (December 26, 1983).
24. Ibid.
25. Thomas, *Trinidad Express,* p. 10.

26. Don Rojas, interview, *Inter-Continental Press* 21, no. 25 (December 26, 1983):758.
27. "Report by Anonymous Nurse," p. 4.
28. Belmar, *Trinidad Guardian*, p. 6.
29. Thomas, *Trinidad Express*, p. 5.
30. Ibid.
31. "Report by Anonymous Nurse," p. 6.
32. For court proceedings see successive issues of the *Grenada Newsletter*, throughout 1984 and 1985. See also Anthony Payne, Paul Sutton, and Tony Thorndike, *Grenada: Revolution and Invasion* (New York: St. Martin's Press, 1984), p. 136; and Kai P. Schoenhals and Richard A. Melanson, *Revolution and Intervention in Grenada: The New Jewel Movement, the United States, and the Caribbean* (Boulder, Colo.: Westview Press, 1985), pp. 90–91. For the evidence of Joseph St. Bernard see *The San Juan Star* (San Juan, Puerto Rico), May 9, 1986, p. 13.
33. "Statement Broadcast by General Hudson Austin on Radio Free Grenada, 19 October 1983" in *Documents on the Invasion of Grenada*, pp. 11–12.
34. Belmar, *Trinidad Guardian*, p. 7.
35. Thomas, *Trinidad Express*, p. 6.
36. Dwight Wiley, quoted in interview, *Trinidad Express*, October 31, 1983, p. 14.
37. Als, *Trinidad Express*, p. 3; Editorial Statement, *Trinidad Express*, November 7, 1983, p. 6; Stanley Lumsden, letter, *Trinidad Express*, November 24, 1983, p. 9.
38. Trevor Munroe, secretary-general, Workers party of Jamaica, press release, *Daily Gleaner*, October 20, 1983.
39. Dr. Jensen Otway, *Trinidad Express*, January 5, 1984, p. 28.
40. Edmund Burke, "Letters on a Regicide Peace, 1796," in *Burke's Works* (London: G. Bell and Sons, 1914), vol. 5.
41. Friedrich Engels, "Introduction to the Class Struggles of France," in *A Handbook of Marxism*, ed. Emile Burns (London: Victor Gollancz, 1937), pp. 89–90.
42. Ibid., pp. 95–96.
43. G. K. Chesterton, *Stories, Essays and Poems* (London: Everyman Series, 1935), p. 116.

10 Bishop, Coard, the Ultraleft Faction, and the Military

1. "Statement by General Hudson Austin on Behalf of the Revolutionary Council Monitored on Radio Free Grenada, 10:00 P.M., October 19, 1983" and "Statement Issued by Major Christopher Stroude, Member of the Grenadian Revolutionary Military Council on October 20, 1983," in *Documents on the Invasion of Grenada*, pp. 11–15.
2. *Latin American Regional Reports: Caribbean* (London), November 4, 1983.
3. Michael Als, *Trinidad Sunday Express*, November 6, 1983, pp. 14, 15.
4. "Last Words of Radio Free Grenada," *Everybody's Magazine* 7, no. 7 (November 1983):25.
5. Kendrick Radix, statement presented at Second Conference on Culture and Sovereignty in the Caribbean.
6. Conversations with author throughout 1984 in Trinidad and Puerto Rico.
7. May Greaves, "Interview with Angela Bishop," *Sunday Sun* (Bridgetown, Barbados), November 13, 1983.

8. Don Rojas, interview, *Inter-Continental Press* 21, no. 25 (December 26, 1983):762.
9. "Inside the NJM," by an Insider, *Trinidad Express,* November 17, 1983.
10. Gabriel García Marquez, "Bishop," *Claridad* (San Juan, Puerto Rico), Supplement, November 4–10, 1983.
11. George Chambers, prime minister of Trinidad and Tobago, in *Trinidad Express,* July 12, 1983.
12. "Maurice Bishop Speaks to U.S. Working People, June 5, 1983," in *Maurice Bishop Speaks,* pp. 287–312.
13. Ernesto Cardenal, *En Cuba,* Serie Popular Rea (Mexico City: Serie Popular Rea, 1977), pp. 147–48.
14. Graham Greene, *Getting to Know the General: The Story of an Involvement* (London: Bodley Head, 1984).
15. "Inside the NJM," p. 60.
16. "Report by Ex-Prisoners of the People's Revolutionary Government," *Trinidad Express,* January 15, 1984, pp. 18–19.
17. "Inside the NJM," p. 24.
18. "Report by Ex-prisoners: The Great Escape," *Trinidad Express,* February 13, 1984, pp. 15–16.
19. Sunshine and Wheaton, *Death of a Revolution,* p. 10.
20. Don Rojas, interview, Inter-Continental Press 21, no. 25 (December 26, 1983):610. See also remarks in "Inside the NJM," p. 24.
21. *Everybody's Magazine* 7, no. 7 (November 1983):35.
22. Letter of Prime Minister Bishop to President Reagan in *Caribbean Contact* (Caribbean Conference of Churches, Bridgetown, Barbados), March 1982, p. 7.
23. *Maurice Bishop Speaks,* passim.
24. See *Trinidad Express,* December 14, 1983, p. 16. For a different view see Kari Polany-Levitt, "Special on Grenada," *Bulletin Centre de Recherches Caraïbes* 3, no. 2 (Fall 1983):11.
25. Anthony Payne, "The Foreign Policy of the PRG," conference on Grenada sponsored by the Caribbean Institute and Study Center for Latin America, Inter-American University; and Gregory Sandford and Richard Vigilante, *Grenada: The Untold Story* (Lanham, Md., Madison Books, 1984), p. 106.
26. *Grenada Documents,* Document 105–3.
27. Rojas, Interview, December 26, 1983, p. 715.
28. *Grenada Documents: An Overview and Selection,* Document 112–14, 15. See also "Lessons in Marxism, 4."
29. Jacobs and Jacobs, *Grenada: The Route to Revolution,* pp. 32–33.
30. Selwyn R. Cudjoe, *Grenada: Two Essays* (Tacarigua, Trinidad: Calaloux Publications, 1984), pp. 12–13.
31. "A Permanent Standing Commitment to Freedom of Worship and Religion, February 15, 1980," speech of February 15, 1980, in *Maurice Bishop Speaks,* pp. 60–69.
32. The Reverend Leslie Lett, *Grenada: A Challenge to Caribbean Theology* (Bridgetown, Barbados: Caribbean Conference of Churches, June 1984), p. 4. See also *The Grenada Invasion: A CCC Perspective* (Bridgetown, Barbados: Caribbean Conference of Churches, December 1983).
33. Don Rojas, interview, *Sunday Sun,* October 30, 1983, pp. 9–10. See also Harold H. Sandstrom, "Grenada's Revolution: The Drift to the Left," paper delivered

at Conference on Grenada, University of Connecticut at Storrs, April 14, 1984.

34. Tim Hector, *Outlet* (St. John's, Antigua), reprinted in *Antilla Special*, December 1, 1982, pp. 27–29.
35. Cudjoe, *Grenada: Two Essays*, pp. 4–9.
36. Eric E. Williams, "Perspectives for Our Party" (Port-of-Spain, Trinidad, 1958), in *Forged from the Love of Liberty: Selected Speeches of Dr. Eric Williams*, comp. Paul K. Sutton (London: Longman Caribbean, 1981), pp. 111–15.
37. Cudjoe, *Grenada: Two Essays*, p. 7.
38. Diederich, "Interviewing George Louison," p. 18.
39. Russell Tyson, *The Bomb* (Port-of-Spain, Trinidad), August 3, 1984, p. 15.
40. Lloyd Noel, *Grenada Newsletter* 11, no. 15 (November 1983), pp. 4, 5.
41. *Covert Action Information Bulletin* (Washington, D.C.) 20 (Winter 1984):4–9.
42. Ibid., p. 10.

11   The Counterrevolution Prepared: The Role of the Caribbean Bourgeoisie

1. Justice Aubrey Fraser, article in *West Indian Law Journal* (May 1979), reprinted in *Trinidad Express* December 16, 1983.
2. "Treaty Establishing the Caribbean Community (CARICOM), 1973," in *Documents on the Invasion of Grenada*, pp. 119–27; and "Treaty Establishing the Organisation of Eastern Caribbean States, 1981," ibid., pp. 129–39.
3. "Declaration of Heads of State, Ocho Rios, Jamaica," *Caribbean Contact*, December 1982, pp. 13, 14. Sol Linowitz et al., *The Americas in a Changing World* (Commission on United States-Latin American Relations, Washington, D.C., 1976).
4. For the general problem of the Caribbean Community process, see W. Andrew Axline, *Caribbean Integration: The Politics of Regionalism* (London: Francis Pinter, 1979); and Anthony J. Payne, *The Politics of the Caribbean Community, 1961–1979* (Manchester: Manchester University Press, 1980). For the details of the 1983 trading difficulties between member states, see the regional press throughout January–June 1983. See also Ramesh Deosoran, "Nationalism vs. CARICOM," *Caribbean Contact*, April 1984, p. 7.
5. See the Caribbean press for January–June 1983.
6. Chris Searle, *Grenada: The Struggle Against Destabilization* (New York: published by the author, distributed by W. W. Norton, 1984), pp. 52–53.
7. Ibid., pp. 60–67. See also Charlie Cobb, "Securing Independence: Grenada Faces Massive Resistance from the United States," *Trans-Africa Forum* (New York) 1, no. 2 (Fall 1982):8, 9. For the similar case of Nicaragua see Ana Marin Ezcurra, *Ideological Aggression and the Sandinista Revolution: The Political Opposition Church in Nicaragua* (New York: CIRCUS Publications, 1984). For further on the Jamaica case see Michael Manley, *Jamaica: Struggle in the Periphery* (New York: Third World Media Ltd., printed by Oxford University Press, 1982).
8. Searle, *Grenada: The Struggle Against Destabilization*, p. 156.
9. For example, interview with Maurice Bishop, *Trinidad Express*, March 27, 1983.
10. For the Jamaican press assault on the Manley regime in Jamaica, see *Psycholog-*

ical Warfare in the Media: The Case of Jamaica (Kingston, Jamaica: Press Association of Jamaica, n.d.).

11. "Interview with Robert Coard," *Boston Globe,* November 3, 1983, p. 6.

12. Senator John Donaldson, minister of external affairs, Trinidad and Tobago, "Statement," *Trinidad and Tobago Review* 3, no. 1 (May 1979):21–22.

13. "Address to the Nation on 25 October 1983 by His Excellency L.F.S. Burnham, President of the Co-operative Republic of Guyana," in *Documents on the Invasion of Grenada,* pp. 63–65.

14. Trevor Farrell, *Trinidad Express,* December 13, 1983, p. 6.

15. A.N.R. Robinson, chairman, Tobago House of Assembly, *Trinidad Express,* November 13, 1983, pp. 4–6.

16. Lloyd Taylor, "The Oligarchs Against the People," *Trinidad Express,* March 8, 1984, p. 8.

17. Trevor Farrell, *Trinidad Express,* November 4, 1983, pp. 8–9.

18. Ibid.

19. Statements by the prime minister of St. Lucia, John Compton, and the prime minister of Dominica, Eugenia Charles, *Barbados Advocate,* October 22, 1983, p. 19.

20. Statements of the prime minister of Trinidad and Tobago, George Chambers, *Trinidad Express,* October 24, 1983, pp. 3, 4.

21. Statement to the nation by the prime minister of Jamaica, Edward Seaga, October 25, 1983, in *Documents on the Invasion of Grenada,* pp. 67–73.

22. Statement by the president of Guyana, L.F.S. Burnham, in *Documents on the Invasion of Grenada,* pp. 63–65.

23. Statement by the prime minister of Trinidad and Tobago, George Chambers, to the House of Representatives, October 26, 1983, in *Documents on the Invasion of Grenada,* pp. 75–80.

24. Ibid., p. 79.

25. "The Pitt Recall," statement by the prime minister of Barbados, Tom Adams, *Trinidad Express,* November 9, 1983, p. 1.

26. Statement by the prime minister of Trinidad and Tobago, George Chambers, to the Annual Conference of the People's National Movement (PNM) Women's League, *Trinidad Express,* November 7, 1983. Full text of address published by the PNM Information Centre, n.d.

27. Anonymous sources cited in *Trinidad Express,* November 26, 1983, pp. 1–6. See also comments of Dr. Patrick Solomon, *Trinidad Sunday Express,* December 11, 1983, p. 7.

28. See statement by L.F.S. Burnham, president of Guyana, *Guyana Chronicle* (Georgetown, Guyana), November 6, 7, 1983, pp. 3–5.

29. Statement by the prime minister of Jamaica, Edward Seaga, cited in *Trinidad Express,* November 1, 1983, p. 1, and November 2, 1983, p. 15.

30. Statement by the prime minister of Dominica, Eugenia Charles, cited in *Trinidad Sunday Express,* December 11, 1983, p. 2.

31. Statement by the prime minister of Barbados, Tom Adams, cited in *Trinidad Express,* November 30, 1983, p. 60.

32. Statement by L.F.S. Burnham, president of Guyana, *Guyana Chronicle,* November 30, 1983, p. 14.

33. For general comments on all this, among much else, see Michael Manley, "The Seaga-Reagan Agenda," *Trinidad Sunday Express,* November 13, 1983, p. 7;

and Michael Baptiste, "The Grenada Situation: Chambers' Greatest Hurt," *Trinidad Sunday Guardian*, November 13, 1983, p. 7.

34. Prime Minister Tom Adams, "Text of Address to the Nation, 27 October 1983," in *Documents on the Invasion of Grenada*, pp. 35–39.
35. Prime Minister Edward Seaga, *Trinidad Express*, November 1, 1983, p. 1.
36. Prime Minister Tom Adams, *Barbados Advocate*, October 29, 1983, pp. 1, 2.
37. "Steps Behind Invasion," *New York Times*, October 30, 1983, p. 20.
38. Prime Minister Edward Seaga, quoted in *Washington Post*, October 30, 1983, p. A14.
39. Statement by Prime Minister Eugenia Charles, cited in *New York Post*, October 27, 1983, p. 5.
40. Interview with Sir Paul Scoon, governor-general of Grenada, in *Trinidad Express*, November 13, 1983, p. 2.
41. Austin Clarke, "Scroon's Call to Eugenicus," *Weekend Nation* (Bridgetown, Barbados), January 20, 1984, p. 11.
42. "Joint Press Conference with the President of the United States, Ronald Reagan, and the Prime Minister of Dominica, the Rt. Hon. Eugenia Charles," in *Documents on the Invasion of Grenada*, pp. 31–34. See also *Barbados Advocate*, October 26, 1983, pp. 7, 8.
43. Prime Minister Tom Adams, statement in *Barbados Advocate*, October 16, 1983. See also *New York Times*, October 30, 1983, p. 20.
44. Cited in report by Stuart Taylor, Jr., *New York Times*, November 6, 1983, p. 20; and in *Trinidad Express*, October 27, 1983, p. 24.
45. Remarks of Commander Hudson Austin in *Washington Post*, October 30, 1983, p. A14. See also *Grenada: Whose Freedom?* (London: Latin American Bureau, 1984), p. 83.
46. Sir Shridath Ramphal, secretary-general of the Commonwealth, in *Trinidad Express*, November 29, 1983, p. 18.
47. A.N.R. Robinson, chairman, Tobago House of Assembly, interview in *Trinidad Sunday Express*, November 13, 1983, p. 14.
48. Dr. Jeff Davidson, deputy chairman, Tobago House of Assembly, in *Trinidad Express*, November 29, 1983, p. 7; and December 11, 1983, p. 7.
49. Dr. Brinsley Samaroo, opposition leader, in *Trinidad Express*, October 26, 1983, p. 3.
50. Dr. Ritchie Haynes, opposition spokesman, in *The Nation* (Bridgetown, Barbados), November 16, 1983, p. 21.
51. Errol Barrow, leader of the opposition, Barbados, "The Danger of Rescue Operations," *Caribbean Review* 12, no. 4 (1984):52.
52. *The Decision to Assist Grenada* (Washington, D.C.: U.S. Department of State, Bureau of Public Affairs, January 24, 1984), p. 2.

12   October 25, 1983: The Empire Strikes Back

1. Hugh O'Shaughnessy, "The Sledgehammer and the Nutmeg," *Observer Review* (London), March 4, 1984, p. 17; *New York Times*, October 26, 27, 1983, pp. 21–22; *Miami Herald*, October 26, 27, 1983, pp. 4, 5, 6.
2. O'Shaughnessy, "The Sledgehammer and the Nutmeg," pp. 17–18.
3. Fidel Castro, *Una victoria militar pírrica y una profunda derrota moral* (Havana:

Editora Política, November 14, 1983), pp. 9–10. For the full record of the Cuban response see Fidel Castro, *Conferencia de Prensa, Granna, Resumen Semanal,* Havana, Cuba, November 6, 1983; *Statements by Cuba on the Events in Grenada, October 1983* (Havana: Editora Política, 1983); also included in *Documents on the Invasion of Grenada,* items XII, XIII, XIV. See also Fidel Castro, farewell address to Cuban soldiers, *New York Times,* November 20, 1983, p. 60.

4. *New York Times,* October 29, 1983, p. 6.
5. William S. Lind, *Report to the Congressional Military Reform Caucus: The Grenada Operation* (Washington, D.C.: Military Reform Institute, April 4, 1984); Representative James Courter, Release no. 8412, Washington D.C. For the Beirut episode, see report of House Subcommittee, in *New York Times,* December 20, 1983, pp. 1–12.
6. *Grenada: Whose Freedom?*
7. *Covert Action Information Bulletin* 20 (Winter 1984):14.
8. Bernard Weintraub, *New York Times,* October 29, 1983, pp. 1, 7; Stuart Taylor, Jr., *New York Times,* November 6, 1983, p. 20; Heath Meriwether, executive editor, *Miami Herald,* October 20, 1983, p. 4C.
9. Vice Admiral Joseph Metcalf, quoted in *New York Times,* November 6, 1983, p. 20.
10. Dan Bohning, *Miami Herald,* October 30, 1983, p. 40.
11. *New York Times,* November 7, 1983, p. 23.
12. Peter G. Bourne, *Los Angeles Times,* November 6, 1983, part 4, pp. 1, 3, 4.
13. *Covert Action Information Bulletin* 20 (Winter 1984):8–10.
14. Peter G. Bourne, *Los Angeles Times,* November 6, 1983, part 4, p. 4.
15. Ken Kurze, reported in *Barbados Advocate,* October 24, 1983, p. 4; see also *Grenada: Whose Freedom?* pp. 83–87; *Covert Action Information Bulletin* 20 (Winter 1984):8–10; Sunshine and Wheaton, *Death of a Revolution,* pp. 11–14.
16. *Everybody's Magazine,* 7, no. 7 (November 1983):14, 15.
17. Ron Kephart, "Some Personal Observations on the Grenada Intervention," mimeo, (Gainesville, Florida, February 1984), p. 3.
18. West Indian Jurist, not named by request, in "The Grenada Situation: Invasion . . . Legal or Not?" *Trinidad Sunday Guardian,* November 13, 1983, p. 5.
19. Mike Royko, in *Chicago Sun-Times,* November 1, 1983. See also Jorge Dominguez, "U.S. Fears Not Well Documented," *Boston Sunday Globe,* October 21, 1984; see also Associated Press Report in *Trinidad Guardian,* November 11, 1983, p. 5.
20. Remarks of Colonel Ken Barnes, in *New York Times,* November 7, 1983, p. A-14.
21. Wendell Bell, "The Use of False Prophecy to Justify Present Action," paper delivered at Conference on Grenada, University of Connecticut at Storrs, April 14, 1984.
22. "United Nations General Assembly Resolution," *New York Times,* November 4, 1983; "United Nations Security Council Resolution," *New York Times,* October 29, 1983.
23. Statement by the prime minister of Great Britain, Margaret Thatcher, reported in *The Times* (London), October 31, 1983. For criticism of the United Kingdom record from a Caribbean source, see remarks of Ron de Lugo, territorial delegate of the U.S. Virgin Islands, cited in Ronald Walker, "Grenada and Britain," *San Juan Star* (Puerto Rico), November 10, 1983, p. 43. For criticism from the

British parliamentary opposition, see remarks of David Steele, Liberal party leader, cited in *Trinidad Express,* December 16, 1983, pp. 11, 13. See also Tony Burton in *Daily News,* October 30, 1983, p. C-2. See also "British Government Policy on Grenada," in *Grenada: Whose Freedom?* Appendix 1, pp. 105–10.

24. "Treaty Establishing the Organization of Eastern Caribbean States," in *Documents on the Invasion of Grenada,* Article 8, pp. 113–34.

25. Report in *The Guardian* (New York), November 16, 1983, p. 16.

26. "U.S. Lawyers' Views of the Legality of the U.S. Invasion of Grenada," in *Grenada: Whose Freedom?* Appendix 4, pp. 125–27.

27. I. Brownlie, *International Law and the Use of Force by States,* quoted by Dr. R. D. Moodhoo, "Letter," *Trinidad Express,* December 20, 1983, p. 8.

28. Remarks of Prime Minister Thatcher in *Documents on the Invasion of Grenada,* item XX, pp. 87–88.

29. Anselm Francis, "Legal Implication of United States Intervention in Grenada," paper delivered at the Conference on the Grenada Revolution, 1979–83, Institute of International Relations, University of the West Indies, St. Augustine, Trinidad, May 24–25, 1984, pp. 5–9.

30. William Clay, "The Grenada Diary of Congressman Louis Stokes," *The Congressional Record: Proceedings and Debates of the 98th Congress,* Washington, D.C., November 16, 1983, vol. 129, no. 159. Louis Stokes, "New Human and Civil Rights Dilemma in Grenada," ibid.

31. Representative Ronald V. Dellums, Press Release from the Congressional Office (Washington, D.C., November 9, 1983).

32. For representative samples of West Indian opinion supporting this position see, among much else, Ken Boodhoo, "Letter," *Trinidad Sunday Guardian,* November 13, 1983, p. 8; Neville Linton, "Letter," *Trinidad Express,* November 4, 1983, p. 7; H. Singh, "Letter," *Trinidad Express,* November 15, 1983, p. 8; Christian D. Periera, "Letter," *Trinidad Express,* November 16, 1983, p. 8; Oswin Avery, "Letter," *Trinidad Express,* December 3, 1983, p. 8; Harry Turner, "Using the Big Stick Again," *San Juan Star* (Puerto Rico), November 5, 1983, p. 31; Report of the Board of Social Responsibility of the Anglican Church, *Trinidad Express,* December 9, 1983, p. 3. For dissenting opinions see, among much else, Roland Perusse, "Grenada Invasion . . . a Legal Act," *San Juan Star,* November 5, 1983, p. 30, Alfred Farah, "Letter: The Law as a Convenience," *Trinidad Express,* November 16, 1983, p. 8; and successive editorial columns in the *Jamaica Daily Gleaner* and the *Barbados Advocate* for November to December 1983.

33. D. J. Harris, *Cases and Materials on International Law* (London: Sweet and Maxwell, 1979), p. 676; referred to in Francis, "Legal Implications of United States Intervention in Grenada," pp. 16–17.

34. *Reports of International Arbitral Awards* (Geneva, 1925), pp. 5–6; referred to in Francis, "Legal Implications of United States Intervention in Grenada," pp. 7–8.

35. Ibid. For a somewhat different opinion see Sir Archibald Nedd, chief justice of Grenada, "The Doctrine of Necessity," *Trinidad Guardian,* October 17–18, 1985.

36. Sunshine and Wheaton, *Death of a Revolution,* p. 13.

37. Clay, "The Grenada Diary of Congressman Louis Stokes."

38. Cited in *Daily News* October 27, 1983, p. C-2.
39. *Latin American Regional Reports: Caribbean,* November 4, 1983, p. 3: James M. Anderson, quoted in *Commonwealth Journal* (Somerset, Ky.), November 6, 1983, cited in *Cuadernos del Tercer Mundo* (Mexico) 6, 66 (1984):96–100.
40. Interview with Jean-Luc Pepin, minister of external affairs, Canada, in *Documents on the Invasion of Grenada,* item XXII, pp. 91–93.
41. Michael Manley, *Trinidad Sunday Express,* May 6, 1984, p. 2.

13   The Imperialist Ideology and Mentality

1. Of the vast literature on all this see, as examples only, William Appleton Williams, *Empire as a Way of Life* (New York: Oxford University Press, 1980); Richard E. Feinberg, *The Intemperate Zone: The Third World Challenge to U.S. Foreign Policy* (New York: Norton, 1983); Tom Buckley, *Violent Neighbors* (New York: Times Books, 1984); Raymond Bonner, *Weakness and Deceit* (New York: Times Books, 1984); Jenny Pearce, *Under the Eagle: U.S. Intervention in Central America and the Caribbean* (London: Latin American Bureau, 1982); Stanley Hoffman, *Dead Ends: American Foreign Policy in the New Cold War* (Cambridge, Mass.: Ballinger, 1983); Walter LaFeber, *Inevitable Revolutions: The United States in Central America* (New York: Norton, 1983).
2. U.S. Department of Commerce, *Economic Study of Puerto Rico,* 2 vols. (Washington, D.C.: U.S. Department of Commerce, December 1970); Jorge Heine, ed., *Time for Decision: The United States and Puerto Rico* (Lanham, Md.: North-South Publishing, 1983).
3. "A Plan for the Caribbean," *New York Times,* February 25, 1982, p. 3. For critical commentary on the Caribbean Basin Initiative, see *Report of Meeting of Ministers of Foreign Affairs, CARICOM, Belize, 1982,* CARICOM Secretariat, Georgetown, Guyana; and J. Edward Green, "Perspectives on U.S.–Belmar, Caribbean Relations in the Mid-Eighties" (San Germán, Puerto Rico: Caribbean Institute and Study Center for Latin America, Inter-American University, 1984), pp. 11–12. For a supportive view see *Report of Conference on Business and Investment Opportunities Under the New Caribbean Basin Initiative, San José, California, 21–24 May 1984,* sponsored by San José State University School of Business and the Caribbean Basin Initiative Center.
4. Representative Thomas J. Downey, "The Price of Force, the Promise of Diplomacy," *Miami Herald,* November 13, 1983, p. 6-C.
5. José Arsenio Torres, "Reagan's Imperial Democracy," *San Juan Star,* May 3, 1984, p. 38.
6. Juan Bosch, *Pentagonismo: Substituto del imperialismo* (Mexico City: Siglo XXI, 1968); translation, *Pentagonism: Substitute for Imperialism* (New York: Grove Press, 1968).
7. Review of the Month, "Where Are We Going?" *Monthly Review* 35, no. 7 (December 1983):5.
8. Lind, *Report to the Congressional Military Reform Caucus,* passim. See, more generally, Edward N. Luttwak, *The Pentagon and the Art of War* (New York: Simon and Schuster, 1985).
9. Representative James Courter, *Release no. 8412.*

10. Will Elsworth Jones, *Trinidad Express,* November 14, 1983, p. 19.
11. Larry Speakes, cited in *Covert Action Information Bureau* 20 (Winter 1984):16.
12. President Ronald Reagan, "Remarks," noted in Sunshine and Wheaton, *Death of a Revolution,* p. 30.
13. U.S. Secretary of State George Schultz, quoted in *Trinidad Express,* February 9, 1984, p. 48.
14. "Yanks Seize Terror Island," *New York Post,* October 26, 1983, p. 1.
15. Charles Krauthammer, "Grenada and the End of Revolution," *New Republic,* January 30, 1984, p. 16.
16. Barry Levine, "The Alienation of Leninist Group Therapy," pp. 14–15, 48–58.
17. Arthur Schlesinger, Jr., "Grenada, Without Warning," *Wall Street Journal,* November 9, 1983, p. 17.
18. Max Lerner, "Reagan Had Rendezvous with History," *New York Post,* October 27, p. 39.
19. Norman Podhoretz, "Proper Uses of Power," *New York Times,* October 30, 1983, p. E-19.
20. Sally Shelton, interview, *New York Times,* November 5, 1983, p. B-12; *Boston Sunday Globe,* December 18, 1983, p. A-17.
21. Bill Reel, "Backward Christian Soldiers," *Daily News,* October 27, 1983, p. C-16; see also Beth Fallon, "So Tell It to the Marines," *Daily News,* October 28, 1983, p. C-16.
22. Reported in *Trinidad Express,* October 23, 1984, p. 25.
23. William González, "Letter," *San Juan Star,* November 14, 1983, p. 29.
24. Representative Thomas P. O'Neill, interviewed by James Reston, *New York Times,* November 1, 1983. Press Release in *San Juan Star,* November 13, 1983, pp. 16–17.
25. *Covert Action Information Bulletin* 20 (Winter 1984):8–10.
26. Ibid. See also Peter Bourne, *Los Angeles Times,* November 6, 1983, part 4, pp. 2–4.
27. *Covert Action Information Bulletin* 20 (Winter 1984):9. For Pastor's interviews on the Grenada matter, see his paper "The Impact of Grenada on the Caribbean: Ripples from a Revolution," presented at the Conference on the Grenada Revolution, 1979–83, Institute of International Relations, University of the West Indies, St. Augustine, Trinidad, May 24–25, 1984.
28. *Covert Action Information Bulletin* 20 (Winter 1984):20.
29. For the typology of this phenomenon in American public affairs see, for example, Michael Wright, "National Security's New Insiders," *New York Times Magazine,* March 3, 1985, pp. 58ff.
30. Albert K. Weinberg, *Manifest Destiny: A Study of Nationalist Expansionism in American History* (Baltimore: Johns Hopkins University Press, 1935). See also Nathaniel Peffer, *America's Place in the World* (New York: Viking Press, 1945).
31. Weinberg, *Manifest Destiny,* p. 432.
32. Jeane Kirkpatrick, U.S. ambassador to the United Nations, interviewed by George Urban, *New York Post,* October 27, 1983, pp. 37, 39.
33. For the liberal critique of all this, with particular reference to the Grenada affair, see, for example, Tom Wicker, "Unsettling Questions," *San Juan Star,* November 21, 1983, p. 30; Flora Lewis, "Grenada Isn't Lebanon," *San Juan Star,* November 8, 1983, p. 14; Anthony Lewis, "What Is Reagan Hiding?" *San Juan Star,* November 7, 1983, p. 30; remarks of Senator Daniel Patrick Moynihan,

cited in Anthony Lewis, "Historical Insight," *San Juan Star,* June 6, 1984, p. 37; and Professor David E. Apter, Yale University, "Letter," *New York Times,* October 23, 1983.

14   The Dependent Colonial Ideology and Mentality

1. U.S. Department of Commerce, *Economic Study of Puerto Rico.* Raymond Carr, *Puerto Rico: A Colonial Experiment* (New York: New York University Press, 1984); Jorge Heine and Juan M. Passalaqua, *The Puerto Rican Question* (Washington, D.C.: Foreign Policy Association, 1983).
2. Franklin W. Knight, *United States Cultural Influences on the English-speaking Caribbean During the Twentieth Century* (San Germán, Puerto Rico: Centro de Investigaciones del Caribe y América Latina, Inter-American University, 1983).
3. Of a large literature on this topic see, for example, George Lamming, ed., *Papers of the Second Conference of Intellectual Workers* (Mount St. Benedict, Trinidad, January 13–14, 1984).
4. See, for example, C.L.R. James, "The West Indian Middle Classes," in C.L.R. Jones, ed., *Spheres of Existence* (Westport, Conn.: Lawrence Hill, 1980). For Memmi see Albert Memmi, *Retrato del Colonizado* (Buenos Aires: Ediciónes de la Flor, 1975). For Fanon, see Fanon, *Studies in a Dying Colonialism;* and B. Marie Perinbam, *Holy Violence: The Revolutionary Thought of Frantz Fanon* (Washington, D.C.: Three Continents Press, 1982).
5. Wendell Bell, "Equality and Social Justice: Foundations of Nationalism in the Caribbean," *Caribbean Studies* 20, no. 2 (June 1980):5–36.
6. Carlos Buitrago Ortiz, *Ideologia y conservadorismo en el Puerto Rico de hoy* (Río Piedras, Puerto Rico: Ediciónes Bayoan, 1972), cited in Gordon K. Lewis, *Notes on the Puerto Rican Revolution* (New York: Monthly Review Press, 1974), p. 77.
7. David Lowenthal, *West Indian Societies* (New York: Oxford University Press, 1972), p. 136.
8. U.S. State Department spokesman, quoted in *San Juan Star,* August 14, 1984, p. 23.
9. Prime Minister Tom Adams, "Remarks in Parliamentary Debate," *Barbados Advocate,* November 18, 1983, p. 1; and in *Trinidad Express,* November 18, 1983, p. 6.
10. Archbishop Anthony Pantin, statement in *Trinidad Guardian,* November 11, 1983, p. 1.
11. Letter of Prime Minister Bishop to President Reagan, *Caribbean Contact,* March 1982, p. 7; and remark of the U.S. State Department official in *Trinidad Express,* November 14, 1983, p. 39.
12. *South Magazine* (London), reprinted in *The Bomb,* January 20, 1984, p. 6; and "Report," *The Economist,* October 31, 1983.
13. Dean Harold Critchlow, "Statement" reported in *Trinidad Express,* November 8, 1983, p. 29.
14. Kurleigh King, "Statement" reported in ibid., November 29, 1983, p. 24.
15. *Grenada and the Eastern Caribbean: A Report of a Delegation Visit* (Philadelphia: American Friends Service Committee, January 1984), p. 12.

16. "Pen Portraits of the Governor-General and Council: Sir Paul Scoon," *The Grenada Voice,* November 26, 1983, p. 4.
17. Prime Minister Tom Adams, "Remarks in Parliamentary Debate," *Trinidad Guardian,* November 17, 1983, p. 5.
18. Prime Minister Edward Seaga, "Statement to the Nation," in *Documents on the Invasion of Grenada,* item XVI, pp. 67–73.
19. Joint Press Conference with the President of the United States and the Prime Minister of Dominica, in *Documents on the Invasion of Grenada,* item X, pp. 31–34; the prime minister of Dominica, Eugenia Charles, interview, *Trinidad Sunday Express,* December 11, 1983, p. 2. See also Michael J. Belrin, "Portrait of an Ally in the Grenada Move," *New York Post,* October 26, 1983, p. 35.
20. Prime Minister Eugenia Charles, interview, *Trinidad Sunday Express,* December 11, 1983, p. 2.
21. Address to the nation by President L.F.S. Burnham, interview, *Trinidad Sunday Express,* December 11, 1983, p. 2.
22. Prime Minister Tom Adams, comments reported in *Barbados Advocate,* November 17, 18, 1983.
23. Remarks of David Steel, Liberal party leader, Great Britain, *Trinidad Express,* December 16, 1983, pp. 11, 13.
24. Eric E. Williams, "Epilogue," in Sutton, ed., *Forged from the Love of Liberty,* pp. 438–39.
25. Alain Blérald, *Histoire économique de la Guadeloupe et de la Martinique de XVIIe siècle à nos jours* (Fort-de-France, Martinique: Editions Karthala, 1985). See interview with Blérald in *Antilla,* March 10–16, 1986, pp. 39–40.
26. "Bibliografía de J. Benjamin Torres," *Claridad,* Supplement, April 18–24, 1986, pp. 25–26.

15 The Lessons for the Caribbean State System

1. Of the extensive literature on this topic see, for example, Carl Stone, "The Caribbean and the World Economy: Patterns of Insertion and Contemporary Options" (San Germán, Puerto Rico: Centro de Investigaciones del Caribe y América Latina, Inter-American University, 1983); George Beckford, ed., *Caribbean Economy* (Mona, Jamaica: Institute of Social and Economic Research, University of the West Indies, 1974); H. Brewster and C. Y. Thomas, *The Dynamics of West Indian Economic Integration* (Mona, Jamaica: Institute of Social and Economic Research, University of the West Indies, 1967).
2. For one example of this general phenomenon see Vaughan Lewis, "The Small State Alone: Jamaican Foreign Policy, 1977–1980," paper presented at the Seventh Annual Conference of the Caribbean Studies Association, Kingston, Jamaica, May 25–29, 1982.
3. Anthony Gonzales, "Superpower Rivalry and Caribbean Freedom," *Caribbean Contact,* April 1984, p. 14.
4. Frank Taylor, "Militarization of the Caribbean Basin," *Caribbean Contact,* March 1984, pp. 14–16.
5. Nizam Mohammed, "Parliamentary Debate, House of Representatives, Trinidad and Tobago," *Trinidad Express,* October 27, 1983, p. 24.

6. *The Caribbean Community in the 1980s,* report by a Group of Caribbean Experts (Georgetown, Guyana: Caribbean Community Secretariat, 1981), pp. 102–25.

7. Patrick Solomon, keynote speech, Organisation for National Reconstruction, *Trinidad Express,* November 12, 1983.

8. Neville Linton, "Facing Up to Ideological Pluralism in CARICOM," *Caribbean Contact,* July 1983, p. 2; and Frank Taylor, "Transnational Violence in the Caribbean," *Caribbean Contact,* January–February 1984, p. 7.

9. Lloyd Good, "Grenada: A Crisis of Moral and Intellectual Insight," *Trinidad Express,* February 3, 1984, p. 8.

10. Lloyd Taylor, "The Limitations of West Indian Independence," *Trinidad Express,* March 7, 1984, p. 7.

11. *The Caribbean Community in the 1980s,* p. 7.

12. Statement by Senator Basil Ince, minister of external affairs, Trinidad and Tobago, at the Thirteenth Regular Session of the Organization of American States, in *Documents on the Invasion of Grenada,* item XVIII, pp. 81–83.

13. Thomas Enders, assistant secretary of state, quoted in Helen McEachrane, "Collective Security Action . . . Myopic U.S. View," *Trinidad and Tobago Review* Independence Issue (1982):7; Undersecretary of State Robert Olds, "Statement of 1927," quoted in "Timetable of War," *South-Third World Media* (London) 14, no. 6 (1984):13–17.

14. "1981 Resolution, Caribbean Conference of Churches," in Lett, *Grenada: A Challenge to Caribbean Theology,* pp. 23–24.

15. Linton, "Facing Up to Ideological Pluralism in CARICOM," p. 2.

16. *The Caribbean Community in the 1980s,* pp.3–4.

17. Report of the National Bipartisan Commission on Central America, Chairman, Henry Kissinger, Washington, D.C., 1984. *The Americans at a Crossroads,* report of the Inter-American Dialogue (Washington D.C.: Woodrow Wilson International Center of Scholars, 1983), reviewed by Neville Linton, in "A Classic Case of Enlightened Self-Interest," *Caribbean Contact,* October 1983, pp. 14–15. Report of the Inter-American Dialogue, excerpted in *Herald International Tribune,* April 15, 1986, p. 6.

18. David Scott Palmer, "U. S. Policy Issues in the Caribbean Basin in the 1980s: Economic, Social and Political Aspects," mimeo (Baltimore: Foreign Service Institute and School of Advanced International Studies, Johns Hopkins University, 1983).

19. Edward Gonzales, "U.S. Strategic Interests in the Caribbean Basin" (San Germán, Puerto Rico: Centro de Investigaciones del Caribe y América Latina, Inter-American University, 1983).

16   The Lessons for the Caribbean Left

1. For examples of the response from all points of the Caribbean left-wing compass see *Grenada: Our Position* (San Fernando, Trinidad and Tobago: Oil Workers' Trade Union, 1984); *Tribune* 3, no. 7 (November 1983), published by the February 18th Movement, Petit Valley, Port-of-Spain, Trinidad; *Grenada and the Caribbean* (Georgetown, Guyana: Working Peoples' Alliance, March 13,

1984); "Focus on Grenada: Special Issue," *Friends for Jamaica Newsletter* 3, no. 2 (1984); "Granada: Porqué de la pequeñez salen gigantes," *Claridad,* November 4–10, 1983; Alberto L. Marquez, "La invasion de Granada," *Claridad,* December 20, 1984; Gabriel García Marquez, "Que pasa al fine en Granada?" *Claridad,* December 2–8, 1983; Marica Rivera Quintero, "Granada: Masacre e invasion en la isla de la fantasia" (San Juan, Puerto Rico: Ediciones de Paz y Justicia, n.d.); *Statements by Cuba on the Events in Grenada;* "Editorial," *Barricada Internacional* (Managua, Nicaragua) 4, no. 131 (December 1984). See also "Granada, l'espoir assassine," *Antilla Special,* December 1, 1983.

2. Perinbam, *Holy Violence: The Revolutionary Thought of Frantz Fanon.*
3. Lord Acton, *Letters of Lord Acton to Mary Gladstone,* ed. Herbert Paul (London: George Allen, 1904), p. 142.
4. Friedrich Engles, *Revolution and Counter-Revolution* (London: George Allen & Unwin, 1896).
5. D. Sinclair Da Breo, *Of Men and Politics: The Agony of St. Lucia* (Castries, St. Lucia: Commonwealth Publishers International, 1981).
6. Singham, *The Hero and the Crowd.*
7. John Henry Newman, *On the idea of a University* (Dublin: Catholic Publishers, 1873), p. 143.
8. Cudjoe, *Grenada: Two Essays,* pp. 9–10.
9. Dick Howard, ed., *Selected Political Writings of Rosa Luxemburg* (New York: Monthly Review Press, 1971), pp. 289–90.
10. Rosa Luxemburg, *Die Russische Revolution* (Berlin: n.p., 1918), p. 113. For the recent growth of interest in the life and work of Rosa Luxemburg in Third World circles see, for a Caribbean example, José Echevarria, "Rosa Luxemburgo, Polemista critica," *Sin Nombre* (San Juan, Puerto Rico) 13, no. 3 (April–June 1983):23–26.
11. Tony Thorndike, "Revolution and Reform: The New Jewel Movement in Theory and Practice," paper presented at the Conference on the Grenada Revolution, 1979–83, Institute of International Relations, University of the West Indies, St. Augustine, Trinidad, May 24–25, 1984, p. 42. For a recent Puerto Rican critique of the form of centralized *partido-estado,* see Anonymous, *Manifiesto de autogestion* (San Juan, Puerto Rico: n.p., April 1984).
12. Tony Thorndike, comment made in discussion at the Conference on the Grenada Revolution, 1979–83.
13. Thorndike, "Revolution and Reform," p. 46.
14. Richard Hart, *Grenada: An Assessment of the Revolution* (Mona, Jamaica: University of the West Indies, March 21, 1984), pp. 18–21.
15. Don Rojas, interview, *Inter-Continental Press* 21, no. 25 (December 26, 1983):7. The reference to Webbs is to Sidney and Beatrice Webb, *Soviet Communism: A New Civilization* (London: Victor Gollancz, 1935).
16. Jean Girard, "The Assassination of Hope," *Caribbean Contact,* April 1984, pp. 6–7. For further comments see articles by Gordon K. Lewis, Vaughan Lewis, Richard Hart, and Clive Thomas summarized in *Bulletin d'Information* 4, no. 3 (1984):13–15.
17. Henry S. Gill, "The Grenada Revolution: Domestic and Foreign Policy Orientations," Conference on the Grenada Revolution, 1979–83, Institute of International Relations, University of the West Indies, St. Augustine, Trinidad, May 24–25, 1984.

18. Ibid., pp. 25–26.
19. Paul W. Ashley, *Jamaican Foreign Policy in Transition: From Manley to Seaga* (San Germán, Puerto Rico: Centro de Investigaciones del Caribe y América Latina, Inter-American University, 1983), p. 10.
20. Henry S. Gill, "The Foreign Policy of the Grenadian Revolution," *Bulletin of Eastern Caribbean Affairs* 7, no. 1 (1981):3.
21. W. Richard Jacobs, confidential letter, "Relations with the CPSU," January 1983; and confidential letter, "Grenada's Relations with the USSR," July 1983; both cited in Thorndike, "Revolution and Reform: The New Jewel Movement in Theory and Practice," pp. 26–27.
22. Trevor Munroe, *Revolution, Counter-Revolution* (Kingston, Jamaica: Vanguard Publishers, 1984), pp. 95–100.
23. Perry Mars, "Destabilization, Foreign Intervention and Socialist Transformation in the Caribbean," *Transition* (University of Guyana, Georgetown, Guyana) 7 (1983):21–32.
24. Aimé Césaire, *Lettre à Maurice Thorez* (Paris: Présence Africaine, 1956), pp. 12–13.
25. Statement of Working People's Alliance of Guyana, in *Friends for Jamaica Newsletter* 3, no. 11 (1984):7.
26. Rupert Roopnarine, statement in ibid., p. 8.
27. Klaus Mehnert, *Stalin versus Marx* (Port Washington, N.Y.: Kennikat Press, 1971).
28. Leon Cornwall, *The Grenada 'Elections': An Analysis from Behind Prison Bars,* mimeo (London: Caribbean Labour Solidarity with the NJM, n.d.). .

17   1984: The Orwellian Aftermath

1. *Public Opinion Survey* (St. Augustine, Trinidad: St. Augustine Research Associates of Trinidad and Tobago), reported in the *Weekend Nation* (Bridgetown, Barbados), January 20, 1984, p. 1.
2. Statement by Paul Adderly, foreign minister of the Bahamas, to the General Assembly of Organization of American States, reported in *Trinidad Guardian,* November 17, 1985, p. 5. See also statement by Rashleigh Jackson, foreign minister of Guyana, reported in *Trinidad Express,* November 12, 1983, p. 3.
3. Lloyd Noel, "The Legal and Constitutional Position Under the Governor-General," *The Grenadian Voice,* November 20, 1983, p. 16.
4. *Covert Action Information Bulletin* 20 (Winter 1984):19–20. See also "Islanders in Shocked Dependence," *Latin American Regional Reports: Caribbean,* December 9, 1983, p. 6.
5. Sunshine and Wheaton, *Death of a Revolution,* pp. 22–23.
6. Case of Donald Foster, reported in the St. Louis Post-Dispatch, April 17, 1984.
7. *Jamaica Committee for Defence of Human Rights in Grenada* (Kingston, Jamaica, n.d.), passim.
8. The comparison with post-1965 Santo Domingo is drawn in Sunshine and Wheaton, *Death of a Revolution,* pp. 21–26. For the Dominican Republic as a whole, see, for example, Carlos María Gutierrez, *The Dominican Republic: Rebellion and Repression* (New York: Monthly Review Press, 1972).

9. Christian Girault, "Gulf et Western en la République Dominicaine: De l'enclave sucrière au controle d'une partie de l'économie," *L'Espace Geographique* 24, no. 24 (1983):223–29.

10. For the Club Med type of tourist operation see, for example, report in *Trinidad Express,* November 1, 1983, p. 19.

11. *Grenada and the Eastern Caribbean* (Philadelphia: American Friends Service Committee, 1984), p. 26.

12. Ibid., pp. 20–22.

13. Ernest Harsch, "Bitter Fruits of Revolution's Defeat," *Inter-Continental Press* 22, no. 17 (September 17, 1984):543–49.

14. Pam Girton, *Trinidad Express,* October 30, 1984, p. 6.

15. Andy Johnson, *Trinidad Express,* October 27, 1984, p. 11.

16. See *Inter-Continental Press* 22, no. 17 (September 17, 1984).

17. Peter Noel, "The Ambitious Exiles," *Trinidad Sunday Express,* March 4, 1984, p. 39.

18. Pam Girton, *Trinidad Express,* October 26, 1984, pp. 16, 17. For the return of Eric Gairy and its implications see Dan Sewell, "Eric Gairy Seeking a New Image Now," *Trinidad Guardian,* January 27, 1984; Robert Hardman, "Grenada: A Year After the Invasion," *Boston Sunday Globe,* October 21, 1984, p. 14; interview with Eric Gairy, "The Grenada Elections," *Trinidad Sunday Express,* October 7, 1984; "Gairy May Rise Again," *Insight* (London) 14, no. 5 (August 1984):4–5.

19. Statement by Rashleigh Jackson, foreign minister of Guyana, in *Trinidad Express,* November 12, 1983, p. 3.

20. The Rickey Singh matter is briefly narrated in Milton Young, "Letter," *Trinidad Express,* December 30, 1983, p. 9. For Singh's record see "Rickey Singh and the Caribbean Media," Caribbean Conference of Intellectual Workers, Havana, Cuba, 1984.

21. Statement by Prime Minister Edward Seaga, *Jamaica Daily Gleaner,* July 10, 1984, p. 16.

22. *State Security and Treason Acts,* reported in *The Sun* (Port-of-Spain, Trinidad), January 20, 1984, p. 5; *The Nation,* January 19, 1984, p. 4; *Voice of St. Lucia* January 18, 19, 20, 1984.

23. See, for example, *Revo,* by playwright Shango Baku, reviewed by Kathy Ann Waterman, *Trinidad Sunday Express,* June 10, 1984, p. 34.

24. Barbara Gelb, "Grenada: A Traveler's Briefing," *New York Times,* February 5, 1984, Travel Section, pp. 19, 48.

25. Ernest Tracey, "U.S. Professor Runs into Hostile Audience," *Trinidad Guardian,* July 31, 1984, pp. 12, 15.

26. "Une interview de l'ambassadeur américain en France à l'occasion de sa visite en Martinique," *France-Antilles,* July 26, 1984, p. 5.

27. See KNT International, "Many More U.S. Officials in East Caribbean," *Trinidad Express,* April 27, 1984, p. 49.

28. This process culminated in early 1985 with the announced intention of the U.S. government to place emergency nuclear weapons in Puerto Rico, see "Puerto Rico dentro del sistem a nuclear militar de los Estados Unidos," *Claridad* February 22–28, 1985. For the growing militarization of the English-speaking Caribbean, see Humberto García, "Apuntes sobre la política militar de los Es-

tados Unidos en el Caribe anglo-parlante," mimeo, ponencia, seminario, Las Amenazas a la Paz en el Caribe y Centro América, Aguas Buenas, Puerto Rico, October 2–7, 1984.

29. For the continuing debate on the Barbados Defence Force see the press—*The Nation* and the *Barbados Advocate*—throughout February, March, April 1984.

18　Some General Observations

1. Joseph Schumpeter, *The Sociology of Imperialism* (New York: Meridian Press, 1955).
2. George Lichtheim, *Imperialism* (New York: Praeger, 1971).
3. "Unidad y diversidad de las Antillas en América Latina," *Caribana* 3 (February 1984):8, 9. Traducido del frances de un Grupo Interdisciplinario de Investigación y documentacion Sobre América Latina de la Universidad de Burdeos, p. 11.
4. Jacobs, *The Grenada Revolution at Work*, p. 10.
5. Chou En-lai, *Report on the Question of Intellectuals* (Peking: Foreign Languages Press, 1956), p. 43.
6. *Statement Delivered by H. E. Unison Whiteman, Minister of Foreign Affairs of the People's Revolutionary Government of Grenada to the Second Special Session on Disarmament,* at the United Nations, June 23, 1982.
7. Lasana Sekou, *Maroon Lives* (Kingston, Jamaica: Lasana Sekou, 1984).
8. George Kennan, quoted in Gaddis Smith, "The Legacy of Monroe's Doctrine," *New York Times Magazine,* September 9, 1984, p. 126.
9. Senator Frank Church, "Thoughts on the Limits to American Power," *New York Times,* April 15, 1984, p. E-19.
10. "Unidad u diversidad de las Antillas en América Latina," p. 11.
11. V. S. Naipaul, article, *Harper's Magazine* (March 1984) quoted in the *Trinidad Guardian,* July 29, 1984.
12. Bill Riviere, "The Collapse of the Grenada Revolution and the Road Ahead for the Caribbean Struggle," mimeo of address presented at City College, New York, March 14, 1984, p. 17.
13. Working Peoples' Alliance, *Grenada and the Caribbean* (Georgetown, Guyana: Working Peoples' Alliance, March 13, 1984), pp. 5–6.
14. Clive Thomas, "Hard Lessons for Intellectuals," *Caribbean Contact* September 1984, p. 12.
15. Ibid.
16. Mandle, *Big Revolution, Small Country.*
17. Payne, Sutton, and Thorndike, Grenada: Revolution and Invasion, pp. 221–24.
18. Colin Henfrey, "Between Populism and Leninism: The Grenadian Experience," *Latin American Perspectives,* issue 42, 2, no. 3 (Summer 1984):34.
19. Sandford and Vigilante, *Grenada: The Untold Story.*

19　1986: Denouement

1. *Daily Express* (Port-of-Spain, Trinidad), December 5, 1986, pp. 1, 3. *Trinidad Guardian* (Port-of-Spain), December 5, 1986, p. 1.

2. *The Nation* (Bridgetown, Barbados), August 9, 1984, p. 5.

3. Ibid., October 1, 1985, p. 6; October 2, 1985, p. 7; May 9, 1985, p. 8; March 14, 1986, p. 10; May 17, 1986, p. 4.

4. Ibid., May 28, 1984, p. 4; June 1, 1984, p. 9; June 2, 1984, p. 8.

5. Ibid., March 19, 1984, p. 15.

6. Ibid., June 29, 1985, p. 21; June 30, 1985, p. 32; July 7, 1985, p. 43; August 30, 1985, p. 27; September 4, 1985, p. 22; April 29, 1986, p. 11.

7. Ibid., July 4, 1986, p. 27; July 5, 1986, p. 13.

8. Ibid., April 18, 1986, p. 17.

9. Ibid., July 24, 1986, p. 23.

10. Ibid., August 1, 1984, p. 23.

11. Ibid., August 20, 1986, p. 33.

12. Ibid., June 29, 1986, p. 12.

13. Ibid., August 20, 1986, p. 33, for Bernard Coard's professed love of Bishop.

14. Ibid., August 8, 1986, p. 1.

15. Ibid., September 4, 1986, p. 17.

16. Ibid., June 17, 1986, p. 29.

17. Ibid., September 2, 1986, p. 15.

18. Ibid., July 18, 1986, p. 32.

19. Ibid., September 11, 1986, p. 23.

20. Ibid., June 13, 1986, p. 29.

21. Ibid., May 9, 1986, p. 19.

22. Ibid., May 11, 1986, p. 15.

23. Ibid., April 25, 1986, p. 12; April 30, 1986, p. 12; May 4, 1986, p. 18; May 8, 1986, p. 1; May 13, 1986, p. 6; June 4, 1986, p. 14.

24. Ibid., October 29, 1986, p. 27.

25. *The Grenada Newsletter* (St. Georges), vol. 14, no. 17, November 8, 1986, p. 2.

26. Ibid., p. 4.

27. Ibid., p. 3.

28. *The Nation,* October 23, 1986, p. 22.

29. Abraham Lincoln, "The Gettysburg Address," in *American Issues. Volume I: The Social Record* (Chicago: J.B. Lippincott Company, 1944), p. 552.

Index

About the Author

GORDON K. LEWIS is professor of political science at the University of Puerto Rico. His previous books include *Main Currents in Caribbean Thought: The Historical Evolution of Caribbean Society in Its Ideological Aspects, 1492–1900.*